Advance Praise for *Rising to Power*

"Don't even think about taking a promotion to any type of 'Vice President' job or any role that starts with 'Chief' unless you have read this book first. There isn't anyone who has moved into an executive role that hasn't faced challenges brilliantly articulated and addressed in this book—the struggle to balance risk taking and decision making with confidence, patience, and trust without becoming completely paralyzed by the newfound power and magnitude of the issues at hand. If you want your leadership to effect remarkable good in the organization and lives of those you lead, start reading."

—MEGAN BILSON, Vice President, Global Head of Learning,
American Express

"*Rising to Power* unmasks the trials and triumphs of climbing the executive ranks. Based on a decade-long study and their extensive consulting experience, Ron Carucci and Eric Hansen show why some leaders flounder and others flourish."

—ADAM GRANT, Professor, Wharton School of the University of
Pennsylvania, and bestselling author of *Give and Take: A Revolutionary
Approach to Success*

"Be prepared to see your own power-deflating behaviors reflected back from the pages of this gorgeous and deeply impacting book. You'll learn quickly from every page of *Rising to Power*. Carucci and Hansen combine the best new thinking on leadership with practical accounts of how hundreds of top executives have failed to get anywhere near their aspirations, and then identify what sets apart those who exceeded their aspirations. The result is the best book on using organizational power in years: a roadmap to broad, contextual, connected—and wise—executive leadership. Read *Rising to Power* this weekend! You'll begin a new, more impacting journey on Monday."

—DAVID FOSTER, CEO, BVR, LLC

"*Rising to Power* is a must read for all aspiring executives and those who support them. This practical yet impactful study of executive power takes the mystery out of how to become a successful leader in today's organizations. Those responsible for equipping their organizations with the best leadership talent will also gain valuable insight as to why some leaders succeed and others never make the grade. And, for executives looking for sound advice on how to take your leadership to the next level, you will find yourself wishing you had read this book years earlier in your career, saving you from the pitfalls of learning how to lead through trial and error!"

—LORI J. KELLEHER, Chief Human Resources Officer, Black & Veatch

RÎSING

POWER

RÎSING

to

POWER

The JOURNEY *of*
EXCEPTIONAL EXECUTIVES

Ron A. Carucci | Eric C. Hansen

FOREWORD BY PAUL MAASS

GREENLEAF
BOOK GROUP PRESS

Published by Greenleaf Book Group Press
Austin, Texas
www.gbgpress.com

Distributed by Greenleaf Book Group

For ordering information or special discounts for bulk purchases, please contact Greenleaf Book Group LLC at PO Box 91869, Austin, TX 78709, 512.891.6100.

Design, cover design, and composition by Greenleaf Book Group

For permission to reprint copyrighted material, grateful acknowledgment is given to the following sources:
Forbes Magazine: From "Netflix CEO Reed Hastings Blew $12 Billion in Market Cap. Why We Should Listen to Him About Education" by James Marshall Crotty from *Forbes Magazine*, May 3, 2012. Copyright © 2012 by Forbes Magazine.
Fortune Magazine: From "How Netflix Got Started" from *Fortune Magazine*, January 28, 2009. Interview by Alyssa Abkowitz. Copyright © by Fortune Magazine.

Cataloging-in-Publication data
Carucci, Ron A.
  Rising to power : the journey of exceptional executives / Ron A. Carucci, Eric C. Hansen ; foreword by Paul Maass. —First edition.
    pages ; cm
  Issued also as an ebook.
  Includes bibliographical references and index.
  ISBN: 978-1-62634-108-1
  1. Executive ability. 2. Executives — Training of. 3. Career development. 4. Leadership.
I. Hansen, Eric C., 1961 — II. Maass, Paul. III. Title.

HD38.2 .C37 2014

658.4/09   2014936357

Part of the Tree Neutral® program, which offsets the number of trees consumed in the production and printing of this book by taking proactive steps, such as planting trees in direct proportion to the number of trees used: www.treeneutral.com

TreeNeutral®

Printed in the United States of America on acid-free paper

14 15 16 17 18 19   10 9 8 7 6 5 4 3 2 1

First Edition

For

Trevor, Blythe, Chandler, Micah, Cecily,
Matthew, and Rebecca

As you rise up in life and take your rightful places in the world,
may you never forget your ultimate source of power
as you learn to use it for a greater good.

You have made us proud fathers.

CONTENTS

DESPITE THE BAD ODOR THAT CLINGS TO the very notion of power because of the misuses to which it has been put, power in itself is neither good nor bad. It is an inescapable aspect of every human relationship . . . to a greater degree than most imagine, we are all the products of power. . . . We live at a moment when the entire structure of power that held the world together is now disintegrating. A radically different structure of power is taking form. And this is happening at every level of human society. In the office, in the supermarket, at the bank, in the executive suite, in our churches, hospitals, schools, and homes, old patterns of power are fracturing along strange new lines. . . . There is strong reason to believe that the forces now shaking power at every level of the human system will become more intense and pervasive in the years immediately ahead. Out of this massive restructuring of power relationships, like the shifting and grinding of tectonic plates, will come one of the rarest events in human history: a revolution in the very nature of power.

A "powershift" does not merely transfer power.

It transforms it.[1]

—Alvin Toffler, *PowerShift*

ACKNOWLEDGMENTS

As is the case with any major writing endeavor, this has been a multiyear journey and a labor of love and sacrifice. We've been fortunate to have the good work of a wonderful team join us on this expedition.

To all our clients, past and present, for everything you've taught us about rising to power, for the private places you've invited us to step into with you, and for the exceptional way you have modeled learning to lead, we thank you deeply, and hope you find your stories in between the lines of these pages in a way that honors your rise to power.

And very special thanks to Paul Maass, for allowing your story to inspire and challenge many others to consider theirs in the Foreword. You are an uncommonly good leader, and an even better man. Your partnership and friendship are a great gift to Navalent.

An immense shout-out to a world-class editorial and research team; Mina Samuels and Michael Russell, your magic on these pages made them oh, so much better; you are delights to work with. Emily Powers, your brilliant statistical knowledge and tireless poring through piles and piles of data helped us discover and synthesize the story we wanted to tell. And Ellen Maag, your literary brilliance amplified our voices in ways we'd never have been able to do on our own—your work unquestionably made this book possible.

To our reader group—Michele, Ken, Toby, Devin, Lisa, Jeff, Evan, Gail, Josh, Susan, and Dave—thank you for your candid (sometimes a tad too blunt) feedback and the benefit of your varied perspectives, for your willingness to immerse yourself in the draft material, and, ultimately, for your amazing encouragement to help us refine the message for the world of your peers.

You are each rising to power in exceptional ways of your own, and those you lead are fortunate to have you to follow.

To the team at Greenleaf, thanks for your great partnership and belief in the project, and us, from the outset.

To our colleagues at Navalent, thanks for being the greatest bunch of co-conspirators with whom to transform the journeys of leaders and organizations.

To our wives, Barbara Carucci and LeAnne Hansen, our lives are blessed by your unconditional support, love, patience, and partnership as we do what we do in the world.

FOREWORD

AT THE END OF MY JUNIOR YEAR of college I made the decision to run for senior class president. I can't explain the reasons, but something within made me believe I could make a difference. I wanted to have an impact on my school. The odds were stacked against me. My opponent was far more known and popular. I would be the underdog. Still I felt compelled to try, knowing that if I lost, I'd have at least given it a strong try. The evening following the election (back then we took calls on the lobby pay phone), I received a call from the outgoing president telling me I'd lost. I was deeply disappointed as I hung up the phone, but not for very long, because a few seconds later he called back and said, "Just kidding—you won!" That moment of disappointment following the first call was a personal reminder of how badly I wanted to win. In hindsight I realized it is something that defines leadership for me. Fundamentally, it is something you genuinely must *desire*; it's not something you just "do."

One of my responsibilities was to raise significant funds for our senior class gift—an endowment fund to the university. Our team put extensive effort into that project, and together we raised $250,000—nearly 30 percent more than any other class had ever raised. From that experience I learned a critical lesson: Harnessing a group of people and their passion toward a common goal can bring unimaginable results, but to do so, you have to want to be more than average. You have to *want* to excel.

Nearly a quarter century later, I lead a team of more than fifteen thousand people who deliver $11 billion of revenue for ConAgra Foods each year, feeding countless millions of consumers. The journey has been full of lessons, many I wished I hadn't had to learn the hard way or that someone had advised me about before jumping in, but some lessons can only come with time and experience. I feel extremely grateful to have worked alongside amazing people who have taught me valuable lessons about leadership, with whom I have seen great achievement, and without whom my leadership would have amounted to much less. Daily, they remind me of how privileged I am.

I began my career as a commodity trader. As an individual contributor, I thrived in an environment conducive to fast, fact-based decision making and results. As a trader, you are constantly looking for risks and evaluating options. Endless calculations have enormous implications for the potential upside any given trade might yield. I had no idea how well this experience was preparing me for future leadership. I learned to see a business from end to end, understand how to weigh risks and trade-offs against opportunities, and how to make decisions in the service of a greater good. I was also fortunate to have a boss who role modeled what it meant to make split-second decisions, stand with courage behind them, and keep commitments once you make them. Those formative years were more valuable to me than I could have possibly realized at the time.

Having done well as a trader, I was invited to take on the running of a sizable portion of our trading business. I quickly learned this was a business that had been done the same way for many years. The business had underleveraged its potential over time with a static business model and I believed that changing the game could lead to significant benefits. Against a chorus of *"that's never been done before"* and *"we don't do it that way"* voices, I began the uphill climb of leading substantial change. Within a year, our revenues had grown tenfold, and within two years, they'd grown twentyfold. The profound learning for me over this period was how self-imposed constraints can cause people not to see beyond "what is" to "what could be" and the game-changing results that too often go unrealized because we so readily accept the status quo as "the way it's done."

Next, I was offered the opportunity to run the ConAgra Foods flour milling business. The business had been a revolving door for five presidents over the previous decade. Nothing much had happened to improve the business and I was told not to expect to do more than "keep the seat warm." Growing up on a farm, I learned early on that it's not OK to just be OK when it comes to work. I am fortunate that my dad instilled in me a staunch work ethic that would not let me settle for just OK. I was determined to do far more than just keep a seat warm. I would make a difference.

I do wish someone had taken me aside and said, "Paul—running a milling business is a whole lot different from running a trading desk . . ." I had to discover that on my own. Early on I realized I was spending all of my time doing nothing but firefighting. My days were an endless stream of crisis management, people bringing me problems and me dispensing solutions. I'd never taken a professional management class before then, but soon, something instinctively told me there had to be more to the job. I felt that for me to truly lead the company forward, and help it reach its full potential, I needed to devote a significant portion of my time to strategy and positioning the company to win. However, the daily grind was eating up so much of my time, it left me little time for strategic work. Yet I had been well conditioned to lead this way in my role as a trader. An endless stream of split-second decisions and problem solving—an ongoing series of calculations. "If XYZ is true, then do ABC." Of course I've since realized that leadership is anything *but* a formula. What I could not see at the time was that I was failing miserably, and without the good fortune of a comprehensive 360-degree assessment that came at the right time, I seriously doubt I would be where I am today. This far-reaching and extremely personal forty-five-page assessment revealed that I was suffocating my people. I was pulling them all toward me and as a result, driving all decisions my way. Uncertain of who I was, they were coming to me for help and I was giving them answers. I thought I was helping them to solve their problems, but they were feeling crippled by my problem solving. And worse, they were feeling alienated, as if they didn't matter, and that I was disempowering. The result couldn't have been further from my intentions, yet there it was, in black and white. It never occurred to me before that moment that it was possible, despite genuinely good intentions, for my actions and my beliefs to be completely disconnected. It was a painful moment for me, and I knew I had hard work ahead to repair what I had done, and to learn what I needed in order to be more effective running a business. That was a defining moment for me, one that changed the course of my career and the ConAgra Mills organization.

Every year I get the wonderful opportunity to spend time with younger leaders from across ConAgra Foods in one of our leadership programs and I tell them this story as they are receiving their first 360-degree feedback assessments. I remind them that inherent in any hard message is a great gift—in my case, an invitation to a future I might not otherwise have ever realized.

With a new lease on leadership and redoubled effort to fundamentally adapt to the needs of the business, I set out to drive what had historically been a static milling business toward success. Taking my lessons from the trading business, I believed that there had to be a way to drive growth and make ConAgra Mills a more relevant contributor to overall enterprise growth. Consumers had been asking for years for a product that had all the nutritional value of whole grains without the loss of the taste and texture of refined flour. More than a decade earlier, our R&D team had developed a product that could fulfill this unmet consumer demand, but it had never been commercialized. I knew if we could successfully launch it, we would have a blockbuster product, and we could change our relationships with our customers by better enabling them, in turn, to succeed with their customers. Today, this product line, sold under the brand name Ultragrain, is a far more meaningful contributor to the ConAgra Mills portfolio, and we successfully shifted our relationships from flour supplier to strategic partner. Once again, seeing potential possibilities enabled us to achieve something we hadn't before imagined, simply because we decided not to accept conventional thinking as the only way to view the future.

As I'm sure is the case with you, my career has been a collection of experiences through which I struggled and learned. Some were proud achievements and others were dismal failures. There are stories where those I led made me enormously proud and others where they frustrated the dickens out of me. Yet each successive story played an important role to prepare me for what came next. That is what leadership is. In my career and in yours, leadership is a collection of stories that both define and reveal who you are first as a person and then as a leader. The rise to power isn't a single, one-way event, but an ongoing process of learning and adapting.

Each time my career has progressed I have faced the challenge of "starting over." Each role has brought a steep learning curve with a healthy level of intimidation, but I have consciously pushed myself to begin each assignment with a posture of curiosity and "I don't know," rather than "Oh, I've got this" and "I already know." Had I taken the time to step back and been more curious about the milling business, and the dramatic difference between the role of a trader and an executive running a business, I would have avoided some of the distress I caused myself and my team.

I also learned from growing up and working on a farm that the decisions I make are mine to own. Today, I am aware that I have a CEO, a board of directors, and shareholders who must live with the implications of my decisions, and I respect their authority to trump my choices at any time. However, I have been entrusted with a role and am expected to act within the authority of my role and own the consequences of my decisions. I expect the same of those who work for me. As a result, when people come looking for me to make their decisions, even under the guise of "just getting alignment," I am quick to push those decisions back their way. The distance between alignment and permission is far greater than you may realize, and the cost of granting permission disguised as alignment comes with a hefty price when you train others to over-rely on you instead of gaining the needed confidence to own the implications of their choices. I'm happy to help, offer a perspective, challenge an assumption, but I'm not willing to suck the energy out of those I lead, deplete them of passion by unburdening them from the responsibility of their decisions, and perpetuate the illusion that it's safer to have your boss decide for you. Far from "safe," nothing could be more dangerous than to push decisions up in an organization. I suspect many of you have experienced the bitter taste of having your decision-making authority taken from you by an ego-laden boss who swelled with a sense of importance at the chance to have all the answers. Years back, I did, and I never want to be "that guy." And I certainly don't want them working in my organization!

When I promote and hire executives into my organization, I pay particular attention to two important qualities. First, I look for their level of curiosity. Those who show up with answers and a toolbox of successful solutions from their past track record ready to deploy in my organization are likely to wreak havoc. Second, I look for evidence of managerial courage. If I suspect they are someone who will overly seek my permission or approval, they won't succeed in my organization. I want to work with leaders who never stop learning, and who make and own the implications of their decisions.

When I was six years old, my mother was diagnosed with cancer. Yet she was determined to see me graduate from high school, and for years I watched her fight for that dream. It meant leaving before sunrise to travel to cancer treatments. It meant a great deal of suffering to a depth and degree I will never understand. Still, she fought for her dream, and she fought for her family. Through her force of will, she beat the odds, and watched me graduate, though she never beat her cancer. For all of those years, I had a front row seat to a master class of a leader showing me what it meant to fight passionately for something they believed in. Though I couldn't fully appreciate it at the time, I was being trained through tragedy that if you stayed focused on an outcome so important that you were willing to literally fight for your life to achieve it, that you indeed could. Fighting tenaciously for those principles and goals I most believe in has become foundational to who I am as a man and a leader. (And, yes, sometimes that same tenacity has a downside, showing up in the form of stubbornness. As they say, too much of a good thing. . . .)

Today, I am blessed with a wonderful wife and three great kids. My wife, Julie, is my "Chief Strategy and Sanity Officer" because of the tremendous sounding board she is. She listens and knows me better than anyone else. She sacrifices tremendously to enable me to do my job. As I hope is the case with you, I am ever mindful that all I get to do requires a supporting cast of many. I am a grateful man for the amazing people at my side, and whatever my weaknesses, I'm certainly not foolish enough to think I did any of this on my own.

I bet that when you look back on the story of your life, you will also vividly remember many experiences that have shaped you as a leader. You will see formative seasons where you were conditioned to view the world in a particular way, to act around certain kinds of people, to believe certain things, and to desire certain outcomes. Like mine, over time, you probably can recognize how your story has shifted and adapted. I share my story as a leader not so that you will be impressed with me, but so that you will be drawn to more deeply understand your own story, the part that has already happened, and, more importantly, the part that is still ahead. If you have recently been appointed to an executive role, you have my hearty congratulations for reaching such a worthy milestone. If you have been an executive for many years, then I hope I have at least intrigued you with the possibility that there is more to your story than you may have thought.

On the pages ahead, you will find time-tested wisdom that has been gleaned from both successes and failures of rising executives—about what it means to become an executive whose story leaves a great mark on the world around them. Read it slowly, and see the pages as a reflection of what is possible in the unwritten parts of your story that live in the months and years ahead. And as you consider this next chapter of your story, I hope . . .

> That you will discover leadership as something you genuinely *desire.*
>
> That the goals you have set are privileges worthy of harnessing the energy of others to reach and exceed, and that you inspire in them the passion to make a difference, to matter.
>
> That whatever your status quo, you not readily accept it but find healthy ways to question it enough to see beyond what is, to what is possible, and that you stretch for the game-changing results somewhere within your reach.
>
> That you will embrace the need to learn, however steep the curve, and that you remain open to what *you don't yet know* long enough to learn more than you know now.
>
> That when you look around your life, you readily see the amazing supporting cast of family, friends, and colleagues who enable you to do all you do, and that you are filled with gratitude and never take them for granted.
>
> And mostly, I hope that you see your story, which is part of a much greater collection of stories that include those you lead and the future of your organization, as a dream worth passionately fighting for.

Strive to become the kind of executive others will want to emulate and that your organization is proud to have leading—worthy of the legacy you want to leave. That is the ultimate test of your rise to power. That when finally done, the story of your leadership is revealed on the faces of passionate, courageous, curious, and tenacious leaders who've come behind you to take up the mantle of leadership, and guide your organization to heights even you never imagined. If that is the dream you have for your leadership, don't waste a minute putting off what you need to do today to make sure that's where you end up. Candidly, if you have no such dream, or if you are intending to just keep the seat warm, hoping you merely don't fail while avoiding any defining moments, joining the gravitational push of upward decision making, then I ask that you reconsider whether or not you should play the role of an executive. Too many corporations are jam-packed with such leaders and seem resigned to accept their mediocrity. Sadly, we are all paying a high price for it.

You get to decide *now* that you are *not* going to be such a leader. You get to commit to becoming an executive worthy of the trust bestowed on your role. And you get the humble privilege of making an impact on the lives of many for the years you remain leading. If that is what you desire, and I sincerely hope it is, I'm confident *Rising to Power* can help you get there.

Paul Maass, President, ConAgra Foods
Omaha, Nebraska
January 2014

PRE-FLIGHT

THE RAIN PELTED AGAINST THE windshield so hard that even the wipers on high barely created a few feet of visibility. *"How fitting that we're having a monsoon on a day like today,"* Jordan Neffron thought to himself. Many of the mourners at the graveside funeral service for Mackenzie "Mac" Jacobs—all dressed in fine attire, now soaked despite umbrellas—dropped the last of their flowers and turned to make their way toward their cars and limousines. Susanna Jacobs, Mac's wife of nearly thirty years, and their two sons, Steven, a junior at Yale, and Cameron, married with a baby of his own and working in the business, were among the last to leave.

Mac had been the Huntington Industrials CEO for nearly fourteen years. He'd started at Huntington right out of college and had grown up there. His father, Linton, had started the company when Mac was a young boy. He'd seen the company through major growth, setbacks, several key acquisitions, and changes of all kinds during those years. He'd been a fearless champion of innovation and technology and had taken some daunting risks. Some of those bets had failed, but a few took Huntington to market leadership positions in several of the categories they pioneered.

No one on the leadership team would ever forget the day Mac came into the executive conference room where his entire team waited anxiously. He didn't sit down in his usual chair. He just stood—long faced and somber. He uttered two words that brutally changed not only his but everyone else's lives: "Stage four." Everyone knew he'd been sick, and when the initial diagnosis came through, they all just assumed Mac would beat the odds like he beat everything else—with staunch determination and optimism. But tragically, that wasn't to be the case.

The dubious way this revered man's life came to such an abrupt ending, not due to the disease that ravaged him but by his own hand, only added to the tension hanging over the day's memorial activities. Mac had lived a life full of extraordinary accomplishment and goodness. To have his humanity suddenly exposed—skeletons that he had worked to keep closeted soon to be revealed—made for an unsettling eulogy. It was a rude awakening to a Mac none of them ever knew. This venerated man would now be remembered not just for his greatness, but for his failures of leadership and character as well, failures that had not yet fully come to the public's light. How the world would reconcile both remained to be seen. But one thing was sure. Regardless of whether Mac's final choice was driven by the fatigue of his physical suffering or the torture of his public shame, Jordan now had a colossal cleanup on his hands. The media, shareholders, and all of Huntington's employees would be demanding answers and accountability while the person ultimately responsible was now dead. Not the ideal way to step into a new job.

Kyle Morgan, Huntington's CFO, longtime business partner, and friend of Mac's, stood at the back of the crowd. It was uncharacteristic for him to stay separated from everyone, and he was eerily stone-faced and somber. Nobody could imagine what he was feeling, but if anyone knew what had been going on, it was him. Kyle seemed to be avoiding everyone as the crowd broke. As he headed toward the parking lot alone—not even his wife was with him at the funeral—two gentlemen in suits headed him off. From a distance it looked like he was caught off guard and impatiently wanted to take the conversation somewhere else; it was clear something was wrong. Jordan turned to Elise and quietly asked, "Any idea who those guys are?"

Watching the awkward interaction, she responded in a monotone voice, "SEC, I'd guess."

"Geesh. They don't waste any time, do they?"

Jordan had been at Huntington for about twelve years. The fair-haired boy since his arrival, Mac had groomed him for "great things," though no one thought that meant being his successor so soon. As chief marketing officer, Jordan had reinvented Huntington's brands and corporate reputation and had single-handedly been seen as the "hero" behind much of Huntington's growth over the past five years. Sentiments throughout the last week were universal. "I thought we'd have much more time with him." "How are we going to make it without him?" The one that chilled Jordan most was "Wow—those are big shoes to fill."

Now, just shy of ten months after Mac's diagnosis, hundreds drove away from his funeral wondering if Huntington's best days were now over, and if it was just a matter of time before some large competitor swallowed them in a leveraged buyout. Several of the departing mourners gathered around Jordan to wish him well, but every supportive word pushed on Jordan's flight impulse. *"Get out while you can,"* shrieked the voice in his head. *"These people all clearly think you're doomed!"* Jordan tried to find the right platitudes—"There's no way I could ever fill Mac's shoes . . . well, it's hard to come to terms with . . . I mean, we're all human . . . and . . . I know we will all pull together and make him proud. I will need your help to do it, and I know Mac . . . I know we can get the job done." The words left a bitter taste on Jordan's tongue and it was clear everyone tasted it.

Finally, the last of the mourners drove away and Jordan was left alone. The deep sadness from losing a man who had changed his life so profoundly, the terror of taking on a job he wished he'd had years more to prepare for, the excitement of the once-in-a-lifetime career opportunity, the outrage and shock at what he now had to step into, and dread of the strain he knew this would put on his family all converged in an emotional downpour. Jordan found himself standing alone in front of Mac's gravesite, immobilized and feeling an unbelievable confluence of devastation and hope.

He wept. The flood of memories of all the happy and challenging times they had shared made Jordan ache all the more. From the golf course to high-risk top-to-tops to family gatherings, he ached for the conversations that would never take place, the explanations to these painful new discoveries he would never get, and all the inevitable questions he would now have to field with no one to turn to for help.

Huntington's new leadership regime was being ushered in under brutal circumstances. While it was a group full of energy, promise, enormous talent, and a deep pride in the company that had raised them, it was also an untested team with little experience in making the big decisions and lacking the full confidence of the organization. Jordan, and the other leaders who were now arriving into roles for which they weren't fully prepared, had no idea what lay ahead. They were stepping into a chapter of Huntington's story they never could have imagined.

The reality of all of this haunted Jordan as he stood before Mac's grave. Turning to go, Jordan whispered the only thing he could think of—"I'll try not to let you down, Mac."

INTRODUCTION

WING WALKING: AN EXECUTIVE'S SUDDEN RISE TO POWER

An ABRUPT ARRIVAL INTO THE CEO ROLE, like Jordan's, with the corresponding chain reaction of elevating other executives is fast becoming the norm of organization life. According to Booz & Company's 2011 survey of the world's 2,500 largest public companies, 14.2 percent of their CEOs were replaced, a rate substantially higher than 2010's turnover of 11.6 percent.[2] And incoming CEOs are younger than ever before. A recent article on the failure rate of CEOs says:

> Two decades ago, the research examining the CEO's career path concluded that around 90 percent ended their careers due to natural causes such as retirement, lack of fitness or death. Hence, only 10 percent were unexpected. . . . Over the past few years . . . shorter, less stable incumbencies lasting between three and five years . . . [have] resulted in CEO turnover being twice that seen during times of prosperity. . . . These days CEOs are younger, less experienced, and the skills expected of them are no longer honesty and excellence but rather charisma and decisive leadership.[3]

Today executives are moving into senior and C-suite roles at an alarmingly fast pace, often under extreme circumstances and with less tenured experience than ever before. Prepared or not, organizations are placing bets on younger leaders in an attempt to achieve better strategic results. And with opportunity coming well in advance of the experience, knowledge, and relational and emotional maturity necessary to sustain success, failure rates are astounding but predictable. The costs and frequency of failed executive transitions have been chronicled by many. Corporate Executive Board, in their research, estimates that 3 percent of executive transitions "fail spectacularly" while nearly 50 percent "quietly struggle" in the first eighteen months, leading to either slow death or suboptimal effectiveness.

The ripple effect of the leader's underperformance creates significant risk and cost for the entire business. The direct reports of a struggling transitioning leader perform, on average, 15% worse than those who report to a high-performing one. And those direct reports are 20% more likely to be disengaged or leave the organization. Add to this the set of executive colleagues whose productivity suffers because they depend on a struggling transitioning leader and missed business opportunities and stalls in critical new strategies or business launches, and the negative impact can quickly balloon to tens of millions of dollars a year, or more, based on the scope and scale of the leader's role and organization. This easily dwarfs the leader's direct recruiting, onboarding, salary, and outplacement costs.[4]

"Wing walking" is the act of moving across the surface of an airplane wing while the airplane is in flight, and it is an apt metaphor for the process of executive transitions. This stunt was common in the aerial circuses of the 1920s, when people flew biplanes with struts and wires between wings that provided handholds. Still, wing walking seemed to be a lunacy to most people. But insane as it may sound, this risky stunt was not just about satisfying the needs of thrill seekers, or those who paid to see someone risk death. Beyond the entertainment value for local county fairs, pioneer wing walkers were instrumental in completing the first in-flight refueling maneuvers, advancing the cause of distance flight and modern aviation at great personal risk. Successful wing walkers all followed the cardinal rule of their art: do not let go of the wing post you're holding until you have a firm grasp of the next. Foolhardy wing walkers who ignored this rule were killed, while those on the opposite end of the spectrum failed by completely losing their nerve, clinging desperately to the first post and never risking to venture across the wingspan once in flight.

The act of transitioning to executive roles in organizations is fraught with many risks similar to those faced by the wing walkers of the 1920s. You are being watched by countless thousands. The balance of holding on, letting go, and trusting elements beyond your control are all essential to success. The stakes are high, even potentially career-fatal. The timing of each decision you make is crucial. You are likely terrified while having to look confident. And some of those watching would love to see you fail. Sadly, many executives make the same lethal mistakes failed wing walkers did. They impulsively and prematurely leap for the reins of leadership without ensuring they—or the organization—are ready. Others, paralyzed by the magnitude of the challenges facing them, freeze up and try desperately to hold on to the work they should relinquish to others, never fully embracing the more ambiguous, risk-ridden, strategic work of the role they have taken on. There are many factors underlying these two forms of executive transitional failure, and many gradations of failure between them.

Over the last ten years we have invested a great deal of effort into better understanding the emerging generation of leaders. Nearly a decade after our original research, some of the people that we studied during their earliest leadership transitions are now positioned as today's executives. And as gifted and eager as many of them are, their lack of readiness for the broad responsibilities they face suggests that, unless we radically change how we approach preparation for and appointments to executive roles, failure rates will increase.

TALES OF TRAGEDY

We've each enjoyed a rich portfolio of consulting experiences over the course of our careers, helping gifted executives take on challenging roles and make great differences, as well as watching ill-prepared executives go down in flames with needless organizational wreckage left behind.

Ron had the privilege of working alongside a young, promising executive at a global pharmaceutical powerhouse. He was the company's rising star by all accounts. He worked his way through functional assignments in finance and marketing, and found his way to leading critical business units for the pharma giant and turning them around. When the incumbent CEO of nearly two decades named him as his successor, it was a bit of a surprise given his young age, but most believed he had the talent to do the job despite having big shoes to fill. He inherited an enterprise with a track record of success in several blockbuster drugs. He began to adjust the company's portfolio of businesses to bring more focus to its core capability, selling off ancillary businesses and acquiring complementary businesses. Some early big bets didn't pay off as well, and after his first year, a few missteps had him on his heels. Patent wars, a perennial industry risk, were heating up, further exposing his lack of experience in big pharma. His demeanor began to shift. What had felt to me like a strong relationship, a rich exchange of ideas and debate, a full exploration of alternatives, and openness to feedback, including hard views of his leadership, now began to feel distant and impervious. When Ron raised this with him, he would joke and say, "Oh, you're just feeling unloved today. I'm up to my ears, give me a break." The banter felt familiar, so Ron thought nothing of it. Then bigger missteps came, resulting in federal investigations and negative press in business journals. The shadow of scandal caused him to be defensive and curt which alienated his team. Feedback became increasingly unwelcomed. The more the headlines, the analysts, and the public questioned his decisions, the more entrenched he was in his views, and the more irrational his attempts became to stem the tide with big bets. This was a side of him Ron had never seen in the years he'd known the executive. He was grasping at straws and not at all leveraging the very talents of measured leadership that distinguished him. After a tragically short tenure the board was forced to oust him in the face of allegations of misstating company financials. It was devastating to watch this promising career rise to well-deserved power and influence only to see it quickly tumble tragically in the face of strategic and competitive pressures that, ironically, he likely had the skill to successfully endure had he approached them differently.

Eric recently worked with a rising executive whose tragic demise happened in less than a full year at her new company. In addition to leading the portfolio of growth brands, she was hired away from another CPG organization to help build out an enterprise marketing capability, and to support changing the company's operating environment toward greater internal collaboration and speed in service to increased market responsiveness. Having lived it previously, she understood the strategic playbook and how to execute it well, perhaps too well! Her reputation preceded her as "one of the best marketers we've ever had" and "head and shoulders above what we've known and just what we need." However, the initial halo too soon became a noose. As she proceeded to make her leadership presence felt, and in her focus and resolve to live up to expectations, she quickly but unwittingly managed to offend and alienate most everyone she needed to help her succeed. Serious about her mandate, in meetings with senior executives where others held their tongues she voiced disagreement and suggested an alternative approach or, even more egregiously, claimed the decision authority she felt she needed to drive business results. Unfortunately, she reported to someone who was highly paternalistic and unwilling to have his expertise or authority challenged in any way. In meetings where she disagreed with peers, she openly and directly challenged—unfortunately too often unaided by relational intelligence or political savvy. Her display of what others interpreted as fierce independence and countercultural style raised eyebrows and created a strong opposing coalition. In her previous organization such behavior wouldn't have been given a second thought; however, in this organization, unfamiliar with such leadership, especially from women, it was perceived as offensive and charged as insubordinate. Her offenses were only partially redeemed by strong performances at top-to-top customer meetings and by the clear plans and growth commitments she presented. Still it was insufficient to compensate for damage already done and put her squarely in the crosshairs of powerful people. The downward spiral was in motion. By the time Eric began working with her, she had realized that things weren't working and that she desperately needed help. A strong set of feedback data confirmed the dimensions of her challenge. She listened and took them to heart, but her best efforts to acknowledge, apologize for, and act to rectify past sins was too little, too late. Superiors, peers, and subordinates had circled the wagons. Standing outside, she could see more clearly that her wounds were, in part, self-inflicted. Sadly, she had played into a leading role to help this organization successfully repel yet another attempt to introduce well-intended but poorly orchestrated change.

It is personally painful to watch such primitive behaviors play out so needlessly and far too frequently. Our deeper frustration is that the aftermath is most often avoidable. For now, the full destructive impact to this leader's emotional well-being and career remains unanswered but not unpredictable. And, the same is true for the impact to the broader organizational psyche and the wasted capacity expended in pursuit of such an outcome. Will organizations ever become places where people thrive instead of merely survive?

What's most tragic about these two stories isn't just the carnage to two careers and organizations. It's that they are not isolated. In fact, they are already too commonplace in our corporations. Instead of addressing the core, under-lying issues, we have constructed brilliant ways to normalize such failure and institutionalize leadership mediocrity that we rarely have a broader vision for much more than "as few of these as possible."

We believe *much more* is possible, and necessary. Corporations' ability to sus-tain and advance competitively advantaged positions will be directly predicated on their ability to not just minimize organizational failure, but to create organi-zational communities radically different from today's—places people can't wait to go to, where they are passionate about contributing and personally thriving, and where as a matter of routine rather than exception say, "I love working for my boss . . . best leader ever!" Cynics roll their eyes at such revelry, not having to look beyond the neighboring office or cubicle, or mirror, for mounds of organizational nonsense suggesting "this is as good as it gets."

Well, not us. Troubled by the consistent failure of executives and their transitions, and deeply hopeful for so much more success than we're seeing, we set out to better understand how to help organizations more effectively ensure executive preparation and appointments prosper more consistently. Since it is unlikely that the velocity of earlier executive career transitions will change, learning to make these transitions effectively is vital. Our research was extensive, and included two primary sources. For over a decade, we have collected diagnostic data in nearly fifty different organizations ranging in size and industry. With the help of IBM's Watson, the powerful cognitive content analysis computing system, we conducted a statistical analysis of the more than 2,600 interviews of managers to C-suite executives to identify the stron-gest correlating factors of leadership behavior on company performance. We isolated the diagnostic initiatives expressly focused on individual executives in transition to new roles, and the factors that enabled or impaired the success of transitions as experienced and reported by the executives themselves as well as twenty to thirty of their colleagues (boss, peers, direct reports) whose views were also included in the assessment. Over this longitudinal study, the factors most influential to executive performance were remarkably consistent despite changing market dynamics.

Second, we surveyed approximately one hundred executives who had transitioned to their first executive role within the last three years. We asked them to identify the factors that most impacted the effectiveness or ineffectiveness of their transition, what they wish they'd known before they assumed their new role, how their organizations had helped or hindered their transition, and how different their entering assumptions were from what they actually experienced after taking the role (see Executive Transition Survey instrument in appendix). These two sources of primary research, combined with critical secondary sources, form the basis of our conclusions.

STARTING HUNCHES

We began our research with several hypotheses about what factors influenced the success and failure of executive transitions. These hypotheses were based on decades of direct experience working with hundreds of executives and hearing their first-hand accounts of the harsh realities of their transitions. These included:

FAULTY ASSUMPTIONS
Reconciling the difference between leaders' *assumptions* of what their executive role would be like and what it was *actually like* can be brutally sobering. The grim discovery of "it isn't at all what I thought . . . nobody told me" has a hampering effect on transitional effectiveness. Often it results in early discouragement, self-doubt, regret and cynicism, and, for some executives, depression that must be masked with a face of staunch confidence. Nearly half of the respondents in our study indicated their assumptions were not realistic about what an executive role entails.

GULLIBLE EXPECTATIONS
The pressure to perform, to exhibit confidence and speed in decision making despite often high levels of ambiguity, and misconceptions about the degree of

autonomy they will have—can lead to impaired judgment, shortsightedness, feelings of isolation, and sometimes harsh treatment of self and others. "I had no idea it would be like this" is an all-too-common gripe of executives shortly into their tenure.

POLITICAL CURRENTS

Young executives often dismiss the *political implications* of life at or near the top of an organization. Some newly minted executives try to ignore or dismiss the competitive realities, the lack of transparency and trust, and the pressures to conform to certain norms. Many start out declaring they will "rise above" these factors. That is, until they actually face them. The discouraging and disorienting effect of political factors can result in insecurity, paranoia, and the endless second-guessing of self and others.

INTENSIFIED RELATIONSHIP DEMANDS

New peer sets and an almost instantaneous demand for greater emotional and social intelligence often expose previously hidden pathologies and emotional immaturity that were more easily contained in less demanding roles. Leaders often feel socially off balance and isolated. The wide-ranging implications and importance of executive relationships we heard about is reflected in our extensive discussion about them throughout *Rising to Power*.

TENSIONS OF INCREASED POWER

Finally, the realities of attaining greater degrees of *power* as executives rise can bring otherwise unseen character flaws sharply into focus. Some leaders shy away from the power they must exercise. Others indulge their power in excessive and self-interested ways. Power is a beautiful and dangerous component of executive leadership, and there is generally little in a leader's experience that prepares them to be responsible with the nitroglycerin-like properties that positional, relational, and informational power hold.

While we held these hypotheses and assumptions loosely as we began our research, we believe that the implications of such factors are the "wings" across which new executives must successfully learn to walk.

THE FLAWED DESIGN OF THE "RISING" JOURNEY

Since the dawn of the industrial revolution, organizational hierarchies have defined successful career paths in a linear, hierarchical fashion. The singular upward rise toward larger roles of increasing responsibility and power accompanied by increasing compensation has defined the corporate organizational dream for more than a century. It is a well-entrenched paradigm of how the world has defined "career." Throughout much of the twentieth century, this type of upward career path was largely predictable. The National Bureau of Economic Research documents that between 1969 and 2002, the average job tenure was about twenty years with one company suggesting that this paradigm is still alive and well.[5] While some statistics between the late '90s and early '00s suggested loyalty to companies was decreasing as seasoned leaders were more willing to defect from long tenures for better opportunities, current research from the Bureau of Labor Statistics suggests that the recent recession may be causing the reverse of this[6], with the most recent recession driving a more conservative attitude among older employees, who are beginning to "nest" in jobs. With fewer older executives willing to take career risks, it seems likely the people most willing to change jobs are younger—they appear to be our willing "wing walkers"—whereas their older peers appear to be clinging to the struts.

Many progressive organizations have tried to make multiple channels of advancement available to talented younger leaders by broadening the definitions of career paths, delineating management from technical careers, and instituting the notion of the "lateral" move to broaden aspiring executives' knowledge and experience bases before elevating them. HR systems tried to adapt as economic growth permitted increased shuffling between organizations. Unfortunately, while talent development processes have made incremental progress, compensation practices have gone the other way. The disproportionate degree of money allocated to those at the top of organizations has become an attractive nuisance for those looking to accelerate their careers. Perceived shortages of leadership talent needed to fuel global growth have persisted despite the huge pool of talented young leaders eager to find opportunities. So reflexively, they are also accelerating young leaders' upward movement into roles for which they have little preparation. In our study, 76 percent of respondents indicated that the formal development processes of their organization were not, or were at best minimally, helpful in preparing them for their executive role; 55 percent indicated that they had minimal, if any, ongoing coaching and feedback to help them refine their ability to perform in an executive role; 45 percent indicated they had minimal understanding of the challenges they would face in an executive role. The twenty-first century has ushered in an era of less experienced, younger leaders who are taking on executive roles sooner and getting paid more than their predecessors a generation earlier ever dreamed of. There is a bizarre and growing disconnect where the pipeline from the general population into the avenues of executive development in organizations seems somehow sharply narrowed. Our traditional notions of career preparation and advancement are failing us and there is a growing disconnect between readiness and expectation among new executives.

This disconnect is just one of several indicators that the definition of "rising" is dangerously flawed. The notion that executive preparation comes from a cumulative set of linear job experiences of proportionately increasing degrees of responsibility is, frankly, unsound thinking. What we learned in our research and have observed in executives for nearly three decades is that the preparation of a successful executive—the foundational requirements that separate those who can thrive at higher altitudes from those who fall off the wing—begins much earlier in life. It is the result of far richer experiences than an MBA and a solid career profile can provide. Many students of leadership are observing the dramatic shifts in how leaders are rising and the requirements for success. Bob Johnson and Rob Oberwise, authors of *Developing Global Leaders*, have concluded:

> What would constitute "high" human capital maturity? We would say it was a matter of a staff having three attributes: savvy understanding of the business, high emotional intelligence, and strong aptitude for continued learning. These would be evident in the high-potentials any multinational organization would entrust with managerial roles. And for that cohort, they would be attributes they had learned to take

for granted in their peers. . . . In fact, it is possible to get a false reading of overall maturity from a strength in any of the three areas—business savvy, emotional intelligence, or learning aptitude. For instance, employees may be unusually empathetic and communicate clearly and even eloquently, but so acculturated to showing esteem for superiors and for traditional methods that they are averse to learning new ways of doing things. Just because a workforce is mature in one category, it doesn't mean it's mature in all three ways. . . . The bad news is that global leadership training and development programs fail to prepare people to assess human capital maturity. That should change.[7]

BECOMING EXCEPTIONAL: TRANSITIONING TO AN EXECUTIVE ROLE AND THRIVING ONCE THERE

Building on Johnson and Oberwise's observations, let's consider some of the known components of executive success we have observed, and to which those we studied readily attribute the success they have realized:

- **Learning.** The world has spent billions trying to predict what will make a successful executive. Several multi-decade studies of leadership effectiveness going all the way back to Lewin, Lippitt, and White in the 1930s have revealed how a person's capacity to learn is a direct predictor of success on many fronts of leadership. The ability to adapt to new circumstances, acquire skills and knowledge, and apply these things to new demands is at the heart of learning. Entering a role with a posture of curiosity and suspended disbelief enables executives to gain critical views of their new context, not just their new role.

- **Understanding business systems.** Recognizing the need to broaden executives' systemic understanding and providing them with multifunctional experiences, choreographing a series of assignments around the organization to deepen their knowledge of how businesses truly work in an integrated and systematic fashion, has definitely enabled those leaders who've benefited from such development to succeed in broader roles because they inherently can see the interdependent nature of how one part of the organization directly affects another, factors that those within those functions are not as inclined to recognize. Additionally, they gain a much stronger appreciation for how *their* business competes and makes money, how solutions and ideas apply to *their* environments, and how to effect change more readily within the unique characteristics of their own organization.

- **Emotional intelligence.** Not surprisingly, the rise of a truly global economy has amplified the need for greater emotional and social intelligence. At the same time, the increased recognition of relational failure as a career derailer has called into question the fundamental emotional and psychological health of leaders as they assume broader roles. As *Emotional Intelligence* author Daniel Goleman says, "You can be the most brilliant innovator, problem-solver or strategic thinker, but if you can't inspire and motivate, build relationships or communicate powerfully, those talents will get you nowhere . . . 'interpersonal skills'—and what I call social intelligence—are the secret sauce in top-performing leadership."[8]

- **Character.** The decade of moral and ethical failures polluting our newspaper headlines has certainly raised the question of leadership *character* and called the fundamental definition of leadership integrity into question. Regaining and retaining the trust and credibility of the organization has become the burden of newly minted executives who are sometimes being painted with the cynical brush of distrust their predecessors earned for them.

- **Clarity of aspiration.** Simply put, the executives garnering increasing levels of power must know what they want from the experience of broader assignments once achieved. If they remain on the organization's upward conveyor belt, simply taking on the roles they are offered without deep reflection on what they desire, and what they *don't* desire, from the experience, they run the risk that their aspirations will be extrinsically formed by the organization rather than intrinsically formed by and for themselves. By default, self-protection, survival, "taking what I can get," and failure avoidance become common struts to cling to and leaders miss the opportunity to embrace the upsides and possibilities such expanded influence might bring. By contrast, a rising executive who (1) is clear on his or her personal and organizational aspirations, (2) chooses the career path that fulfills those aspirations, and (3) intentionally uses influence to achieve something greater than his or her own pursuits is far more likely to blaze a sustainable trail of executive success.

Each of these components of executive success has great merit. And each has been *individually* substantiated in management literature. As Johnson and Oberwise suggest, even great strength in any one of these at the expense of another may still result in eventual failure. What remains missing is a holistic look at how each of these elements of success *fits together* with the others. By the conclusion of *Rising to Power*, we will show you how they do, and, moreover, how in combination they can make you exceptional.

Recently, during a working session with a newly appointed general manager to a business unit of a large financial services company, the GM stopped cold in the middle of the meeting in which we were helping to design his first six months' plan. He became very quiet. After shaking his head a few times, he said,

> This sucks. I had no idea it would be this hard. I honestly thought I wanted this job. I thought I was ready for it. Now I look around and under every rock I find another mess to clean up, another challenge I feel ill prepared for. I feel like a complete imposter. And I feel like everyone is just waiting for me to tank. I don't think I've ever felt so alone or up against a wall before. People I thought had my back suddenly don't have the time of day for me. Data that seemed reasonably reliable now barely qualifies as fiction. No matter how much I try to rally people around a plausible vision for turning this thing around, they are still defecting. I've had to work most weekends just to keep up with emails and make sure people in the field stay engaged. Just what the hell did I get myself into here?

He inherited a business that was failing badly. It needed major investment, was starved for talent, its reputation in most of its market segments was gravely tarnished, and it was losing money. The board had agreed to breathe life back into the business one more time before deciding to shut it down and sell off the assets. Several market studies indicated there was still some runway left in the brand, and a few of the service lines in which they competed still had some regional advantages to exploit. In essence, though a long shot, there was still a viable business there that if turned around could be successful and even realize meaningful growth. What is fascinating is that all of this was known by this leader *before he took the job*. He was well aware of the business's challenges and struggles. He knew its leadership team was weak—he'd even advocated "cleaning house" a year earlier. When he was offered the job, he was told he would be given only limited investment resources. As he considered the position, several of his close colleagues expressed strong concerns for his career and the high probability of failure, urging him to turn it down—concerns he dismissed as overdramatized pessimism. He'd faced turnaround situations in his career, and though none this dire, he somehow felt confident he could do it. He figured that someone was going to turn it around, so it might as well be him. And he loved the idea of the challenge, knowing that if he did pull it off, it would be an instant career-maker. He wasn't arrogant about it, but rather assessed the risks as he understood them and believed they were worth taking. He even had genuine compassion for the nearly 3,500 employees of the business, some of whom had given their career to the company and deeply wanted to see it survive. He believed they deserved a shot at turning it around. His wife asked him to carefully consider the cost to their family of the three to four years he expected the turnaround to take. Again, he reassured her they could manage it, and the upside far outweighed the costs. This was the biggest opportunity he'd ever been offered, and he wasn't sure when the chance to make such a major difference would come along again.

From that side of the decision, those seemed like reasonable conclusions to draw. All things considered, it was worth going for. So why now, just three months into the assignment, did things seem so drastically different? Nothing much had changed, other than the continued discovery of just how badly broken the business was. And looking ahead at just how rocky the journey would be, he had begun to question whether it actually was all worth it.

These seismic doses of reality are dealt to newly appointed executives every day. Assumptions are upended and careers are destroyed. Intense investments in leadership development for "high potential" executives are flushed as the rising stars are put into untenable situations for which little has truly prepared them. They reach back in desperation to classroom knowledge from the executive programs and action-learning task forces, the past successes that propelled their career, or tidbits of advice they got from "mentors," grasping at any straw they can get their hands on to prevail in the face of tough and unforeseen realities.

Here is the harsh truth about executive leadership most career and leadership development literature won't acknowledge. If you aspire to executive-level work and succeed at attaining it, you will inevitably suffer. Those roles come with a substantial cost that is rarely known going in. Looking only at the upside and never considering the pain only exacerbates a leader's transitional shock once this reality is discovered. But you must equally embrace the fact that extraordinary privilege also accompanies these roles. This is not only in the perks and compensation package that come with the job, but also in the power and influence you will have to make tremendous impact on the organization and hundreds if not thousands of lives. The pain is necessary—it is the crucible that helps forge you into the executive you must become to serve the context in which you are leading. It also provides the needed humility to treat the privilege as just that. Together, the pain and privilege reveal great possibilities for both you and the organization. They combine to ensure that with those possibilities you are opportunistic without self-interest and ambitious, resilient, and able to persevere without bitterness or at others' expense.

So why, with the potential perils and costs of executive leadership so prevalent, would you ever aspire to rise to such roles? You must resolve this question above all others before you begin your ascent, lest it get answered for you haphazardly on the way up. How you answer has profound implications both for you and those you will lead. What did we learn from those who have successfully made the journey? They wanted to make the journey, and were able to withstand the cost because they had a deep desire for their lives to *matter*. They wanted to know they made a lasting difference for the people, the organizations, and the world in which they lived. And it stands to reason the higher up you go in an organization, the more lives you can impact, and the more good you can do. That certainly isn't to say those in the organization with less span of control, or even individual contributors, aren't making a meaningful difference. But leaders who rise to executive roles have the opportunity to effect sweeping, even global change for a greater good. You must be clear as you make your ascent what fingerprint you want to leave on the world on your way up. And you must reach for that vision—which is often on the other side of the wing—at all times. It must be what compels you to persevere through the opposition, risks, and setbacks that are inevitable parts of your walk across the wing. The size of your organization ultimately doesn't matter. If you are a manager of a department in a retail store with twenty employees and aspire to become the store manager with fifty employees, if you are an aspiring senior pastor of a local community church or an aspiring executive director of an NGO, if you are an assistant principal aspiring to be a superintendent of your school district, or if you are a vice president aspiring to be the CEO of a multinational corporation—the rise must have meaning for you. Maintain a clear line of sight to the difference you are hoping to make, and hold fast to that dream as you face the costs of the rise to power. Your life as a leader will matter not to the extent that you garnered power and its perks, but to the extent you used it to effect remarkable good in the lives your broad influence reached.

If you can accept these truths as part of the journey toward executive leadership, then you have a much better chance of success. The transition to executive leadership, regardless of the circumstances under which it happens, does not have to be devastating or debilitating, as we saw in the story above. That is not to say there is a panacea out there to ensure smooth, undisruptive transitions of ease and glory. Hardly. There will be unexpected struggles and moments that will test the limits of your character, knowledge, and emotional fortitude. Making a far-reaching difference as an executive always comes with such a cost. You must see it as a journey worth fighting for. We do. After decades of walking across the wing with executives, and because of the hundreds of executives whose transitions we've studied, we are certain that greater success navigating transitions to executive roles and succeeding in realizing your dream of lasting impact is far more attainable than the current results indicate.

And for the remainder of this book, we're going to show you why.

RISING TO POWER

Instead of addressing the elements of executive success one at a time, we've put all the pieces *together* and present an integrated picture of success. *Rising to Power* provides a comprehensive profile of what makes an exceptional executive who can assume broader leadership roles at an accelerated pace and effectively use the power inherent in the role for broader good. It also offers a way to navigate the otherwise perilous factors that derail someone's transition into an executive role. One very important note about the concept of *transition*: for the purposes of this book, it is not defined as a one-time event. In fact, treating it as such is part of the problem. Transition, for us, means an ongoing adaptation of one's leadership, one behavioral choice at a time, to the context and circumstances in which one is leading. Keep that in mind as you read on.

This book is divided into four sections that help organize what we've learned through our practice as well as our research. Section I, *Ascend*, looks at the disorientation, or altitude sickness, which too often afflicts executives as they arrive in top leadership roles. We'll look at the different levels of organizations and how they work interdependently. We will distinguish the Strategic system, where executives must lead, from the more execution-focused work of the Coordinating system, which executives must learn to let go of in order to fully embrace executive leadership. Section II, *Adjust*, offers a concrete blueprint for planning your shift to the Strategic system—how to enter and rise within an organization—distinguishing the new altitude from the former. We also examine the typical distortions we hear about most frequently from our research participants—how data and information get sifted and how challenging it becomes to get others to share honest feedback, how relationships shift with new and former peers, and how time horizons and systemic perspectives must change from this new perch.

In Section III, *Assert*, we look closely at what kinds of influence get extended at the executive level, and the typical abuses and perversions of power that lure executives. We study what the productive use of power requires and offers. And, we look at some of the unrealistic expectations followers often have of leaders, including perfection, equity and fairness, transparency and justification, clairvoyance, accessibility, inspiration, and hope.

We will readily acknowledge that the first three sections of the book may feel sobering—a "realist" vs. "idealist" view of rising to power. Our intent isn't to paint a dismal picture of executive transition, but an honest one. If you can steel your way through, we're confident that the noble promise of the rise to power will be that much more inspiring in the concluding section.

Finally, Section IV, *Affect*, looks at the lasting impact executives can have. We offer what we believe to be the holistic blueprint of what executive effectiveness requires—the exceptional executive—and we will distill from our research a profile of what an effectively transitioned executive looks and acts like. We also look at what is required to sustain executive effectiveness at the highest altitudes in organizations and explore how organizations must systemically build systems that proliferate exceptional executives. Figure 1.0 illustrates the journey on which *Rising to Power* will take you.

We've organized these concepts in a user-friendly, practical way so you can quickly apply them to wherever you are in your transition. Don't read the structure as a "formula" for transition or executive effectiveness. Read it with the unique context of your own journey in mind. Use the parts that are most

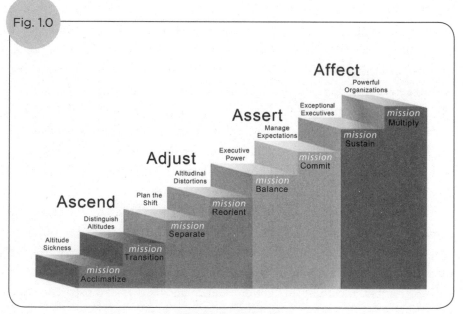

Fig. 1.0

The rise to power

helpful and set aside the parts that don't apply now. We have protected the identity of our friends and clients in rich, detailed cases in order to fully illustrate the concepts we are exploring while not indicting or exploiting anyone. And along the way, we will revisit the newly appointed executives at Huntington Industrials, the fictitious company we described earlier in this introduction. Huntington Industrials is an archetype that represents patterns revealed in our research and consulting experience, and is meant to vividly show you executive "rising" in action—serving as a mirror of sorts. It is not an allegory or parable—merely our way of illustrating what we think. The characters, the challenges, and the flawed and ingenious choices and behaviors are all very real. Our hope is that by being drawn into that story, you will in turn be drawn safely into your own story for the purposes of learning, discovery, and the possibility of transformative change.[9]

Welcome to your journey toward exceptional.

IN FLIGHT

JORDAN ENJOYED THE EMPTY PEACEFULNESS of Huntington's parking garage at 6:30 in the morning. He'd started arriving this early when he'd become CMO—it was the best time to catch some private time with Mac. Now he arrived alone. The only adjustment to his routine was the time he now spent looking in his rearview mirror at Mac's empty parking spot. Just as he couldn't quite bring himself to move into Mac's office, he also hadn't been able to take down Mac's name on the revered parking spot and replace it with his own.

Finishing up in the washroom, Jordan zipped open his leather Tumi bag—Mac had given everyone on the executive team one—and took out a prescription bottle. "Three months ago it took an act of Congress to get me to take an Advil. Now look at me!" An avid runner and health enthusiast, Jordan was always baffled by how people allowed themselves to become hooked on prescription sedatives, justifying their choices with excuses like, "I just need them to cope for now. I can stop anytime I want." After the last few months, he had deeper sympathy, having told himself he would stop after the intense stress and mayhem of the transition was over.

As Jordan sat down at his old desk he began looking over the report, now in its fifteenth draft, being prepared for the board on the SEC investigation. His elbows rested on piles of documents awaiting his signature, responses to questions people were asking on various strategic initiatives, approvals being sought, and a variety of other business awaiting his attention. Most of it was probably stuff that never should have hit his desk. But Mac's proclivity to "get into the details" had trained the organization to escalate more issues and decisions than was necessary or helpful. Retraining the organization to think and act more independently would be one of the many challenges Jordan would have to contend with as he established his own CEO voice.

He recalled the mandate he'd been given at the board meeting two months earlier. "First, get us out of this SEC mess with as little PR damage as you can. Just tell the reasonable truth, pay the damned fines, and move on. Second, make sure we have no unwanted defections. We need everyone on board and can't afford any distracting exits now, especially of our key people. We want people feeling confident, despite the blow that we know Mac's death dealt. And finally, close the Newrizon deal, and try and do it before any of this other crap hits the newspapers." No small task, he thought to himself, as he cynically remembered feeling like the underlying message was, "Do what we tell you, don't screw it up, and we'll have your back."

Jordan's reverie was interrupted by Kyle Morgan, the guy the SEC had been talking to at Mac's funeral. Kyle had become Huntington's CFO soon after Mac himself had joined and was Mac's go-to advisor on most decisions—for good reason. He was a brilliant CFO and businessman and he and Mac had had a close bond. Jordan knew he would never have that same relationship with Kyle and, given Kyle's role in the earnings restatement that had attracted the SEC's interest, he wasn't sure he cared or if he even wanted Kyle to stay at Huntington. Jordan wondered if receiving Mac's dedicated attention, and being declared the "heir apparent" so soon in his Huntington run, had made Kyle envious. Had the CFO wanted a shot at the throne and never gotten it?

Sailing into Jordan's office, Kyle didn't waste time with a greeting. "Jordan, have you looked at those Newrizon numbers yet?" he asked impatiently. He glared at the pile of papers on Jordan's desk that he assumed held the data in question.

"Uh, yeah, I've taken a first pass through them but I'm not quite finished—I had some questions. . . ." Jordan stumbled through his response, knowing full well he wasn't convincing Kyle that he'd even opened the file despite the fact he had—Kyle's eye roll gave that away.

"Look, Jordan, I'm trying to be patient here, cutting you some slack after all . . . well, all that's happened. But you know there's a lot riding on closing this deal at the right price point, and Newrizon is expecting your direct involvement in negotiations. If you aren't prepared, they'll know it. We really need your head in the game here, man."

Jordan couldn't help being a tad defensive. "My head IS in the game, Kyle, you don't need to worry about that. You'll have my input back on your desk tomorrow morning. Now if you'll excuse me . . ."

"That's what you said last week, Jordan, and it didn't happen then either," Kyle interrupted abruptly.

Offended by the blatant disrespect, Jordan stood up. "Look, Kyle, I get that you're frustrated, and I'll admit I'm not quite as caught up as I want, but that's no excuse for not showing me the same respect you showed Mac. I deserve at least that. Now if you'll let me get back to what I was doing, I can make sure that tomorrow . . ."

"Deserve??" Kyle blurted out. "Listen Jordan, just so we're clear, you don't deserve *this job*, much less a fraction of the respect Mac earned. I get that he anointed you, so we're all going along with the plan here because the board has backed you. But what we're all waiting for is for you to actually start *doing the job*. You've been walking around here moping for almost three months now while everyone is desperate for someone to lead. In case you haven't noticed, you're not the only one that's dealing with Mac's death, and the aftermath of it. You don't get to crawl into a cave until you *feel like* leading. You need to step up. If you want to earn the respect of a CEO, then start being one."

As he reached the door, Kyle stopped. "Oh, and one more thing." He pulled a document out of his pocket while he walked back toward Jordan's desk. Slamming it down, he said, "You might want to tell your personal pharmacist with all the tattoos not to park his motorcycle in the visitor's parking spot when he makes your deliveries. I'd suggest you have him bring those to your home. With everything this company's been through, we don't need any more drama." Tapping the document he'd slammed down, he finished, "Get it fixed." And with that, he stormed out.

Jordan looked down at the document in his shaking hand and read, "Huntington Employee Assistance Program." Uncertain whether to be enraged or terrified that his inner struggle was exposed, all of the words he wished he'd said to Kyle came flooding to his brain.

"Who the hell are you to tell me to do MY job? Where were you a year ago when Mac started inflating our earnings to drive up our share price, huh? Thinking he was doing us all some kind of favor to avoid having the analysts downgrade us when he died? I'll tell you where you were, you bastard, you were helping him do it!!! The SEC has all of the documents, all of the proof that you helped with the scam. YOU SIGNED THEM, you moron! And you have the balls to question whether or not I'm doing MY job?"

"You winning?"

Jordan was jarred out of his fantasy.

"Excuse me, Carolyn?" he said.

"I said, are you winning? Every time I come in here, you're having some argument in your head with someone. I just hope you're winning." Her concern was genuine. Whatever Kyle had said had clearly rattled Jordan. She said in her spry, warm way, "Mac never would have picked you if he wasn't absolutely sure you could do it. You don't have to be him. He would want you to be better than him. At one time or another every person on this floor will challenge, frustrate, and irritate you. He let it roll off his back, and you'll learn to do the same. You're a good man, Jordan—we all know it.

We believe in you because we know Mac did. Mac never lost sight of the passion he had for Huntington, or the difference he knew he could make for our people, customers, *and* industry. You can fill Mac's shoes, but you have to fill them in your own way. Everyone knows you can make an extraordinary difference here. Do you believe that? What do you want it to be? Figure that out and you'll be fine." Carolyn paused for a moment and then said, "Now take a breath, get some coffee, and shake it off. The lawyers are waiting for you in the conference room."

SECTION I

ASCEND

CHAPTER ONE

ALTITUDE SICKNESS

ACCLIMATIZING TO THE REALITIES
OF EXECUTIVE LEADERSHIP

THINNER AIR AT THE TOP

ACUTE MOUNTAIN SICKNESS IS THE TERM USED to describe the debilitating impact of high altitudes on the human body. The scientific reason is clear: as you ascend, the atmospheric pressure decreases and the air is actually thinner. One breath at this altitude delivers one-third less oxygen to your bloodstream, which diminishes both mental acuity and physical agility. Shortness of breath, flu-like symptoms, and something akin to a drunken stupor—including disorientation, torpidity, and clumsiness—are common effects of altitude sickness. Persistent exposure left untreated can result in more serious and potentially fatal complications.

The onset of altitude sickness is primarily driven by the rate of ascent in combination with the altitude attained. The best safeguard is a slow, deliberate climb, giving the body time to adjust to decreasing oxygen levels at higher elevations in order to avoid altitude sickness. This methodical process of altitude acclimatization cannot safely be rushed, and it is the reason experienced climbers spend significant time on a mountain preparing before attempting to conquer the most challenging peaks.

The parallels to overly accelerated organizational ascents are obvious. Leaders who climb rapidly to the summit of an organization often suffer from similar disorienting and debilitating symptoms. Whether it's a physical or career summit, those who ascend too rapidly ultimately cry out, "Help me, I can't breathe!" Jordan's newfound reliance on meds is just one example.

Everyone who travels to high altitudes is at risk of acute mountain sickness, but part of the mystery of the illness is predicting who will become affected and to what degree. Expedition journals recount many instances of apparently fit and healthy climbers becoming severely impaired by high altitude symptoms, while their less fit and older companions remain largely unaffected. This is true for career summits as well. Predicting who and how individuals will respond in the rarified air of the executive suite is only partially a function of technical preparation but must also consider psycho-emotional and behavioral preparatory factors as well.

THE HIGHER THE RISE, THE HARDER THE FALL

A few years ago, we worked with a highly talented and well-respected marketing executive who was a rising star in every regard, but one who ultimately failed to acclimatize and then fell ignominiously from her perch atop one of America's prominent consumer packaged goods organizations. She was aggressively recruited directly from college by highly respected consumer-brand businesses, ultimately choosing to go to what she proudly referred to as "THE premier global marketing company." Her career certainly benefited from the technical development offered there, but she further distinguished herself early by coupling the training with her natural, intuitive understanding of the power of brands and how to build them. She proved time and again that she had insight into the consumers she served and showed particular brilliance at pulling the right levers to influence purchase behavior and drive consistent increases in financial performance in whatever business she touched. With a strong support infrastructure in place, she created an admirable track record of success, rising steadily through the ranks to claim a vice president role over a global brand portfolio at a relatively young age. Then, after a few years of success in this position and a remarkable turnaround of one of her struggling portfolios, she became impatient. Sure that her ambitions would not be met on the timeline she wanted, and not one to wait for opportunity, she set out to find her next career summit.

She soon found herself with a president's title and responsibility for a product portfolio that generated the majority of enterprise revenue and profits at another premium consumer packaged goods organization. Her reputation preceded her. Many assumed she would be a marketing messiah. As it is for most executives, the organization initially gave her the benefit of some time to assess the business and make needed adjustments. Even with that benefit, however, she soon started to gasp for air. It quickly became apparent that the organization she inherited didn't think about marketing in the same way she did. And, for all the brilliant ideas she offered, her people pushed back claiming that those things may have worked at her *prior company*, but they certainly wouldn't work *here*. The markets, consumers, and distribution channels operated from a different set of assumptions, each presenting a set of less familiar complexities to manage. The business operated at an unusual pace that felt frustratingly sluggish, but no one else seemed to notice. The functional structure denied her access to many of the levers she had previously been able to pull on directly. Access and decision making now required partnering with peers in unfamiliar and uncomfortable ways. She recommended restructuring to address it, but the substantive changes she proposed were ultimately diluted. This company had an illustrious history of effectively engaging their consumers, with an abundance of advertising awards to prove it, and they didn't need an outsider stepping in, so her attempts to gain traction early by offering a perspective on advertising strategies were politely acknowledged but largely ignored. And finally, she concluded that much of the talent she inherited was substandard. She rectified this a bit by bringing some of her own people in. For some this was a welcome development, but for others it felt superior, judgmental, and unappreciative. The more she asserted herself, the more passivity turned into subversive resistance.

Disoriented by the new surroundings, her initial enthusiasm and confidence devolved to frustration then panic and eventually settled on overt contempt toward the organization. She had too little oxygen in her new environment, and little in her past experience had prepared her for it. The pressure was on her to reverse the chronic, downward top- and bottom-line performance trend, but little felt familiar or natural in the new organization. With the mandate looming over her and everyone expectantly watching, but few stepping in to really help, she became overtly directive and dogmatic. She brought outside resources in to help and demanded that others listen and do it her way. She had turned around a floundering business before and she would do exactly the same here! Instead of partnering, she criticized. Instead of developing, she fired a few more people—a clear shot over the bow to emphasize expectations. Each of her actions served to further alienate her team and isolate her.

The rest of this story is predictable, with each side overestimating what was possible and underestimating what was required—especially for one person. For those who were resentful or lacked faith when she entered, she effectively proved them right. She failed to learn the business because she didn't ask and they didn't volunteer to teach her and give her the benefit of their institutional knowledge. She drew premature conclusions about the new business and its needs, based on her prior experience, without really understanding its relevance in this different context. She was clear that turning the business around was her mandate, but she mistakenly assumed the answer was to *replicate* and not *adapt and apply* her past experience. The promise of possibility ended prematurely and left both an organization and the leader worse for the experience. This is an all-too-common story of rapid ascent and failure that this book is intended to help prevent.

SUMMIT SHOCK: RECONCILING IDEALS WITH REALITY

Many rising executives feed on the adrenaline, affirmation, and increased privileges of upward mobility and advancement. The reality for most people, though, is that the uncertainty associated with most change creates degrees of discomfort most of us generally try to avoid. Whenever we decide to take an advancement opportunity, it is typically because our current level of satisfaction is less than the perceived net satisfaction—including any stretch or pain—associated with the change. In order to effectively cope with anticipation of the pain associated with change, humans rely on idealization.

Idealization is a cognitive-emotional process that calms your anxieties and steels your confidence to move forward with a decision by focusing on, reinforcing, and even exaggerating the positive qualities and potential of our choices. We amplify the list of benefits of our future opportunity while downplaying any known or potential negatives. Further, ascending executives too often underestimate the actual work required to be successful in the role to which they aspire. They often see the incumbent as incompetent and assure themselves comparatively that "it can't be that hard if he's doing it!" In this way, they choose to discount what they *do* understand as the demands of the role and its associated challenges while assuring themselves they can overcome and conquer them, too often underestimating the actual degree of difficulty.

In research studies conducted in the late 1950s, Leon Festinger[10] introduced the term *cognitive dissonance.* He concluded that humans possess a powerful motive to maintain cognitive consistency that can ultimately trigger irrational and sometimes maladaptive behavior. According to Festinger, we each hold varying attitudes, opinions, and beliefs about the world and ourselves; when they clash, a state of tension known as cognitive dissonance occurs, and because the experience of dissonance is unpleasant, we are motivated to reduce or eliminate it.

This idea plays a big part in what happens when we move into a new role and reality comes crashing in. Things rarely turn out to be as we initially envisioned. And, while some show an uncanny ability to live in denial for protracted periods, at some point you must inevitably confront and reconcile your preconceived notions with reality. Cognitive dissonance refers to a situation involving conflicting attitudes, beliefs, or behaviors that produce feelings of discomfort that ultimately lead to a modification of one or more of the factors to restore balance.

To better understand how people manage the tension of dissonance, Festinger studied members of a particular cult that believed that the earth would be destroyed by a flood at a specified time. He was interested to know the effect on cult members when the flood did not happen as predicted. The study concluded that, while fringe members were inclined to acknowledge that they had made fools of themselves and chalk it up to experience, those who were really committed to the cause—meaning those who had given up their homes and jobs to work for the cult—were more likely to reinterpret the evidence to support their beliefs. They rationalized that, in fact, the flood was avoided and the earth was not destroyed because of the profound faith of the cult members.

As you ascend you will experience some degree of dissonance, so you must expect and prepare for it. Healthy dissonance presents itself as nervous energy and small nagging doubts: "Can I do this?" "What have I gotten myself into?" "How will they react to me?" or "What if . . . ?" Well understood and productively harnessed, these thoughts and their accompanying emotions can serve to sharpen your learning edge, heighten your energy level, and elevate your effectiveness as you navigate upward. These same thoughts left to fester, however, may trigger a host of counterproductive internal narratives and unproductive, even self-destructive, behaviors. Every leader is susceptible, so you must expect and prepare yourself for that moment when you are confronted by the reality that all you had initially imagined about your new role is, in fact, not the complete story. Your dreams of the accolades, economic gains and perquisites, opportunity for broader visibility, influence and impact, and the idealization of interacting with powerful people must inevitably yield to the honest realization that this role you aspired to is often an unforgiving and punishing job with challenges and limitations you are not fully prepared to deal with. You are well compensated precisely because it is more complex, demanding, and even overwhelming. This reconciliation, while uncomfortable, is healthy. It is the first test of leadership at this elevated altitude.

But, as you work to distinguish fact from fiction, just know that you will feel some combination of surprise, dread, guilt, betrayal, anger, and even hostility. You may find yourself thinking things like, "I knew the business was struggling, but I didn't think it was *this* bad," "The depth of talent is shallow, how can they expect me to succeed when this is all they have to offer," "I know what I'm talking about, so why don't they pay more attention to what I tell them," or "Why weren't they honest with me about how aggressive the objectives and timelines would be?" As you assume your new position, you may face other unexpected circumstances. For example, you may be succeeding a highly venerated leader who retired or, worse, was fired. Or, as in Jordan's case, an admired leader who has left a messy legacy. The leader's departure and the feelings of others about them cannot be easily dismissed or bypassed, and you must deal with the aftermath. Or, you may find yourself in the position of establishing a precedent-setting role. At first the "blank sheet" may seem appealing, but building credibility and rewiring an organization to understand, accept, and effectively use a brand new role or function comes with its own set of land mines to navigate. Regardless of the challenges you uncover as you begin to acclimatize to your new role, remember that all eyes are on you as you make your opening moves.

Depending on your particular circumstances, your instincts may be to criticize and assign blame, as happened with the marketing executive. While you may be justified, resist these urges. Your first impulse will likely be to find external explanations for the anxiety you feel—someone else to blame. However, your first impulse should be to examine your *own* assumptions for flaws.

Ultimately, you can't ignore reality and hope to be successful. You must actively consider how your preconceived notions about the job are constricting your ability to function at this altitude. Consider this your first test and succeed by maintaining as much objectivity as possible. Executives can navigate through this disorienting phase using a simple journaling exercise we call, "*What? So What? Now What?*" illustrated in figure 1.1 below. Throughout the first six to nine months in your role, you will continue to encounter things that surprise and potentially fluster you. By identifying and documenting them, you can effectively avoid more potentially irrational and destructive thoughts that can trigger less productive responses. The act of getting them out into the open and putting them on paper will enable you and others to more reasonably assess and address them. Resist the impulse many organizations impose to complete a "ninety-day transition," dangerously implying that once three months pass, all you need to know will be known.

Fig. 1.1

What did I believe/assume?	What do I now know to be true?	What are the implications?	What are reasonable, available options to move forward?

Journaling Outline for First Six Months

MANAGING SUMMIT SHOCK: HOW TO ACCLIMATIZE

MONITOR YOUR INTERNAL MONOLOGUE ON ARRIVAL

As you arrive at the next career summit, an important first shift is to consciously assess the stories you are telling yourself about why and how you got here. This is vital because how you think about yourself in your new role will trigger the behaviors by which you'll be judged and that will ultimately drive your success or failure.

Muhammad Ali, known for his sense of confidence and ability to turn a memorable phrase, used a simple but consistent personal tagline: "I am the greatest." And he believed it. Those who were alive during the years of his dominance in the ring only have to hear that phrase to be reminded of the former heavyweight champion. Urban legend holds that once, while traveling by plane, Ali was asked by a flight attendant to put on his seatbelt. He replied, "Superman don't need no seatbelt!" to which the attendant wisely said, "And Superman don't need no airplane! Put on your seatbelt please." In a similar way, many rising executives also tell themselves a hero's tale, falling victim to the Superman Syndrome.

If the story that consistently runs through your mind tells you that "I deserve this! I earned this! They are lucky to have me because I have the answers!" then you are setting yourself up for exhaustion and ultimate failure. Left unmanaged, your burden will soon become the self-imposed mandate to single-handedly fix all problems, repeatedly proving your value through endless heroic rescues. Taking on everything is a recipe for failure. Your delusions of grandeur will deceive you into believing that your knowledge and skills are indispensable and are the wellspring from which every success will be realized. That, in turn, causes you to spread yourself too thin, disappointing yourself and others when you can't deliver. Further, it causes you to resent those you lead and weakens their abilities. You end up creating unhealthy codependency by convincing them they can't succeed without you. When you try to be more than you are, you end up being much less than you could be. Yes, fools still rush in, and both you and Ali still need an airplane.

Another story that may surface says, "I'm lucky. Someone gave me a shot, but the rest of the world isn't convinced I deserve this role." Despite clear evidence of competence and legitimate accomplishment, the Imposter Syndrome is a psychological phenomenon in which people are convinced that they are frauds and do not deserve any success they achieve. The tapes in their head cause them to live in fear that others will find out what they secretly believe about themselves, namely, that any success they achieve is through luck, fate, or as a result of deception—somehow they've hoodwinked others into believing they are more intelligent and competent than they believe themselves to be. Burdened with this narrative, executives set out to repeatedly prove to others they deserve to be there. They set impossible standards for themselves and their team to prevent others from discovering "the truth." Their drive and relentless perfectionism leads to more praise and success, which increases personal feelings of fraud and heightens the fear of being "found out." This often leads to feeling disoriented and can result in a loss of confidence.

We refer to these stories as people's *operative narratives*. We delve into this concept in greater detail in chapter 4. For now, it is sufficient to understand that these operative narratives— the stories we tell ourselves about our situation and our personal strengths and failings—have a profound impact on how we show up and react to the challenges and opportunities we are given.

There are countless narratives that create distorted thinking and drive destructive behaviors as leaders reach higher organizational altitudes. If, in your mind, you're tasked with a mandate to fix something, then everyone and everything suddenly appears broken and you must fix them. If you feel compelled to prove your value, then everyone and everything becomes evidence of your success or failure and you will impose your will upon the organization to drive success and eradicate any evidence of your failure or imperfection.

The point is not to name every possible unproductive narrative, but to challenge you to discover yours. Effective acclimatization requires that you become aware of both your internal narrative and its origin in order to productively address and shift it when necessary. In fact, your safe zone and compelling narrative must become, "I'm here to perform in service to larger organizational goals. I'm here to become the best (fill in the blank) I can be and to help others do the same." You must be willing to remove yourself from the center of the story, and stand apart from your role long enough to ascertain what is needed by the enterprise.

With genuine understanding comes an ability to honestly assess what you bring to the role. Don't simply amplify and play to those things you're good at; figure out how to get good at those you're not. Truthfully assess the story and what is required before you start subconsciously responding to tapes that may or may not be relevant or accurate.

CHANGE THE ALTITUDE OF WHAT YOU SEE AND THINK

Take time to survey the landscape from your new vantage point, and make sure you have clearly identified the relevant variables to include as you shape your perspective. The situation that faced the General Motors executives following the successful introduction of the Saturn brand is a nice illustration. Based on the initial success of the Saturn brand, many mid-level executives assumed that if one plant was good, two might drive even more profitability. They set out to repeat this success story. From their vantage point they defined car manufacturing as their domain, and they had successfully proven their ability to compete on different terms. Meanwhile, the executives above them recognized that, in fact, the margins on auto manufacturing and sales were slim and shrinking, irrespective of the Saturn success. These higher-level executives began to think more broadly about their business and to consider alternative paths to growth and profitability. They concluded that the best opportunity was not in manufacturing but in after-market sales. They enlarged their definition of the economic neighborhood to personal transportation and chose to invest instead in satellite technologies from which GM's OnStar annuity was born. While not necessarily related to a new role or the arrival at a higher altitude, the senior leaders in this example took the time to reflect on and understand their situation before making a determination of the right variables to consider in shaping their decisions and actions.

RESIST THE MYTH OF THE MANDATE

As you assume greater levels of power and influence in the organization, you should expect your view of the business and of the competitive landscape to shift commensurately. For many, the increasingly vast view can be overwhelming and difficult to assimilate. Instead of looking up and out, they habitually look down and back. They find it difficult to set aside the comfort and control of the familiar, more constrained view of their former roles, and instead tend to act as if their new role is a mere extension of what they used to do. Hiring managers are too often complicit in this. Instead of pushing to set a broader future vision and higher expectation during the interview process, they reinforce the candidate's history of accomplishments, consciously or unconsciously setting the expectation that repeating the past will lead to success in the future. This is often compounded by apparent urgent circumstances as executives are appointed—"Our supply chain is badly in need of retooling and you've done it before" sets the trajectory of failure in motion. Is it any surprise then that many leaders tend to do what they have previously done and unleash their prepackaged solution on a problem they've yet to understand? Armed with a familiar set of tactics (and some new talent they choose to bring with them) they move forward, intent on execution with little to no consideration for the broader context or nuances. Admittedly, some are successful—for a time. However, too often we see newly promoted executives fall short or completely fail as they attempt to apply past success to new problems. Instead of identifying and carrying forward the principles that can be adapted and applied to new situations, they rely on tools and techniques that don't apply, becoming confused and often belligerent when they don't work. What was once a rewarded skill may not be what is necessary for success in a different context and, in fact, may be a liability. Healthy collaboration in one environment is weakness and indecisiveness in another. Managerial courage in one company plays out as self-promoting individualism in another. Context is everything. If you prematurely apply past approaches in vastly different contexts, you could quickly run headlong into organizational organ rejection before you know it.

Counterintuitive but effective advice for rising executives is to not assume your new role too readily. Instead, take deliberate steps away from the previous role you held. Purposefully let go of what you know and are most comfortable with. Deliberately identify the lenses that will be helpful to you to do this, as well as the blinders that may hinder you in the future. Do this by spending the first six to nine months learning about the broader business, and practice setting aside your functional or business unit biases. If you have been promoted to be the head of Sales, make a concerted effort to spend sufficient time learning about supply chain, finance, innovation/research and development, and human resources. Trust that Sales will continue to run largely as it has in the past, and trust that the time you spend focused away from your new role will pay dividends toward your future success. Let what you learn about and from new peers shape how you define and exercise your role. Focus on understanding what is important to them and understand how their roles impact the top and bottom line. Identify and make notes about assumptions they hold that may be flawed. Then, over time, find ways to partner with them and jointly set your sights on new heights to conquer.

If you discover that you are, or have become, inwardly driven by a sense of marching orders—self- or organizationally imposed—take a moment to untangle yourself from it long enough to recalibrate what you actually believe you are here to accomplish. Be direct. Call the question with whoever hired or promoted you to reset expectations for what you will and won't accomplish. Disconnect your track record of success from the current situation. If there is any notion swirling in your or others' minds about repeating that success here, make it crystal clear that you have no intention of attempting duplication. Instead, let people know that while there is wisdom to be gained from successful experiences that may have *some* similarities, this is a different context that you must deeply understand before knowing precisely how aspects of your past successes may apply. Invite them to join you on the learning journey to discover exactly how to adapt your collective past experiences and what part you and they must play together to win.

REFLECTIONS ON THE RISE

1. What "mandate" do you feel you brought to your role? What operative narrative is reinforcing your compulsion to follow it?

2. How have you seen other successful leaders transition particularly well into more senior roles?

3. How can Jordan best respond to the three board mandates he's been handed? And what narratives of his are interfering with his ability to respond?

EXTEND YOUR SENSE OF TIME AND EMBRACE COMPLEXITY

The fact is, as your role complexity increases—as the set of variables to consider and manage expands—the time horizon for realizing results will also increase. This is just one of the foundational adjustments in thinking that you must make as you rise. The accelerating dynamics of an increasingly global marketplace and advancements in technology both play into this. With all these variables, the ability to make long-term bets for future prosperity and delay gratification becomes your new reality. This can be unsettling. Not only does it place greater importance on your conceptual abilities to identify patterns and proactively plan in the face of longer, more ambiguous timelines, but it also reduces the immediacy of validation to which you've become accustomed.[11] One respondent appropriately expressed this frustration: "The demand for unrealistically immediate results can cause you to lose perspective. I often get mixed messages on the desired speed of change. The number of variables influencing a decision, including the number of people who want a say, can be mind-numbing."

Each level of leadership in all organizations contributes uniquely and substantively toward the success of the enterprise. The major difference is the relative time frame within which their direct impact is realized. Supervisors and managers typically realize the consequences of their actions within days, weeks, or a few months. The time frame for functional leaders and directors may increase to as much as a couple of years as they make efforts to improve the performance and impact of their respective areas. Those at the very top of the organization, however, are making calculated bets the impact of which won't be realized for multiple years into the future. This is a critical adjustment that has crippled many rising executives. The sense of, and need for, immediacy that they carry forward from lower-level roles is frequently detrimental to how they lead. This immature need for immediacy, commonly compounded by their drive to prove themselves with "quick wins," often manifests itself in unproductive impatience and a drive to push the organization for results within unrealistic time frames. In the next chapter, we'll look at the different levels in an organization, and describe the strategic altitude, or system, to which leaders must acclimatize. Jim Collins espoused the concept of the "Big Hairy Audacious Goal" in his bestseller *Built to Last* and talked about visionaries like Henry Ford, who pursued a dream methodically for years to establish a winning product that dominated its market. Doug Ducey of Cold Stone Creamery was inspired by the idea but wanted to do it in a shorter term. He grew Cold Stone from a regional ice cream franchise of 74 stores in 1999 to 1,000 profitable stores by 2004. Stories like these fire up young executives eager to make their mark.[12] But look up Cold Stone today and you'll find that the company only had 1,100 locations in 2011. A 2008 *Wall Street Journal*[13] article and a 2011 CNBC investigative report[14] both looked at the high failure rate of Cold Stone franchises. The moral here is to think not just about the audacious goal you want to achieve, but how you will live with it if you actually get it. Quick wins can be as much of a curse as a blessing.

Suffering from organizational altitude sickness is not an abnormal experience. The most important aspect of acclimatizing to new heights is to see it as normal and preparatory and not let the adjustment period dim your spirit or discourage you. Keep the hope for your success, and a vision of the impact you are passionate about making, front and center at all times. Hold fast to the convictions that you had as you assumed the role, and don't let momentary adjustments that are a normal part of any new role set you back.

IN FLIGHT

NEWRIZON ADVANTAGE MOBILE, ONE OF the leading global providers of cellular services, technology, devices, and accessories, had been one of Huntington's largest customers for the past five years, growing at an average of 7–10 percent each year. About two years ago, as CMO, Jordan saw a major opportunity to pitch Newrizon on a global approach to their branded packaging solutions that would put Huntington in an exclusive provider role. Huntington would be able to provide Newrizon with three-year pricing structures and streamline their supply chain, and it would triple the revenue Huntington derived from Newrizon.

At first, Newrizon dismissed the pitch out of hand—they simply weren't interested in putting so many eggs in one basket; they struggled to see how their cost structure would really be improved and the complexities of transitioning all of their regional suppliers to one global provider seemed daunting. But Jordan and Brandon McIntire, Huntington's executive vice president of Sales, were persistent, and through diligent effort they developed a groundbreaking proposal that would radically change Newrizon's positioning in their own branded device markets. Huntington returned to Newrizon with the deal of a lifetime. Huntington gave a compelling and comprehensive look at how they could rebuild Newrizon's packaging solutions for their branded merchandise with new composite materials and consumer-friendly, far more attractive designs. Newrizon was deeply impressed by the show of commitment, creativity, and genuine partnership displayed by Huntington's efforts. Most convincingly, the cost-saving opportunities were undeniable and greater than anything Newrizon could achieve on its own or with the current portfolio of eleven suppliers. They simply couldn't say no.

The day they got the verbal yes was a blockbuster day in the Huntington offices. Champagne bottles were popping everywhere. Jordan remembered Mac standing on the coffee table in the lobby lounge area where everyone had gathered saying, "This is a big day for Huntington. Not only will this more than triple our revenue with such a key customer, but it will enable us to build capabilities and structure similar deals for other customers that could set us on a growth trajectory we'd never imagined." That was just about a month before Mac announced his illness.

The disruption caused by Mac's death slowed the finalization of the deal by several months. Newrizon was compassionate and patient, but also a bit nervous now that Jordan was on the throne, one step further from Huntington's initial relationship with them. They wanted reassurance that Huntington's ability to execute the deal as pitched had not changed, and that Jordan would personally oversee making sure it was successful.

Though negotiations were fiery, they were in their final phases and the big signing and announcement date were just two weeks out. Newrizon was ruthless in both testing every number in the cost structure as well as pushing for every ounce of savings they could get. To clinch the deal, Huntington also agreed to deliver some prototype designs to Newrizon at the signing as a way to signal commitment to hitting the ground running upon the deal's close. Once the street heard of this maneuver, analysts would be calling and the PR machine would be cranked to high.

Jordan had passed the baton six months earlier to Elise Russell, his successor as chief marketing officer, to finish up the prototypes. This was intended to free him up to play a more strategic role on the project. The design process had not gone smoothly. Elise fired the initial design firm early on when it became clear they wouldn't be able to meet the aggressive time table, and hired a design firm she'd worked with in the past and felt confident could do the job.

Jordan was troubled by some of what they'd produced, feeling like it had strayed too far from the design criteria and blueprints they'd originally pitched to Newrizon. On several occasions he'd felt compelled to step in and provide minutely detailed direction to the team, steering them back toward what he believed Newrizon was expecting. Each time he'd done this, it was clear Elise became frustrated. But Jordan wasn't going to let her petulance or ego stand in the way of making sure the biggest deal in Huntington's history was delivered exceptionally well. His seasoned instincts had always impressed Elise, who had never struggled to take feedback and coaching from Jordan. But now, as CMO, her need for independence and to carry the ball across the finish line made her less open to Jordan's input.

As Elise's team assembled in the conference room for the final showcase, Jordan felt anxious. He was struggling with how to handle his concerns regarding some of the designs during the meeting. He knew instinctively that there were things he needed to let go of and let Elise run with, regardless of how he would have done them. Yet given the magnitude of this deal, separating his "preference" from his "gut instincts" about what would and wouldn't play at Newrizon was proving difficult. He felt like he was walking a tightrope as he tried to establish himself as a credible CEO while knowing that Elise wasn't fully ready to be the CMO. He needed to help Elise get off to a strong start and get out from under his shadow while making sure, as CEO, that the Newrizon deal was executed flawlessly.

During the presentation, Jordan's unease grew. Clear feedback he'd given to the team had not been incorporated. Trying desperately to maintain the norm that Mac had established to keep everything peaceful and polite in front of guests, he held his tongue, but his discontent was palpable. His silence fueled Elise's feeling of being off balance. Unable to stand it any longer, Elise paused, looked at Jordan, and through slightly pursed lips said, "Jordan, you've been rather quiet throughout the conversation.

I know you must have some thoughts on what you've seen so far. I can't imagine you wouldn't, since this is your baby. Care to share any perspectives with the group?"

Jordan knew she was baiting him. He'd hoped his preoccupied restlessness had been less transparent, but it clearly triggered Elise and her irritation got the better of her.

"Why don't we get through all of your content, Elise, and I'll share my views then," Jordan punted.

Elise was politically smart enough to get the hint—he wasn't going there and she should let it go. Unfortunately, she couldn't. "No, really, Jordan, it's pretty clear something's not sitting well with you, and I want the team to hear your concerns directly from you rather than through me, so please, tell us what you are thinking."

Jordan wasn't prepared to be that candid in front of the whole group and he feared losing control. If he shared what he was thinking it could look like he was micromanaging. If he said nothing, he would look like he was hiding something, and that might provoke even more anxious conjecture among the team. Against his better judgment, Jordan let himself get hooked.

"OK, Elise, if that would be more helpful. I'm a tad confused at the two core prototypes. Over a month ago, I gave you clear feedback on the specs and reminded you of the initial commitments to Newrizon, yet here we are, two weeks before we have to unveil this to Newrizon, and we have core prototypes that couldn't be further from what we promised. That's what's troubling me. Can you help me understand how we got here?"

Elise instantly regretted baiting Jordan in front of the executive and design teams. She knew she looked foolish and the design team looked confused—why hadn't she told them about Jordan's feedback? What initial specs was he talking about?

"I guess I'm confused, Jordan, because I thought I was the CMO now. I assumed that this project was under my leadership, and as such, those were my calls to make. I believe this design is a stronger fit to the specs we pitched Newrizon, and I think the data support that conclusion."

Trying to hide his astonishment, Jordan thought to himself, "Did she really just say that in front of the whole room?"

"Elise, if we need to have a role clarification conversation, let's do that offline. In the meantime, can we please get on with the presentation? I'd like to close it out, and then we can let the design team go, and discuss how we get the two core designs back on track."

"So you don't even want to hear the data and my reasoning behind this design?" Elise bit back.

"What I would like is to finish the presentation, and. . . ."

Barry Bostwick, one of the design team members, jumped in, saying, "Let's finish the presentation and then we can step back and recalibrate." It took another forty-five minutes.

Jordan entered his office a little while later to find Elise standing against the bookcase, seething, with her arms folded. "How dare you cut me down in front of all those people!"

"Elise, I tried my damnedest not to go there, but you insisted. Would you have preferred I lied?"

"I would prefer it if you let me do my job!" Elise nearly shouted.

"Are you suggesting that now that you're the CMO, you don't have to take my input anymore?" Elise was taken aback by how dogmatic and obstinate he was being. This wasn't the Jordan who had hired her and worked so well with her all these years. And it wasn't the Jordan who was open to others' ideas and not afraid of being wrong. Elise shook her head in frustration. "You just can't stand the thought that you might be wrong, can you, Jordan? You sold this baby and you don't want anyone raining on your parade. That's why you haven't extracted yourself from any of the design work—you just can't keep your hands out of the game you love. And since you can't catch your breath in this job, you just want to hang on to the job that got you all the glory. Isn't that what's really going on here?"

"What's really going on is you can't stand the fact that you still have a boss, and that you're not ready to be CMO of this company, and that your boss still has more experience and ability than you. Now go and figure out how to get those two prototypes built to the original design specs and have them ready for the launch in two weeks. I don't care what it takes. Just do it." Jordan surprised himself with his degree of assertiveness. *They're kickin' in faster now*, he thought to himself. He wondered if he'd crossed a line.

Elise's tone quieted to one of exhaustion and dejection. "What in God's name has happened to you, Jordan? If this is what this job is turning you into, you should rethink whether you really want it."

She closed with, "Here, read this. If you still want me to rebuild them after you do, email me tonight and I'll get started in the morning if I haven't found another job by then."

It was the data analysis of the market studies defending her design as more aligned to the Newrizon specs. Jordan felt sick. Elise may have been onto something after all. She had spotted some key trends in the consumer feedback, but as he checked the appendix to see the backup data, Jordan realized Elise had missed a key point there. Neither of them was completely right. But truth was, her design was closer to hitting the specs than his. The prototype needed some adjustments for sure, but Elise could easily defend from the data that a complete reversal was unnecessary. Jordan replayed the meeting in his head and realized with chagrin that it had been a complete disaster. How was he going to clean this mess up, save face, and restore the team's confidence in their work, and in him?

On the drive home, he left Elise a contrite voicemail, and asked to see her first thing in the morning.

CHAPTER TWO

DISTINGUISHING YOUR ORGANIZATION'S DIFFERENT ALTITUDES

TRANSITIONING TO THE STRATEGIC SYSTEM

FINDING THE RIGHT ALTITUDE

"SHE PLAYS TOO LOW—LIFT HER UP, GET her out of the weeds!"

"He's always looking over my shoulder! He never seems to trust that I can do the work I was hired to do!"

"If she really wants to do my job, then why did she hire me?!?"

"I have all the accountability and none of the authority."

"We leave meetings having made one decision, but then someone higher up, or lower down, decides to do something completely different."

These comments represent a fraction of the collective complaints we heard during a recent engagement with a large and developing organization in the

Gulf region. Passionate employee interviews revealed a pernicious, but all-too-familiar, pattern of behavior being played out among the leadership ranks. This universal pattern has plagued almost every client system we've been involved with over the past twenty-five years. Regardless of how specific symptoms manifest themselves, the underlying problem is the same: leaders insist on playing "down" in their organizations. Top leaders who should be focused on the strategic challenges of setting direction for the company instead get mired in narrow and often tactical issues. Managers, in turn, become frustrated, begin to second-guess themselves, and are challenged to properly execute on opportunities they were told were theirs to manage. This creates confusion, compression, and constraint within the organization—inhibiting productivity, causing anxiety, and eroding confidence among the broader employee population. It's a universal belief everywhere we work—things would work better if the top leaders limited themselves to doing what they were supposed to be doing. One employee shared, "I get it. Picking stocks is fun. That's why we get into this business! I've been doing it for twenty years and have a great track record. I know what I'm passionate about and have managed my career so I get to keep doing it. If stock picking is what you like, then don't jump on the management track."

We believe that top leaders working at the wrong levels of an organization is a widespread issue for organizations generally—one that needs ongoing vigilance and attention. The direct and opportunity costs of not addressing this pattern are immense. What are the costs of plants that don't keep up with technology and process requirements? What are the consequences to the organization for general managers not thinking through what to do about the coming exodus of experienced colleagues as 50 percent of its workforce retires in the next four years? What are the risks of having to go outside to hire general managers because they are not being developed fast enough internally? What happens when well-intended executives continue to keep their hands in all of the jobs they've left behind, constraining the growth and ability of those appointed to those roles? We saw at Huntington how Jordan's continued involvement in Newrizon constrains Elise. When leaders work at the wrong level, the substantive work needed in support of the future doesn't get done. Talent doesn't get developed, innovation doesn't thrive, the performance culture doesn't get strengthened, and over time the business starts to run out of ways to grow organically and sustainably.

To fully appreciate what executives should and shouldn't be doing, it is important to put into context what *everyone else in the organization* should and shouldn't be doing. So we're going to start with a foundational model of how organizations work so you can locate yourself and your role in the broader context of how others below the executive level are contributing to the organization's performance.

ARE YOU PLAYING YOUR PART?

David O. McKay, an admirable twentieth century leader, often used the quote "What e're thou art, act well thy part!"[15] to guide his personal and professional life. This phrase reminded him to be clear about the role he was expected to play in whatever circumstance he found himself, and to encourage excellence in his contributions. Leaders in twenty-first century organizations are well advised to follow this simple counsel: act well your part, *not someone else's*. There are as many unique excuses for invading other people's parts as there are leaders, but ultimately the reasons fall into one of three categories:

1. Leaders aren't clear about what they are supposed to be doing.
2. Leaders lack the skill to do what they're supposed to be doing.
3. Leaders are simply unwilling to do what they're supposed to be doing.

Ironically, "unclear, unskilled, and unwilling" does *not* sound like most of the top leaders we know. They are smart, hardworking, driven people who care deeply about their organizations and their people. The problems creep in when they don't understand or lose sight of the organization systems at work within their enterprise. Every successful organization has three distinct but interdependent structural systems—a collection of roles and processes—that must function simultaneously to optimize success. These are the Operating, Coordinating and Strategic systems. Understanding how each system works optimally to add value to the organization can go a long way to clarify the discrete contributions that people should be expected to make as they move up and ensure that people are doing no harm as they advance within a company.

THREE INTERDEPENDENT SYSTEMS

The idea of an organization as three interdependent systems is a relatively simple concept, but it is also one that people take for granted until they stop to consciously consider it. However, paying attention to the roles within each of these systems is vital to a healthy organization. It's worth taking a quick look at how each operates and the function each plays. Figure 2.1 below illustrates three interdependent organizational systems.

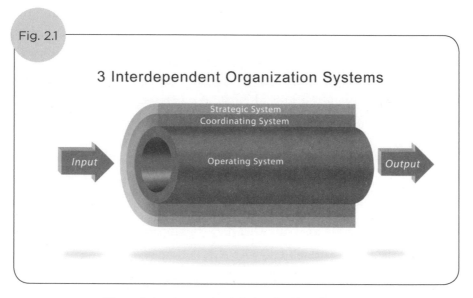

Three Interdependent Organization Systems

If we think in very basic terms, all organizations take inputs and transform them into outputs. Depending on the life-stage and maturity of the organization, an individual role may be required to play in multiple systems, as in start-ups or high-growth environments. In such cases, the need is even greater for leaders to be consciously aware of which role(s) they are acting in and why. Successful companies identify clear and distinct contributions for leaders in the Operating system, Coordinating system, and the Strategic system of the organization. Knowing what these expected contributions are, and demonstrating that knowledge in how you fulfill your role as a leader, is a big part of being an effective contributor in the system in which you participate.

THE OPERATING SYSTEM

The Operating system is all about execution. It plays a central role in the delivery of goods and services to the market. Those participating in this system are responsible for taking raw inputs and converting them into whole, consumable outputs that are valued and used by end-user consumers or by other organizational processes. Ultimately, the majority of the effort and resources of any organization should be allocated to directly support the Operating system, and in return, an effective Operating system commits to the following:

- **Adapt and learn.** Individual and collective effort is expended to acquire competency and increase proficiency to deliver the company's core value proposition to the market.

- **Use resources effectively.** Understanding of the strategy and priority objectives is leveraged to manage and allocate resources to achieve both top- and bottom-line results.

- **Communicate upward.** Given the hands-on connection with the work, the Operating system is uniquely positioned to raise issues and offer insights about the practicalities of executing the stated strategy and objectives.

- **Reinforce desired behavior.** The Operating system has the largest population and therefore exacts the greatest impact on the culture.

For small businesses and start-ups, the primary system in play is the Operating system. There aren't a lot of roles—everyone does what has to be done to keep the business running. A friend of ours launched a business making acoustic guitars with a unique bridge design. At any moment, he could be: master luthier, head of marketing, head of distribution and fulfillment, research and design, facilities management, chief financial officer, materials sourcing, and janitor. He worked ridiculously long hours, but was happy—at least initially. Our friend was a lot less happy a few years later when his guitars were picked up by the Sam Ash music store chain and featured in the Musician's Friend mail order catalogue. When we asked him what the problem was, he said that he had forty employees and forty-one headaches. Like many successful entrepreneurs, he had become impatient with the day-to-day running of a growing operation. When we asked him what his forty-first headache was, he replied the guitars themselves. He was so busy dealing with the minutiae of his business that he hadn't designed anything new in months.

Fast growth often results in muddy roles, and if you're not careful, you'll find you aren't playing the role you most need to play—coming up with the next big idea or changing direction as you see an opportunity in the market. This is why so many entrepreneurs depart as their businesses mature, and are replaced by experienced management teams.

At some point, all organizations must grow up, and part of that process includes parsing out the Operating, Coordinating, and Strategic systems in the organization. Operating system problems aren't limited to start-ups—they manifest frequently in large organizations, too. The business unit head of a large manufacturing company we worked with came to us because his organization had become completely risk averse and incapable of making decisions.

"I have to attend every meeting or nothing gets resolved," he lamented. "We can't work this way. There's no way I can be all over every group in this business. And I don't think I should be. Please help me find out why we're stuck like this."

We interviewed two dozen of his people in various parts of the business and found the same thing: people liked him a lot and were loyal, but they felt he took over all decision making in every room he entered. As we observed him in action and got to know his style, we pointed out that his relentless need to know the facts inadvertently undercut the authority of everyone on his leadership team. No one felt confident to make decisions without him present. This leader was also so interested in his business (a good thing) that he invited himself to every meeting and weighed in on a wide array of topics (a bad thing). When we started talking to him about the different systems in his organization, it became apparent that he was unaware of the effect his leadership behavior was having and what it was costing his organization.

Regardless of whether your organization is new, in a growth phase, or mature and in a sustaining phase, you need effective Operating systems that delineate the unique contribution of individuals who get goods and services to market from the activities that belong in the remaining two systems.

THE COORDINATING SYSTEM

Large enterprises tend not to have the same problem of confusing roles between the Operating system and more senior leadership that smaller businesses and start-ups have. The growing pains of achieving a certain scale and level of success generally occur earlier in the organization's history. The issue for larger businesses lies in the confusion of roles between the Coordinating system and the Strategic system. The way we have drawn these systems in the figure above is quite deliberate—they literally do both wrap around the Operating system, which remains completely central to what the organization does. The Coordinating system has four primary accountabilities:

- **Translate strategy.** Strategies can only be enacted when they have personal meaning for individuals in the enterprise. Coordinating roles ensure that the strategy moves from a theoretical concept into how people must work and add value in order to achieve the strategy.

- **Allocate and manage.** They ensure clear trade-off choices and actively manage how finite resources are used to increase the probability of success.

- **Transfer knowledge and skill.** They elevate and amplify the capacity of the Operating system and develop next-generation talent.

- **Reinforce the operating philosophy.** They enact the desired culture by consciously modeling and holding each other accountable to the values and behavioral standards defined by the company.

We saw an organization with a solid understanding of the role of the Coordinating system when we were asked to design a series of leadership workshops for a consumer electronics company. They had a strong culture of promoting from within and had identified a class of several hundred high-potential sales managers in their US operation. They wanted to move these individuals into more senior management roles in each geographic region, but understood that the very qualities inherent in a successful sales manager could hinder the transition to a regional leadership role. As one of their top leaders said to us, "It's not about rolling up your sleeves and solving problems while others look on and hopefully learn from you. Our managers need to think about arming their people with the tools to make it happen. It's not enough to do the work themselves. They need to work through the system to get the work done." That is a perfect definition of roles in the Coordinating system: working in the system to get things done.

However, not all organizations are as enlightened. The pathologies that impede healthy delineation between the Strategic and Coordinating system are numerous, and getting the boundary conditions right between the two can be more difficult than you might suspect. In large part, that is because the difference between the work of the Coordinating system and the Strategic system is greater than the difference between that of the Operating and Coordinating systems. Compounding the challenge is that those being elevated to the Strategic system have spent years gaining expertise and knowledge, and being rewarded for doing the work of the Coordinating system. Figuring out what parts of that expertise to retain and what parts to relinquish to others can be extraordinarily challenging for newly appointed executives.

THE STRATEGIC SYSTEM

Our client in the consumer electronics business had a real handle on helping high-potential managers make the transition from the Operating system to the Coordinating system. But making the same transition from the Coordinating system to the Strategic system is where a lot of senior leaders struggle. This transition requires an even bigger mental shift in how leaders contribute value. While people in the Coordinating system work *in the system* to get things done, leaders in the Strategic system work *on the system itself.* This becomes apparent when you think about the work of the roles in the Strategic system:

- **Monitor external trends.** Identify opportunities and mitigate threats.

- **Define the competitive position.** Set strategic priorities and define accountability of the company relative to competitors.

- **Secure and allocate capital.** Make the challenging trade-off calls for funding and resource support at the enterprise level.

- **Define corporate values.** Articulate the values and behavioral standards that shape the operating environment for all employees.

- **Define and evolve the organization**. Proactively identify the need to adapt the enterprise to meet strategic objectives and manage change.
- **Develop senior enterprise talent.** Establish and actively manage an integrated talent management system to improve leadership capacity and ensure continuity.

Contributing as a member of the Strategic system requires a mental shift in defining value-adding work, and learning to let go of the "success posts" of the past. The CEO of a media company we worked with promoted one of his best marketing executives to be chief strategy officer. This happened a few months after a major acquisition for the company, and the CEO was eager to have input on strategic direction in a volatile economy. The new CSO was distracted by the post-merger changes in her old marketing department, however, and kept talking in terms of how to adapt existing plans and people to new conditions. She played a big role in developing a traveling workshop that described the new roles people would have in the context of the post-merger strategy. These workshops were a success, but the CEO was intensely annoyed that the CSO was spending a lot of her time designing and rolling them out rather than helping him think about the next major strategic moves the company needed to make. He thought she was playing too low in the organization. She was also frustrated and said that she thought that translating the strategy for heads of accounts and other key players was an important part of her role. "I don't need you to translate strategy," the CEO replied. "We've got people for that. I need you to come up with breakaway ideas that will form the basis of our new strategy going forward. That's what we *don't* have." The CSO was unable to let go of the coordinating roles she knew and as a result she undermined her position and effectiveness. Ultimately, the CSO was unsuccessful in her leadership on the Strategic system and the CEO was forced to replace her.

We had the opportunity to run into her again about three years after this episode. She was herself the CEO of a media company, and, interestingly enough, had contacted us about an executive she had tapped to turn a department around. She was very candid when we met and said that her executive had the same problem she herself had as CSO three years earlier. We were intrigued and asked what she meant. She had been completely overwhelmed by the responsibility of taking on a role in the Strategic system. She thought that she understood it conceptually, but none of her previous experience equipped her for the realities of a position at the top. She felt off balance and found herself continually returning to what had historically made her successful. Now that she had some perspective and had taken on a CEO role herself, she not only understood why she had been unsuccessful three years earlier but also recognized the same problem in one of her senior team members. She was once again playing down a level as she tried to get her direct reports to lead at a more strategic level in the organization. Unattended, history does have a way of repeating itself.

REFLECTIONS ON THE RISE

1. What tempts you to lower your altitude to the Coordinating system? What techniques do you use to recalibrate when you recognize that you are causing compression for those you lead?

2. How would you have coached Jordan and Elise each to act differently? What would it have looked like if Jordan were working at the Strategic level?

3. If you were to transition again from the Operating to Strategic system level, what would you do differently?

FINDING YOUR ROLE IN THE STRATEGIC SYSTEM—FIVE STRATEGIES FOR SUCCESS

We've emphasized the mental shift that has to happen for you to be an effective contributing member of the Strategic system: redefining value-adding work and letting go of the "success posts" of the past. These shifts leave most people feeling off balance. Letting go requires courage and risks failure. At a minimum, it calls on leaders to do more important—yet less familiar—work less perfectly than their own standard of performance would permit, at least for some period of time. And the worst part is that everyone is watching! A principal thing to bear in mind as you transition to and work in the Strategic system is how all three systems in the enterprise work together. One of the many unique aspects of working *on* the system is that you're required to see how all the systems fit together (or don't) to transform inputs into desired results. It is also your responsibility to see the same understanding cascades down through the organization.

The remainder of *Rising to Power* will focus on how to reach the right altitude and manage the challenges you face as you acclimate to new levels of leadership and ultimately establish yourself in the Strategic system. As we've said, it is a monumental shift for most new executives, with some common pitfalls that can be avoided with concerted effort. As you find your center of gravity in a Strategic system role, here are five things you can do, along with some early warning signals to watch out for, to get you started.

GET OUT OF THE WEEDS

A full 59 percent of our respondents indicated they struggled to let go of work they used to do as part of the Coordinating system. The biggest failing of people in the Strategic system is getting bogged down in the minutia of the business. Every large organization is complex, with an almost infinite number of crises competing for your time and having the potential to drag you down and make it hard to see the bigger picture. Most in the organization lack your vantage point, however, and count on you to help them see the bigger picture. If you are down in the weeds then *nobody* has the whole picture, and this can be terribly dangerous for your organization. If, on the other hand, you maintain the appropriate altitude and get involved only occasionally in things you think are important for the big picture, it will send a very powerful message to the rest of the organization. During a series of location visits, the COO of a national restaurant chain disappeared from the group at a flagship location long enough that people went to look for him. They found him in the restroom, cleaning a dirty stall. This COO of a multibillion-dollar company—cuff links in his pocket and sleeves rolled up—was cleaning a stall. He emerged from the stall, washed his hands, and put on his jacket, saying nothing. The store manager and regional vice president were both mortified, but the news made its way coast to coast in no time. A year later, the chain received notice in an industry magazine for having spotless restrooms. If you choose when to get involved instead of living in the weeds, you'll be able to send powerful messages when you need to and you'll avoid paralyzing your whole organization at the same time.

GIVE PEOPLE SPACE

We mentioned the manufacturing executive whose team couldn't seem to make a decision earlier. The real problem was that he was so involved in their day-to-day business that they didn't feel confident making decisions without getting cues from him as to how they should proceed. People need space and autonomy to do their jobs, make decisions, solve problems, generate ideas, make mistakes, and learn from them. It doesn't matter if you think your ideas are "better" or if they come "faster." As long as everyone understands the strategy and is working in the right context, your job is to *let them do their jobs*. Defining the strategy and the context in which they operate *is your job*. You need to support your people without micromanaging. This is harder in the Strategic system than it is in the Coordinating system because your direct reports have far greater spheres of control. The temptation to intervene can be overwhelming. But unless there is a compelling reason for you to get involved, trust your people to do it themselves and support them in their work both in what you do—*and don't*—say and do.

PICK YOUR BATTLES

We once asked a semiretired leader whose judgment we respected how he knew he needed to get personally involved in an issue. He simply said, "Honor necessity." How do you know you've done enough, we pressed. "Honor sufficiency," he replied. We've thought about this over the years, and have come to appreciate these simple measures. There are times when you will need to get involved to resolve issues in the other systems of the organization. Indeed, in some instances, you will be the only one with sufficient perspective and authority to resolve conflicts and find solutions. Do this when it is necessary, and don't flinch from it. If you have picked your battles wisely, your involvement will send a strong message. But bear in mind the dictum "honor sufficiency" as you go. Resolve what must be resolved and then let your people take over the next steps. Remember that you are here to make a difference. You may inadvertently undermine the very impact you hope to make by choosing inappropriate issues in which to involve yourself. When in doubt, ask yourself, "Does my involvement in this issue directly advance the impact I am hoping to make, or just solve a problem more quickly than if I let others handle it?"

CHOOSE YOUR WORDS

Your words have far greater resonance in the Strategic system—and so does your silence. One leader we spoke with was amazed at how quickly the rumor mill took over when he did not provide information. He was preparing to announce a merger and had gone for a few weeks unable to comment on some confidential negotiations under way. He was dismayed by the stories people made up and spread to fill the gaps created by his uncharacteristic silence. Another executive was shocked to find that simple rides in the elevator resulted in multiple people believing they had landed the same top job on his senior team. He actually hadn't promised anyone anything, or at least he hadn't meant to. Another form of word choice comes when you must confront or disappoint, critical at the strategic level. Being direct, never mincing words, and calling hard questions are more critical than ever, less your "smoothing over" or "pulling punches" reinforce actions and beliefs you need changed. Watch what you say and what you omit—there are no "casual" utterances now. Later in chapter 4 we will go more deeply into the realities of leading at higher altitudes and the cues you inadvertently send.

UNDERSTAND THE REALITIES OF SCALE AND ROLE

Understanding the three systems of the enterprise—the Strategic, Coordinating, and Operating systems—is really about understanding the realities of your role in the context of the scale you've taken on. Despite the personal experience and expertise leaders can draw on as they rise to the Strategic system, many find this the hardest transition of their careers, and not all get the hang of it. Your mandate is now quite different. You are not just a Really Big Manager— you are a leader in every sense of the word. You are responsible for creating the strategic context in which the people in the other systems function. You have a broader and longer view than others in the organization and you have the ability to set the course for the enterprise. You can now reshape the organization in ways no one else can. It is important that you keep the scope and scale of your role in perspective. You can do things that no other person can do, which means that if you spend too much of your time on Coordinating system tasks, your job will simply go undone, to the detriment of your business. True, this becomes more challenging when your new organizational peers interpret their strategic roles more tactically than you need to. Still, make the conscious choice to play at the level your organization needs. Your success and the success of all your people depend on it.

We've now laid a foundation for how your executive role in the Strategic system differs from past roles you may have held. In the next chapter we turn our attention to building a transition plan to guide you through your shift into the Strategic system.

IN FLIGHT

About three months before Mac's death, Walt Bergstrom, Huntington's chief human resource officer, retired because of some family health issues. He'd been at Huntington for nearly twenty years. Unfortunately, during that time he hadn't done much to keep the HR function current or build its capability for the future. With all of the mayhem surrounding Mac's death, Jordan had no time to focus on the search for his replacement. The executive search firm had been presenting candidates since before Walt's retirement, but none of them had impressed anyone on the executive team. That is, until Jacinta Williams. She had her first interview the week after Jordan took over as CEO. She was well aware of all that was going on and handled herself magnificently. Her poise, professionalism, articulateness, energy, and strong HR executive track record in some great organizations all spoke in her favor. As a woman of color with fresh thinking, she was a double-diversity candidate who would help put a small dent in Huntington's struggle to attract and retain multicultural professionals. Jordan was thrilled. Outsiders always struggled to gain traction at Huntington, but Jacinta seemed such a good fit that Jordan trusted she'd beat the odds. The entire executive team endorsed her as Huntington's new CHRO and was delighted when she accepted.

During her first six weeks, she dove right in. She used her small group meet-and-greets to help comfort grieving, fearful employees and bolster their confidence in Huntington's future. She came in early and left late, demonstrating a work ethic consistent with Huntington's. She was confident, smart, and adroit at winning people over. She even connected with the usual skeptics who didn't like outsiders.

Imagine Jordan's surprise when he started to hear that it was all going south. Stories of Jacinta's "aggressiveness and lack of sensitivity" began to surface as she challenged her team to think more strategically and bring more value to business partners. She caused friction with peers because she began to bring issues that people would rather not have dealt with to light—like the fact that Huntington's sales compensation model was at the top of the benchmark and encouraged salespeople to sell anything to anyone regardless of profitability. And she was using her past experiences to show people at Huntington all that they were doing wrong and what they needed to do to be more cost efficient or higher performing.

The more stories Jordan heard, the tighter the knot in his stomach got. He knew what Jacinta was likely trying to do, and what message she probably meant to send, but seeing the aftermath of her well-intended efforts was infuriating to him. *"She's an HR executive, for crying out loud; if anyone ought to know better about how to handle these things, it's her."*

Though Jordan had plenty more immediate issues to contend with—the SEC investigation and the Newrizon deal to name just two—he decided to sniff around carefully to see if these issues with Jacinta were isolated, or if there was a growing sense that she was ruffling more feathers. He went to Jason Stillman, who was a great product manager, ran a tight organization, and was deeply connected throughout Huntington. He was a straight shooter and trusted friend and colleague. If there was any noise in the system, Jason would know it, and he'd tell him the truth.

Jason didn't mince words when asked—he said simply, "She's a complete bitch."

"No, really, Jason, don't hold back. What do you honestly think?" Jordan mocked in return.

"She is alienating people by the day. She sent an email to the folks in Supply Chain *whom she'd never even met* with a cost-cutting report and a short note that said, 'Here's what we did at Nokia—it was best-in-class work and we cut some major fat out of the organization, and no black belts either. Would love to meet and discuss—I see some low-hanging fruit we might go after.' Needless to say the Supply Chain folks weren't impressed or interested."

"Please tell me she did NOT do that?"

"Saw the email myself. Wayne forwarded it to me."

"So how bad is this getting?" Jordan asked with growing alarm.

"Lemme put it this way," Jason replied. "You know how much we suck here with outsiders. So we have to own our side of the street. But if you don't turn this around fast, this could be one of the worst ones yet."

He would have simply remained in denial were it not for a disconcerting conversation he'd had with Helen Chandler, a woman who'd been the HR benefits coordinator as long as Jordan could remember. He passed her crying in the hallway and she recounted a conversation she'd had with Jacinta telling her that her work was a waste of time and that she needed to "come into the twenty-first century." Not the kind of message you want to send to a thirty-one-year veteran of the company. If that wasn't bad enough, Jordan returned to his office to find an email from Jacinta outlining her aggressive plans to completely overhaul the entire HR function.

To: Jordan Neffron
From: Jacinta Williams
Subject: HR at Huntington

Jordan—forgive the formality of a memo, but it helps me to some-times jot my thoughts down in preparation for a live conversation. Carolyn is finding us time next week to meet. I've tried to step back and just observe for my first few months and get the lay of the land before making any big moves. You already know that HR at Huntington is at least twenty years behind. There is no infrastructure in place to drive a talent strategy, the generalist talent is weak on its best day, and I don't have a leadership team I can work with to drive transformation. What I've gathered from folks I've chatted with is that they are eager to see change happen. I have felt welcomed into conversations, the ideas I've offered have been graciously accepted with genuine appreciation—they are just starved for a strategic HR perspective here. Everywhere I look I see evidence that HR has been a missing link for too long. And whenever I've pointed out opportunities to see things differently, people are very open and receptive. I think I've gotten enough traction now that I want to talk about accelerating my vision for HR transformation. I've attached a high-level plan that outlines where I want to take the organization over the next three years. The bottom line is this, Jordan: I have to basically start over. There is very little, if anything, here that I can salvage. I see no reason to put this off any longer. I'd like to start scheduling RIF conversations week after next. I know this must be hard to hear, Jordan, but remember—this is why you brought me here. Thanks in advance for your support.

Best,
Jacinta

Jordan's hands were trembling. Understanding, better than she, the havoc her plan would wreak, and the signals she was clearly missing, he simply replied, "Jacinta, this can't wait until next week. I'll have Carolyn find us time tomorrow."

SECTION II
ADJUST

CHAPTER THREE

PLANNING YOUR SHIFT TO THE STRATEGIC SYSTEM

SEPARATING FROM WHAT YOU LEFT BEHIND

GET IN TOUCH WITH YOUR INNER ANTHROPOLOGIST

EVERY ARRIVAL INTO THE STRATEGIC SYSTEM OF an organization is fraught with multiple risks. Earlier, in chapter 1, we explored the risk of believing you've arrived with a mandate and falsely assuming you must repeat past achievements in your new role. Assuming you've avoided that land mine, now you must secure your rightful place at the executive table and leave behind the work of the Coordinating system from which you departed. Your arrival can be further complicated by whether you enter as an outsider or an insider. Each has its own unique challenges. Managing the initial shock of the new altitude is critically important, but it is equally important to be intentional in *planning* your entrance *into* the Strategic system, and *from* the Coordinating system. We'll first talk about how to plan that arrival and simultaneous departure, and then we'll talk about how your work will shift once you're firmly planted at your new altitude. In chapter 4, we'll talk about some of the natural distortions in perspective that happen as you make the shift to higher altitudes.

We've accompanied scores of executives into new executive roles both within organizations and from outside them. To a leader, they all start out with the same well-intended agenda that goes something like, "I'm just going to keep my mouth shut for the first ninety days, really get to know the lay of the land, and listen to people as I get to know them. *Then I'll build my plan.*" Of course, two weeks into their new assignment, the CEO or executive to whom they report is asking, "So, have you built your hundred-day plan and are you clear on what you need to accomplish?" That usually torpedoes the "I just want to listen and learn" approach, which gets hastily replaced with a sporadic set of impulsive moves that support the illusion of progress. Big meetings get called. Decks with "vision slides" are assembled and cascaded in town halls. A few sharp cost-cutting moves are made to signal that the leader "means it" when it comes to big change. Task forces and committees proliferate as ambitious action plans are built. We've all seen this movie. Many of us have lived it.

So much for truly listening and learning.

But it doesn't have to be this way. And, frankly, substantive changes don't come about this way. People usually see right through the faux meet-and-greet lunches and your open-ended questions about the agenda you've already formed. The negative impact resulting from this classic entry strategy can't be underestimated. The leader's loss of credibility compounded by the lost momentum that could have been garnered had the leader simply stayed the course of true learning is immense. Jacinta has stepped right into this morass.

An effective executive enters the Strategic system as a true anthropologist—setting aside preconceived hypotheses about what she will discover and genuinely seeking to "learn" the organization and its people. The relevance of anthropology is significant, because it distinguishes itself from other social sciences through its emphasis on the in-depth examination of context. The way people make sense of the world around them and the relationships they form among themselves are at the heart of social and cultural anthropology. Such a study is foundational to the success of an executive's entry. The notion that this can be done even in ninety days is foolish, but keeping an open mind for at least that long while allowing new ideas and assumptions to form, and building factual conclusions about the context and its people, will take you much further in the long run than "hitting the ground running" with foregone conclusions that later prove unsound. Here's why. A savvy executive understands that she is not just sizing up the organization for what she can or needs to change. She is also sizing up how *she will need to change*, and how the organization *will change her* in the process. Most leaders don't even register that part. They enter under the presumption of change agent, not change beneficiary or potential change casualty. So while clarity of your aspirations will help you stay clear on what your impact will be, prematurely deciding that impact based on what you've been told or what you assume is dangerous. The early days are the time to suspend judgment about what value you came to create long enough to truly learn what difference is possible and what it will require *of you* to make it.

Well-crafted plans to enter higher altitudes have key anthropological elements to them. Some are neutral to your origin as an insider or outsider, while others are specifically tied to it. Figure 3.1 shows these entry plan elements. At the end of the chapter we've provided a simple tool you can use to build out your entry plan.

Fig. 3.1

Every Strategic System Arrival Plan must:	
• Start with a learning plan that targets gathering disconfirming data • Synthesize learning into a shared set of "vital few" priorities • Size up talent and build your team • Solicit and act upon personal feedback at key intervals	
Moving In: Strategic system arrival plan of executives from *outside* the organization must:	**Moving Up: Strategic system arrival plan of executives from *within* the organization must:**
• Help you build authentic relationships and allow people to get to know you • Determine if you are effectively blending in without "going native" • Ensure your diagnosis doesn't become a heavy-handed indictment • Ensure your halo doesn't become a noose	• Re-calibrate relationships with new and former peers • Leverage your knowledge of the organization without your biases • Extract you from the Coordinating system work you'd previously been engaged in, regardless of whether or not you believe others are ready to assume those responsibilities

Strategic System Entry Plan

YOUR ANTHROPOLOGICAL ROAD MAP FOR EXECUTIVE ENTRY

Let's look at each plan element in more detail. All plans for entry into the Strategic system should include these elements.

A LEARNING PLAN THAT TARGETS GATHERING DISCONFIRMING DATA

Regardless of their former role, most executives arrive with a plan for how to assess the organization they are entering and a set of assumptions about what they will find. The headhunter and/or hiring manager has given them data. If they are being promoted from within, they certainly have a sense of the organization's history. That has all informed their thinking. If arriving from outside, they've done their own research with data in the public domain. With such an array of information on hand, it's natural to already have one's mind nearly made up about the state of the organization and what you need to get done.

The obvious problem is that you have likely missed things you weren't looking for—in some cases, critical things. One executive we worked with, who'd been brought in with the express purpose of building out the sales capability of his new organization, got about a year into his journey before things came to a grinding halt. Historically the organization had managed its key customer relationships through very informal and interpersonal means. They had some CRM data to work with, but they weren't very sophisticated and, this executive assumed, not very useful. After spending a lot on a cutting-edge CRM platform to bring the organization into the "twenty-first century," and starting the process of populating it from scratch, many within the organization were clamoring to simply migrate the data they already had to the new platform and avoid the wasteful effort of starting over. At first the leader wouldn't even entertain the idea. Having never looked at the data, he just assumed it was overly simplistic and lacked analytical value. One senior sales executive pleaded with him to simply look at the data and use them to see if they actually had any value. He did and was astonished to find a supply of rich CRM data that had been well maintained, was searchable, and would support reasonable analytics. Migrating it to the new platform would literally save thousands of hours of work. Instead of acting upon his initial conclusion that there would be nothing worth keeping, he should have gone looking for "assets to be preserved for the future." Had he done so, he would have discovered this wealth of information much sooner and avoided offending many of his sales force. The active pursuit of disconfirming data serves as needed "checks and balances" to an entering leader's predisposed assumptions about the organization, and helps guard against missing key information and opportunities that you weren't naturally inclined to look for.

SYNTHESIZE LEARNING INTO A SHARED SET OF "VITAL FEW" PRIORITIES

Having gathered substantive data, including disconfirming data to offset your assumptions, you now need to construct an initial set of priorities around which to focus and align the organization. Newly appointed executives often forget that their arrival is a disruptive jolt for the organization. It sets people off balance as they speculate about what changes the leader will make, how those changes will depart from the predecessor's agenda, and how those changes will affect them personally. Anxious conjecture drains the organization of focus and needed energy for the leader's plan. Leaders who understand the context before they give the organization its marching orders know that less is often more, simplicity equals clarity, and setting up small wins parlays into needed momentum and bigger wins later. Leaders who fail to understand this reveal grand plans that paralyze the organization with too many priorities, and bury everyone under the weight of massive work in addition to their day jobs. Worse, those leaders tend to ignore the organization's indifference to the plan's unrealistic scope and lack of credibility until it is too late.

SIZE UP TALENT AND BUILD YOUR TEAM

One of the hardest aspects of rising to an executive role is inheriting your predecessor's team. It would be great if everyone on the team had to "re-up" for their job, but unfortunately that's generally not the case. A lot of factors influence whether or not the existing team is the right team for you and the direction in which you will take the organization: (1) their track record of performance, (2) how receptive they are to your leadership, (3) how overtly they try to curry favor with you, (4) how subtle they are about throwing their teammates under the bus when sharing their views on "what's got to change,"

(5) how capable they are of delivering against the results you need, and (6) how genuinely they resonate with the vision you are forming. Whatever criteria you use, you must form a systematic way to assess the talent you have against the agenda you are forming to determine who can stay, who can grow, and who must go. Most newly appointed executives are reluctant to make hard calls, especially early in their tenure. They fear alienating their team and sending political shockwaves through the organization by removing people who, though once thought highly of, will clearly be immovable obstacles to change. Whether through a lack of competence, commitment, or both, not everyone will be able to make the journey, and the sooner you are honest about that, the sooner you will get a team around you that is aligned to your vision and willing to lead the required heavy lifting. We are not fond of the "clean house on day one" approach, by any means. The same principle of "taking time to learn" discussed earlier especially applies to assessing talent. But once the data are clear, act.

One CEO we worked with discovered a year after she started that, despite some early changes made upon her arrival, the team she'd kept in place wasn't going to *ever* rise to the challenges the organization faced. She lamented to us, "I just don't have the right team and no matter how hard I try, they don't bring what I need." Yet despite her realization, she waited another twelve months before she started making needed changes. And that intervening year was rife with substantial and needless suffering because she kept rationalizing why it wasn't the right time to pull the trigger. Don't let inadequate talent hold your vision hostage. Get the people you need in place, and get the organization moving in the same direction.

SOLICIT AND ACT UPON PERSONAL FEEDBACK AT KEY INTERVALS

Calibrating how effectively your entrance is going is critical to ensuring it doesn't derail before you know it's in trouble. The lagging indicators for whether or not you are getting traction are insufficient and unreliable for determining if you are "sticking" or not. This is especially important in your first six months, when people are still forming impressions of you and your network is unformed (meaning your data sources are limited). Whether through an online survey tool, or a third party's interviews, you must have a reliable barometer to know if the messages you are sending, the vision you are casting, the leadership you are modeling, the plans to which you are holding people to account, and the changes you are initiating are all being metabolized as you intend. Feedback loops that help you quickly determine where you are on course and where you aren't allow you room to maneuver and course correct. One of the biggest challenges newly arriving executives contend with is how easily their words and actions are misinterpreted. Don't assume that just because you are "new" that people won't be able or willing to provide helpful feedback. True, there may be anomalies in what you hear because some have had less exposure to you than others. Do it anyway. The data will be more than sufficient to help you calibrate. In the next chapter we'll discuss the "megaphone effect" and the reality of how executives are objectified by those they lead. Suffice it to say, if you don't have a way of knowing how far outside your intentions your messages and actions are being interpreted, you'll keep plodding ahead as if everything is fine only to discover you left a large portion of your organization behind. And key to leveraging helpful calibration data, of course, is *acting upon it*. Many new executives graciously invite feedback to establish the look of openness but damage the credibility they gain by doing nothing with it.

REFLECTIONS ON THE RISE

1. In your experience, what has helped or hindered effective entry into new roles? Where have you struggled? In hindsight, would you do anything differently?

2. Why is Jacinta's read of her reception at Huntington so at odds with what Jordan is hearing? In your experience, what causes such disconnects in perception, and how would you coach Jacinta?

WHEN YOU ARRIVE FROM OUTSIDE

In addition to those above, executives arriving from *outside* the organization must also include these elements in their plan.

BUILD AUTHENTIC RELATIONSHIPS AND ALLOW PEOPLE TO GET TO KNOW YOU

Regardless of how much of a "fit" you believed your new organization would be, you are still an outsider. And people will make up things about you as an outsider in the absence of real information. But you have some control over what they make up. The degree of transparency with which you reveal important aspects of your life—your personality, your values, appropriate information about your family, and the degree to which you express interest about those aspects of the lives of others—has a great deal of influence on your credibility and the degree to which people trust you. We've watched several clients effectively use humor to diffuse the awkwardness of getting to know others with "top ten things you should know about me" kinds of lists. Gestures like that signal you are trying to do your part to build a bridge across the divide and both invite them into your life and be welcomed into theirs. There is no shortcut for the time and work it takes to establish deeply formed relationships of trust, grit, and intimacy. But when it comes to organizational entry to executive ranks, there are certainly things you can do to accelerate the process, and, more importantly, circumvent the fabrications about you that people will create in the absence of firsthand knowledge.

DETERMINE IF YOU ARE EFFECTIVELY BLENDING IN WITHOUT GOING NATIVE

Though occasionally executives entering the higher strata can be like bulls in china shops with lots of bravura and declarations of "a new era," most instinctively know those entrances are often short-lived and ill-fated. More commonly, executives default to the opposite side of the spectrum, walking on eggshells: being overly cautious not to ruffle any feathers or "offend" anyone. Ironically, this often has the same consequence as the charging bull—it still offends and alienates people. Leaders get so caught up in trying to "read the environment" that they become excessively inward-focused at the expense of truly "seeing" what is around them. Their self-involved myopia leads them to squander opportunities with those to whom they want to build bridges, and to behave as anything but themselves.

Leaders who are genuinely being themselves don't need to declare it. They can balance "blending in" with keeping a healthy distance from the new environment long enough to get an accurate read on it. One general manager of a large global business unit was so anxious about how he was being received that he ended up burdening the organization with unspoken pleas for reassurance and affirmation. Six months into his new role, the organization had so "reassured" him that he was OK that they turned him into one of them, including all of the dysfunctional and destructive behaviors he'd come to help change. He lasted only a year. We call this "going native"—where you blend in so much with the fabric of the organization that your ability to credibly effect any change is neutered. You must guard against this with clear and objective metrics that gauge how well the changes you are putting in place are progressing and where they are off course. This, along with the personal feedback mechanism discussed above, goes a long way to preventing this form of entry failure.

ENSURE YOUR DIAGNOSIS DOESN'T TURN INTO AN INDICTMENT

Useful diagnostics must be systemic in nature. In other words, they must take into account the context of the organization's competitive landscape, the efficacy of the stated strategy, the "hardware" (the structure, systems, governance, and processes), and the "software" (the culture, people, and leadership). When any of these systemic elements become misaligned from one another, you see unaddressed and persistent performance shortfalls appear. One of the classic pitfalls of executive entry is allowing the diagnosis of one part of the system, even though accurate, to serve as an alienating indictment of another part of the system. It typically looks something like this. An executive enters the organization, having been told "our systems are really outdated and we have no documented processes. And now we're falling way behind the industry and need to leapfrog into the twenty-first century." (We'd love a dollar for every time we've heard newly appointed executives get this speech.) With that frame of reference, the executive typically starts calling in consultants of all kinds—technology and IT consultants, industry experts, benchmarking consultants, strategy consultants, etc.—and a cadre of new leaders to help mount the revolution. With every rock turned over, a new level of antiquated process or inadequate system is revealed, along with the unmitigated risk such discoveries pose, and an increasingly loudening gasp of shock and exasperation from the executive and his newly arrived colleagues. The unspoken insinuation signaled to the veterans of the organization (and sometimes we've actually heard it spoken!) is, "How on earth have you people made it this far? It's a wonder you've gotten anything done or made a penny in this business with this cobbled-together set of nonsense!" The veteran employees—proud of the deeply committed and loyal culture they've been part of for years, and the deep care with which they believed they'd done their work for the customers they serve—feel judged, harshly criticized, dismissed, and even indicted. Not surprisingly, their commitment to helping the new executive realize any of his vision for change disappears, if it was ever there to begin with. Worse, if their anger is aroused enough, they may even set out to actively sabotage the new leader's vision and agenda. It's one of the most painfully common entry stories we see, and is so easily avoidable. The best thing an executive entering under these circumstances can do is to both honor and harness the culture that is there. The last thing you want to do with a set of loyal and committed employees is squelch their commitment and condemn their efforts with unintended acts of public shame. Those cultural norms are one of the greatest assets for change available, and if you squander them, you do so at your own peril. Hold up such a culture as an extraordinary accomplishment. Recognize that those employees are likely all too aware of the inadequacies of the tools with which they've been working, and leverage their commitment and loyalty in the service of needed change that most of them, though perhaps not all, would likely welcome as much as you.

ENSURE YOUR HALO DOESN'T BECOME A NOOSE

Every newly arriving executive enters with some degree of the halo effect. This is intensified when they either arrive behind an exiting leader who was fiercely disrespected or were selected by a predecessor who was especially beloved. You arrive with the status of an organizational savior and to broad belief that your presence equates to the promise of a secure future, until they discover you aren't perfect. We've watched countless executives enter organizations under the heightened sense of anticipation for the greatness they will bring, only to have a slow, low-grade buyer's remorse set in as the inevitable imperfections any leader brings start to appear. Their natural proclivity to compare you with past results becomes an irrational blow to their confidence in your appointment.

Either you "aren't that much better than the last guy, and maybe the devil we knew was better," or "Wow, now I really miss so-and-so; we didn't realize how good we had it." This then distorts their ability to objectively appreciate the very gifts for which you were selected. The predictable pattern then follows as the organization slowly withdraws its support, sometimes irrecoverably, from newly appointed executives whose unaddressed development needs become the magnified distraction of the organization. Totally unaware, and often without the necessary calibration feedback mechanisms, the new executives redouble their efforts in response to the mysterious loss of influence, further broadcasting their warts and obscuring their gifts. The vicious cycle rarely ends well. Again, your best defense is a well-crafted learning plan that acknowledges the areas to which you must adapt your leadership while avoiding the "go native" issue and allowing people to see that the organization has as much to shape in you as you have change to effect in it.

WHEN YOU ARRIVE FROM INSIDE THE ORGANIZATION

Executives arriving into the Strategic system from *inside* their own organizations need to incorporate these elements into their entry plan.

RE-CALIBRATE RELATIONSHIPS WITH NEW AND FORMER PEERS

One of the most perplexing discoveries executives rising into the Strategic system from within their organization make is that of a reconfigured peer set. It can literally make them feel like they've arrived on a different planet. First, those who are no longer peers—some of whom may now be direct reports—treat you differently than they used to, uncertain how much they can now trust whether or not "you're still you." Then there are those with whom you are now a peer, more experienced executives who've learned to navigate the political waters of the Strategic system. These leaders have learned who their nemeses are, who their allies are, and with whom they are competing for the hallowed next rung up that corporate ladder. You feel like the proverbial stranger in a hostile, foreign land, longing for the trusted peers of the land you left behind. You have two dilemmas. Those relationships with former peers can serve you every bit as well as they always have, but you must redefine how they will work in the context of your new role. The relationship with your new peers takes on increased importance, yet is consistently one of the most common derailers of executive careers the higher they rise. Steven Harvard Davis points out that

> [T]he new executive's company usually helps identify the key players within the organization: those people that control budgets and those that supply goods or services. However, to succeed, a new executive also needs to identify the various alliances that exist, the opinion makers, and the people with expert knowledge or influence. All too often, identifying such people is left to the skills of the new appointee, rather than being part of the induction process." Failure to build relationships is one of the key factors Davis cites as driving the 40 percent failure rate within eighteen months among newly appointed senior executives.[16]

Trust at the executive level is extended and withheld on very different bases than it is at the Coordinating system level. The stakes are higher, the wins and losses far more public, and the vying for resources and advancement more ruthless. The rules of the game aren't written anywhere, so most executives just take their cues from whoever appears to be the most successful and from those who have the ear of the CEO. The executives we've seen prevail at this new perch are those with an unwavering sense of self, principles of integrity and courage, whose willingness to acquire knowledge in the service of the greater good of the enterprise is clear, and who are not emotionally unstable in the face of unforeseen setbacks or sophomoric rivalry from their new peers. Because relationship building at the executive level is such a critical determinant of success, the next chapter devotes a significant portion to the work of how relationships get defined, and redefined, upon arrival into the executive ranks. For the purposes of this chapter, what is important to remember is that you have to purposefully plan that transition and thoughtfully construct, and reconstruct, those relationships—it won't happen on its own.

LEVERAGE YOUR KNOWLEDGE OF THE ORGANIZATION WITHOUT YOUR BIASES

As an insider, you have a clear advantage over an entering outsider in the knowledge you possess about the organization—how it works, who to go to for what, how decisions get made and resources get allocated, what is and is not celebrated or punished—and for this reason, executive failure rates are slightly lower for internal rather than external arrivals. As the Booz & Co. 12th Annual Global CEO Succession Study found, though outsider CEO appointments were higher in 2011 than they were five years earlier, insider CEOs continued to perform better and served longer in the role.[17] Equally helpful is the organization's knowledge of you—you are a known entity—and whether or not people believe you deserved the promotion; that you are known can work to your advantage.

Of course this mutual knowledge has a dark side. You and the organization also have biases about one another that may distort the accuracy of your knowledge. These mutual biases, if not carefully deconstructed, can become a liability. You must recognize and address mutual biases with honesty and intention. The newly appointed global chief marketing officer in one of our client organizations had a track record of success across a variety of roles over her seventeen-year tenure. On top of her excellent performance, the organization, for the most part, adored her. When her picture appeared on the cover of *Fortune* as one of "America's most influential executive women," no one was surprised. That is, no one but the chief operating officer, who had never been a fan. Now he was her peer, and his disapproval of her appointment infected the rest of the organization and made it tough for her to influence the very business units she needed to help grow. His bias about her was formed nearly a decade earlier when she was in Europe and he was running the global supply chain. She struggled to gain traction in her first year there due to the learning curve associated with cultural and language barriers, new business lines, and new go-to-market approaches. To him, she was disorganized, was easily flustered, lacked confidence, and was basically ill equipped to "take charge" of situations. In his mind, that's how she remained. He didn't recognize or acknowledge that she had grown and changed. She knew she had never outgrown that reputation with him, and to be fair, she did struggle in new situations to assert her leadership effectively.

As is true with most biases, his was not completely unfounded. It was, however, exaggerated and based on old data. The real problem is that he projected this view of her to the rest of his organization. The result: She was met with uncooperative and resistant behavior from those with whom she—and the other marketing partners—needed to collaborate. In a demonstration of her leadership growth she addressed the issue head-on and got a meeting with the COO. She was direct, forthright, and confident in her approach, and throughout the dialogue remained gracious and collegial. "I understand that nearly a decade ago, you believed my performance fell short and that I was a weak leader. While I may not have become the perfect leader since then, I'm far from the leader I was, and far from the leader I still seem to be in your head, and now in the heads of your organization. If I'm going to help your people succeed—and you know I can—then you're going to need to let go of this image you have of me from years ago and let me be the leader I've become. I'm not afraid of feedback, so if I don't meet your expectations, I want you to tell me, and rest assured when you don't meet mine, I will show you the respect of telling you directly, and only you. You and I need to work together to help these businesses grow." What was scheduled to be an hour-long meeting turned into three. A lot of air was cleared and a number of misperceptions addressed. Their relationship was by no means immediately perfect, but over the coming year, the tenor of how they, and their organizations, worked together dramatically improved. Her knowledge of him, his career, and his businesses, and her understanding of their mutual biases of one another, served to create a game-changing conversation. Had they not had the conversation, their organizational rift would have persisted and severely undermined the company's performance.

EXTRACT YOURSELF FROM THE COORDINATING SYSTEM WORK THAT OTHERS MUST NOW ASSUME, WHETHER OR NOT YOU BELIEVE THEY ARE READY

While this certainly is applicable to executives entering from outside the organization as well, the more common failure is among those from within the organization. Very often we see people rise out of the Coordinating system who neglect to leave their old work behind. Our respondents bemoan, "It's shocking how tentative direct reports can be when empowered to make decisions. Their reliance on me for *everything* is just exhausting. People expect me to make blanket decisions rather than participate in them with me. Trying to help them solve their own problems versus solving them for them is a persistent dilemma."

It is challenging for many to let go of the work they know and that earned them the promotion to begin with, and embrace learning an entirely new role with its associated set of unfamiliar requirements. Often the new role demands that you unlearn what you *were* good at in order to learn what you *now* need to be good at. The most common excuse we hear from executives for failing to let go is that their successors "simply aren't ready to take on the full set of responsibilities," so they feel the need to extract themselves "gradually" so as not to create a huge gap. While there may be some truth to this, the gradual extraction usually stretches into years, with the full transference of responsibility never occurring, and the development of successors in the Coordinating system often arrested. Of course there is no flipping a switch to turn off your participation in Coordinating work and turn on your engagement in Strategic work. A well-choreographed plan, however, that plots your extraction in measurable milestones will help ensure you leave behind a more capable organization that is not dependent on you for their success, while creating sufficient capacity for you to focus on key aspects of your new role.

The rest of this chapter will illustrate in greater detail how the shift from Coordinating to Strategic system is likely to play out. These migration pathways should help you carefully and deliberately plan your own transition.

REFLECTIONS ON THE RISE

1. If your experience of rising is that of an outsider, how did you manage the assimilation process from your side? What could you, or the organization you joined, have done differently? What might Jordan and Huntington have done differently to help Jacinta?

2. If your experience of rising is that of an insider, how did you recalibrate relationships? What challenges did you face in letting go of the Coordinating system?

PREPARING FOR YOUR SHIFT

Arriving at the executive level means leaving behind executional and organizational responsibilities and donning the executive mantle. This requires a substantial shift from tried-and-true methods to new attitudes and ways of working commensurate with your new role. You will definitely experience discomfort, both in giving up what you've used successfully in the past and in getting acclimated to new demands. And most newly minted executives struggle at this pivotal intersection. Fifty-seven percent of our respondents indicated decisions were more complicated and involved than they expected and that those they lead over-rely on them for decisions they should be making on their own. And as previously mentioned, nearly two-thirds of our respondents struggled to let go of work they used to do. The data indicate the shift must be a gradual one, not a cold start. A move into the Strategic system of the enterprise involves a shift in several key dimensions from one way of thinking or working to another. And with each shift, you must have the faith that you are making the organization more, not less, capable by forcing it to rise along with you to fill the gap you leave behind. Accept that each time you choose to regress, you weaken those beneath you.

Here are the shifts leaders most commonly grapple with.

FROM THE TYRANNY OF THE URGENT TO THE ART OF THE LONG VIEW

The Operating and Coordinating systems of the business reward a sharp focus on execution and paying attention to the biggest hurdles to making your numbers. We refer to this as the "tyranny of the urgent." In the Strategic system, the tyranny of the urgent translates into putting out fires without any awareness of a bigger picture. The head of the North American operations arm of a global consumer products company came to us because he was being criticized as being "incapable of action." Yet he was a very busy guy, traveling all over the United States and Canada and making numerous decisions every day. How could he be seen as "incapable of action"? We accompanied him for a few days and took note of what he actually spent his time doing. He was on a dawn-to-dusk fire drill, addressing one small crisis after another all over his organization. He was very popular among all the regional heads. They had a terrific relationship with him and felt they could call him whenever, wherever they needed him. They knew he would bail them out. But this was the head of all North American operations. None of the strategic work the global CEO and board expected of him was getting done. As we dug deeper, we found that many of the function heads also complained of numerous unresolved issues. They couldn't even get on his calendar because he was so involved with addressing smaller "urgent" matters. His inability to shift away from the tyranny of the urgent almost cost him his position.

You need to let other people do things you used to do, and in their own way and style, with your support and encouragement. Many leaders find it hard to "back off," and too often give in to the urge to jump in. As you shift away from the day-to-day running of the enterprise, you shift toward the task of what the organization will do to succeed next year and three years down the road. Determining if there is work that the Coordinating system isn't doing that it should, or if there are too many priorities given what you truly want to achieve, is the work you need to do. Your people need coherent direction from you; that's the best help you can give them.

FROM HYPER-RESPONSIVE TO STEADY AND FOCUSED

Maintaining steady focus instead of being impulsive and reactionary allows you to become the North Star for your people and organization. Your people need to know that the hurdles they're clearing are all aligned and taking them in a direction that achieves the results the strategy calls for. Markets are volatile—people will get knocked off course. You need to keep your sense of direction and your sense of proportion. Again, the speed with which you reacted in a coordinating role can now become a trap. During one of their wars, Hannibal of Carthage faced two Roman generals, Fabius and Flaminius. Flaminius was always eager to defeat Hannibal as quickly as possible, while Fabius preferred to wait, observe changing conditions, and then act accordingly. Fabius may have been unpopular with the Romans who were eager to act, but Hannibal said he feared Fabius more. Flaminius was defeated by Hannibal in battle, but Fabius wore the Carthaginians out over time and ultimately won the war. You need to find a new balance between consideration and action, and you need to include much more information in your decisions. When your organization seems to be pushed off course, you need to find the way back to the path. Quick, sharp turns are disorienting—your people will start to criticize you for your "direction of the week" approach, and they'll become unresponsive. Likewise, your people will lose focus and direction if you don't keep them moving. Providing your people with a steady focus and reserves of energy when they need them—these are key.

FROM SEEING THE PARTS TO SEEING THE WHOLE

Moving from a focus on parts to seeing the whole is deeply embedded in, and a natural part of, all the shifts you have to make. Many executives translate this to mean "I now need to think about all of the units and functions, not just those I used to run." That's true, of course, but "seeing the whole" has to do with *disciplines* as much as it does with units of the business. Seeing "wholes" versus "parts" means understanding the unique interconnections across the breadth of the organization and how value is actually created. No longer should you focus just on marketing or sales or logistics or innovation, but rather on your organization's ability to steward your brands and commercialize successful products. You must now see the "seams" of the organization as the places where competitive distinctions come to life. Seeing the whole means seeing the *broadest picture of the organization* in the context of its capabilities, markets, and strategy. It means enabling all the disparate parts to work together effectively to achieve goals—*not* rolling up your sleeves and doing it yourself. One of our respondents summed this up best in response to the question about which career experience best prepared him to be an executive:

> For me it was important to learn the business with a holistic view from product development to partnering with business leaders to product at shelf. I began my career in visual merchandising, moved purposely to product development, and then held mid-manager positions in two key categories before moving to senior leadership. The range of positions provided a wide view of the company and how organizations work together. It afforded me the opportunity to develop relationships across division lines and helped establish my reputation as a strong partner, honest and nonpolitical.

FROM DOING IT ALL TO PICKING YOUR BATTLES

Of the many challenges our survey respondents noted in their transitional difficulties, the issue of time topped the list. A full 61 percent of them indicated that people wanted more of their time than they had available. The amount of time spent firefighting and fending off the assault of small problems overwhelmed nearly all the executives in the research. One executive lamented,

> Learning to move from the detail or day-to-day operations to a more strategic perspective has been agonizing. Finding quiet time to "think" and "plan" rather than always being stuck in crisis mode has felt impossible. Our organization is very much a working manager / working executive environment that makes it challenging to lift up out of the details. There simply isn't enough time to tend to all the balls in the air. You are responsible for everything you do, and it's difficult to come to terms with how thin you are spread.

Learning to ruthlessly prioritize how you spend your time, and on what, from the get-go is critical to being effective in the Strategic system.

One CEO we knew prided himself on having an empty inbox on his corporate email account. Since everyone in the organization and many outside it—clients, reporters, regulators, and analysts—all had his address, you might wonder if he spent all of his time on email, or none of it because he merely deleted everything unread at the end of each day. In fact, he did neither. He was highly adept at scanning for things he felt needed his attention, responding to them with celerity, and either forwarding or discarding what he felt belonged elsewhere. This is one example of picking your battles. When you take on a top role at any large organization, you cannot expect to deal with even a fraction of the unfiltered demands for your attention that will swamp you every day. We know many executives who are in the same boat. You need to find a way to flag those issues that legitimately require your attention. In some cases, you will be the *only* person able to resolve them. In others, you may choose to intervene, because your presence and action convey a clear message. But your effectiveness wanes as you weigh in on too many issues. Indeed, you can become a terrible bottleneck if you insist on having a say on too much. One executive at a technology company we were supporting had a tendency to weigh in on every decision, even minor ones. The unintended consequence of this is that he divested his senior staff of decision-making authority and ultimately capability. The company quickly determined that it could not make any decisions without him and as a result, had become glacially slow. Get involved where you should—and where you feel you must. But choose wisely.

Strategic System Entry Planning Tool

Learning		
Learning priorities	**Data sources for insights**	**Disconfirming insights/patterns**
Business Context	• • •	• • •
Talent/team— capability; commitment to future	• • •	• • •
My leadership— personal impact; alignment with agenda	• • •	• • •
Priorities & Actions		
Focus	**Priority Issues**	**Actions**
Invest in key stakeholder relationships	• •	• •
Align talent with required capabilities	• •	• •
Establish feedback loops with broad organization • People's alignment with direction (change) • Impact of direction on performance • Experience of my leadership	• •	• •

IN FLIGHT

THE TRIP TO NEW YORK to make the final presentation to Newrizon approached with relentless speed. Despite his attempts to apologize to the design team, and the middle ground he and Elise had reached, Jordan could sense that the team's excitement and passion for this opportunity had taken a hit following the gruesome prototype review two weeks prior. Things were cordial between him and Elise, but she was guarded.

Jordan was getting his first bitter taste of what Mac had always referred to as "the Mac they make up in their heads." With a much thicker skin than Jordan, Mac was always able to joke about the differing versions of him that the organization concocted to decode his behavior. There was the benevolent dictator Mac, the cowboy Mac, the paternalistic Mac, the ruthless winner-take-all Mac, the party-all-night bad-boy Mac, the wise mentor Mac, and countless others. He often remarked that none of these versions were completely accurate—they were simply the way the organization made sense of Mac's words and actions. In truth, he was just a man with a big job—a person with numerous flaws, deeply caring and ruggedly calloused, human and principled, generous and self-interested. "Like all humans, I'm a collection of paradoxical contradictions," he would chuckle. "The difference between me and everyone else," he would explain, "is that while most people get to control which of their contradictions they let the world see, mine are all on public display for everyone to ponder and scrutinize simply because of the role I am in."

Jordan was now realizing just how many "Jordans" he'd helped the organization create in the last couple of weeks. Sadly, most were "Jordans" he never intended to be. Just from the feedback he'd received after that one meeting, there was now the "control freak Jordan," the "scared shitless Jordan," the "threatened by Elise Jordan," the "in over his head Jordan," and the most painful, the "just tell him what he wants to hear so you don't get your head blown off Jordan." He realized that trying to clean up and reconcile all of those misinterpretations could become a full-time job, and, from what Mac had taught him, a futile one at that. While he hadn't intended to be any of those things, he had to contend with the reality that his behavior had contributed to people's perceiving him to be all of them.

The design team was cool but polite as he wandered among them during their final preparations for the flight that evening. He couldn't help but wonder how he was going to put all his awkwardness aside, regain his confidence, and walk into Newrizon the next day portraying a united, optimistic, and energized front with Elise and the team. If there was ever a time Jordan missed Mac, it was now. He remembered his graveside promise to not let Mac down and felt he was precipitously close to doing exactly that.

Mac had an incredible way of mobilizing Huntington at those moments of truth when everything felt like it was on the line. Jordan imagined the final design team meeting Mac would have called just before departing for the airport—the pre-game locker room words of inspiration he would have had for everyone. How he would have helped melt the tensions and mend the inevitable scars accumulated along the way. Jordan couldn't quite imagine himself pulling such a meeting off—he could see the feigned smiles and rolling eyes of the team. He felt like an imposter.

He peeked into Elise's office where she was having a final review with the three product managers who would be joining them in the presentation. Elise looked up and said, "Hey Jordan—do you need something?" Instead of hearing Elise's genuine question, all Jordan saw were the three product managers lowering their heads instead of looking at him. Elise noticed too.

Jordan managed to mutter a reasonable response, "Nope— actually just wanted to see if you guys needed anything from me."

"We're good," Elise assured him. "Just going over some last-minute details. I'll stop over in a little while after we're done."

Jordan waved, and exited.

Jordan stopped by Carolyn's desk and asked for the printout of the final Newrizon presentation, saying "Notes version please—I just want to go over my talking points again."

"I'll bring them right in," Carolyn replied.

Jordan sat behind his desk and began to mindlessly scroll through email.

"Self-pity looks ugly on a CEO," he heard Carolyn say as she placed the talking points and slides down on his desk. He swung his head up to look at her.

"You think I'm feeling sorry for myself?" he countered, defensively.

"In a word, yes. You've been moping around for two weeks since that prototype review meeting tanked." Carolyn laughed. "How is anyone supposed to be excited about tomorrow when it looks as if you feel you're headed to the guillotine?"

"What am I supposed to do, just plaster on a fake smile like everything's perfectly fine when I know everyone is pissed off at me and thinks I'm a jerk?"

"Well, I don't know if that's the best alternative, but I'd take that over this any day," Carolyn stated firmly. "You apologized. How do you know everyone hasn't moved on and isn't wondering why you haven't? Maybe they think you're still mad at *them*. Ever think of that? It's no wonder they are making up versions of you in their heads you don't like when you seem to be going out of your way to be the 'Jordan' you fear they're characterizing you as. They may not be thinking you're a jerk at all, but you acting like one may lead them to."

"She's right, Jordan." Elise had stepped into the doorway. "Sorry for eavesdropping, but I needed to be reminded of that too, Carolyn."

Carolyn grinned.

Elise continued, "Jordan, the truth is that Huntington wouldn't be going to this meeting tomorrow without you. It's a tremendous opportunity for all of us and it was your vision and brilliance that got us here. Yes, you screwed up a few weeks ago. So did I. We both owned it and now we have to move on. People gossiping and chattering about us is part of the territory. Right now this team needs to hear that you are totally sold on this opportunity, and that you believe in them to land it. You walking around sulking only makes them lose confidence in themselves, not in you. No one expects you to be Mac. But we do expect you to lead us. Don't blow this moment, Jordan. There's just too much riding on it."

After a few silent moments, Jordan smiled at Elise. "Thanks. Could you pull the team together in the boardroom in a half hour?"

"You got it." Elise grinned and headed out.

Carolyn crossed her arms in front of her and had a mischievous "it's about time" look on her face. He just shook his head and laughed.

Headed out the door with her, he said, "So Mac told you about his 'Macs they make up in their heads' theory too, huh?"

She gave him a sarcastic look and replied, "Where the heck do you think he got it from?"

CHAPTER FOUR

ALTITUDINAL DISTORTIONS

HOW YOU AND THE WORLD
LOOK DIFFERENT FROM UP HERE

FROM PIXELS TO PICTURES:
THE DISTORTIONS OF HIGHER ALTITUDE

A FEW YEARS BACK, A FRIEND OF OURS went skydiving for the first time. It was on her "bucket list" and so, consistent with her nature, she approached it logically. She gathered detailed information about the mechanics of the dive, risks and probabilities, the equipment, who had the best reputation in the area for instruction, and so on. She made a point of talking to many divers, both experienced and novice. Satisfied with her preparation, she dove. A full week later she was still exhilarated and frankly a bit astonished at what she'd done. Despite being both well informed and well equipped, she said that nothing she had done before prepared her for the actual feeling of falling at well over one hundred miles per hour from thousands of feet above the ground. "I can't really explain what it's like—I can tell you about it, but it's nothing like experiencing it," she said. Taking on one of the top positions in an organization is similar—you can study it, talk to people who do it, and observe it in action, but until you are sitting in the chair it is very difficult to anticipate how you will respond. New senior executives often report feeling this free-fall sensation: Your past experience is all on the ground and doesn't necessarily provide the best guidance for how to "leap from the plane.

Once you are actually in a new role, everything looks and feels different. Most of what you took for granted and relied upon to succeed doesn't work the same way in this new environment. Your senses suffer distortion, old and trusted ways of coping simply don't work, people don't react to you the same way, and you feel surprisingly vulnerable. Many executives don't expect this and are knocked off balance.

Years ago, the autostereogram was popularized by the series called Magic Eye: a 2D picture that if you stared at it long enough, squinted in just the right way, would reveal a magic 3D image from the pixels.

The combination of taking the free-falling plunge and squinting is commonly what it feels like for executives to reorient themselves to the views of themselves and their organization from their new perch.

Of the many altitude distortions executives have asked for our help with, these are the ones that are almost predictable regardless of your role at the new elevation.

LARGER THAN LIFE

Talented cinematographers understand the power of perspective. They exploit the angle of the camera to manipulate our emotions. George Lucas effectively established Darth Vader's menacing character by taking the six-foot-seven David Prowse, who played him, and shooting him from a low angle, amplifying his already imposing presence. Alfred Hitchcock pulled us into the dark world of Norman Bates by consistently shooting the house from a low angle, causing us to feel small and anxious. By virtue of your role and its position in the organizational hierarchy, those at lower levels see you from a similar low vantage point that can distort their perspective of you.

How others see you changes significantly as you rise. You take on the persona inherent to your position, which may or may not reflect who you are or how you want people to see you. Some people will revere you; others will actually fear you. The demands of your job will often make you less physically present and accessible to some, and people will naturally fill in the resulting voids with stories of their own. Many of the senior executives we've coached have been surprised when they realized that people were making stuff up about them. Jordan was at least one step ahead, knowing that people were casting him in roles he had not intended. Remember, by virtue of your role, your presence is felt no matter how accessible, inaccessible, close, or distant you are. This is in part due to the phenomenon of *embodiment*. Sitting atop a function or a business, you *embody* your organization. If you lead Marketing, for example, to the rest of the organization, you *are* Marketing. If you lead the West Division, or the Apparel Division, you *are* the West Division or the Apparel Division. Don't resist this reality; it comes with the territory. Still, don't allow the role or others to completely define you. You must work to prevent a default persona from becoming the way people see you. Be thoughtful about how accessible you are, and when necessary take steps to increase that access with key individuals or groups. Provide insight into what you value and believe; share the essence of who you are and your vision for the role. Consciously incorporate that in both formal and informal meetings, what and how you write, and the stories you tell. As your sphere of responsibility and influence grows, so will your reputation. The higher up you are, the more your reputation matters, and the further outside your direct control it becomes. It will take on a life of its own, entering every room before you do. Your name will be bandied about in offices and break rooms across the company and be on the lips of people you've never spoken to. Rest assured, everyone will have an opinion about who you are. You won't be able to control everything people believe, and you shouldn't make yourself crazy trying; however, if you are not deliberate about what others see and how people experience you, chances are the image they form will be one that you do not intend or desire.

THE MEGAPHONE EFFECT

The larger-than-life view of you has an important corollary that we call "the megaphone effect." Imagine that you speak through a massive bullhorn 24/7. This image is truer than you might realize. The verbal and behavioral messages you send are amplified the moment you step into your new elevated role. Newly appointed senior executives from vastly different industries—one in digital media and the other from a global deep-earth mining organization—said essentially the same thing to us only weeks apart: Both found people kept try-ing to read the future from their off-the-cuff remarks. "I'm just trying to make small talk in the elevator and I've got this creepy feeling they're looking at me like the prophet Elijah," one of them said sadly. "Every time I open my mouth someone attaches meaning to it. I keep hearing people say 'Bill said,' and it is generally to bolster their own case. The 'Bill said' phenomenon is rampant, attributing things to me that I not only never said, but never even thought."

When you are one of the top leaders in your organization—and certainly when you become CEO—there is no "small talk." It becomes difficult for people to separate you from the role. You can certainly still talk to people— don't become stiff and formal—but always keep in mind how people experi-ence you. Try to be as clear as you can about your intentions and as precise as possible in your communication. A little forethought goes a long way. We call this "leading out loud," and we constantly find ourselves coaching newly appointed executives both on the need for it and how to do it effectively. One wise respondent aptly said, "Never take the power of your position for granted. Comments, suggestions, even audible pauses, hold much more weight and meaning now."

Take note: This is very different from "thinking out loud." One senior leader we worked with had a propensity to think out loud about possible direc-tions his group could take. He shared his thoughts about a number of potential opportunities at the end of one particular meeting, but left the room believing everyone had ended with the same "that's nice but now it's back to our day jobs" feeling he had. He was alarmed several weeks later when his group came back to him with a detailed proposal in support of one of the "pipe dreams" he had talked about briefly. They'd researched, developed a presentation, built a budget, and clearly spent a lot of time working on it. He was mortified. He'd had no intention of ever going in this direction and had certainly not wanted people taking up valuable time to explore it. Having to talk his people down from the excitement they had for the opportunity and clarify the mis-understanding was one of his most uncomfortable leadership moments. This is not uncommon. Leaders often launch significant initiatives and work efforts without ever intending to, simply by sharing their musings. If you are not clear in what you are saying, why you are saying it, and to whom, don't be sur-prised when people pick up on fragments and amplify or misinterpret them as directives. As one respondent astutely advises, "I must be careful what I say and in what context. People read more into what I say than I intend. People may drop priorities if I casually express interest in things outside their objectives. My voice must retain focus so they can retain their focus."

SIFTED DATA

The megaphone effect is about the distortions in your messages out to the organization. Just as troublesome is the distortion of message—and data—in to you. It is quite common for new executives to find the information flow on which they have depended dries up the moment they are elevated into their new role.

A former colleague worked in the research and design group of a large technology company. He often mentioned how fortunate he felt to be part of the group. If he needed anything, he only had to reach out and his peers would provide answers and resources. After he was promoted to run one of the core businesses he experienced an abrupt shift in the relationship with his former peers and team. While they expressed support for him, the information he now got from them felt "sifted" and "not as free flowing." He also noticed the nonverbal messages his former peers exchanged in meetings and recognized they were no longer sharing the full story with him. The unexpected experience was troubling and left him feeling off balance. From his perspective he was still the same person and believed his relationships with the group had not changed. Still, his colleagues didn't approach him as often and he found himself increasingly on the "outside." His insight into areas where he previously felt confident was diminished. People reacted to him in ways that were confusing and disconcerting. He came to us because he couldn't seem to find his footing. Stepping into a substantially larger role creates a host of altitude distortions. Accessing and managing the flow of information is one of the most challenging to contend with.

First, level set your expectations. Take stock of how information flows within the larger context of the business. Regardless of personal style or your previous expectations regarding participation, how information flows to and through your new level is largely influenced by a broader set of historic assumptions already in play. If promoted within the same organization, you at least have the advantage of knowing the key hubs of information brokering.

You know the typical conversations that occur before meetings with senior leaders, how information is edited, rationed, and choreographed in the room, and what typically happens afterwards. The difference is that you may now be on the receiving end of this orchestrated behavior. While you may feel uneasy, there is a silver lining in not having access to all that you did previously. It dramatically reduces the risk of your focus being diverted to levels of detail that are now someone else's primary concern. You will need to determine what information is most valuable in light of your new responsibilities and, using prior knowledge, consider how you might influence and work within known organizational patterns to access it.

Information is a currency of influence in all organizations. When you are new to an organization, you must quickly identify the key power brokers and begin to establish a quality working relationship with them. Even from positions of high influence, it is good to recognize you won't have total control over well-established operating norms. We have observed many senior-level executives enter new organizations expecting full access to information, only to find they have access to the data, but those who can bring the nuanced story and understanding to light have gone underground. In the next chapter, we'll explore the important implications of information as a source of executive power.

Mokita is a Papua New Guinean word that essentially means "a truth exists that everyone knows but agrees not to talk about." To varying degrees this type of collusion occurs in most organizations. As a senior executive, a critical role you play is to help eliminate *mokita* and ensure that information flows unrestrained to enable full organizational capacity.

Speaking truth can be risky—especially to those in positions of power. By nature we are predisposed to seek pleasure and avoid pain, and in most companies there is a degree of mythology mingled with reality in the stories told about the negative consequences of telling the truth. Obfuscating truth is a common way of avoiding the pain of a real or imagined negative response from others. Many employees also feel they lack the skill to effectively and directly deliver the message. This is your opportunity.

As an unknown in a new position, recognize that others' fear will stem from your imagined reactions within the context of current mind-sets and practices. Because larger forces are in play, the most meaningful lever you have is your own philosophy and behavior. Find opportunities early and often to prove to the organization that you are trustworthy and able to handle the truth.

People know you have the power to change their careers depending on what they tell you. Are you the kind of leader who shoots the messenger? When you step into your new role, no one understands exactly what you want or need to know. Styles vary widely, and people have to get comfortable with how you will use the information they give you. Many times, data sifting is a relic of your predecessor's time in office. Be up front with your information needs, be mindful of people's concerns, and above all be consistent in your style. Send mixed signals and you too will quickly find yourself struggling to piece together fragments of data.

ALIENS NEXT DOOR

No greater distortion will occur for newly arriving executives—especially those promoted from within—than in their existing relationships with peers and superiors. Former peers may now become direct reports, or at least remain at lower ranks. Former superiors become the new peer set where relational dynamics must also shift. Relationships once characterized by comfortable familiarity may now seem alien and others' reactions to you may be equally foreign and confusing.

Some of your former peers may mock or chide as they view you through the lens of jealousy or hurt, while others will withdraw or become deferent due to uncertainty in the new formal relationship. At times, sophomoric hazing rituals make executive entry painful for newly appointed leaders. A few may see it as an opportunity to leverage greater influence and actively apply pressure for you to act on their behalf. "Finally, now you'll fight for the promotion I've been denied so many times. You'll make it happen!" is an example of lobbied expectations new executives hear upon their arrival. It is also probable that you'll inherit numerous organizational injustices, some of which you too may well have resented, and you may feel pressure to make them right. And still others may simply write you off, believing that you too will soon devolve into one of those leader caricatures you've long complained about together. In fact, you will find yourself in the position of having to now manage the appearance of distorted decision making, as you will certainly carry forward the memory of what it was like to be at the lower level looking up and questioning the sanity of certain decisions. Now you are the decision maker with access to exclusive information and must figure out how to confidently lead without appearing as detached or insensitive as you once accused others of being.

However subtle or pronounced their individual views of and reactions to you are, you should proceed with the assumption that things are not, and will not be, the same. They simply can't be. Even though you won't believe you've changed personally—and you probably haven't—the situation and your leadership responsibilities have; therefore, successful rising executives make a conscious effort to reset expectations and boundaries with existing relationships at each new elevation. They first define for themselves and then deliberately discuss with colleagues things such as new priorities, access, frequency of contact, information flow, confidentiality, and appropriate ways to influence. It may feel awkward, but by resetting these expectations and clarifying boundaries you will free yourself from wondering about and disappointing others' privately held views and expectations of you and your new role. One executive we know was so painfully insecure leading her former peers that she went out of her way to neutralize any sense of hierarchical difference. While well intended, she did such a good job of self-comforting by reassuring everyone that "nothing was really going to change between them"—like the weekly lunch ritual they long shared—that when it came time to make hard decisions and hold volatile information with discretion, she failed. The luncheon became her stage for "going native" and complaining to her old friends with newfound frustrations, burdening them by disclosing highly inappropriate information and colluding with them when it came to justifying underperformance. During enterprise talent calibrations, her team did not fare well, and her attempts to defend them only made her look weak and out of touch. She padded the delivery of hard messages with, "I don't agree with these ratings, but here's where you came out in the mix . . ." Despite her attempts to distance herself from the messages, team members felt betrayed and quickly withdrew their loyalty. Within a year her department had devolved into such chaos that the business unit president was forced to break it up and reorganize the work. She was moved to a smaller role and, though she retained her "rank," her influence and impact were clearly diminished. To date, her career has not regained the momentum it had when she took on her executive role.

You will also confront similar distortions in your new peer relationships. Some will freely welcome you and provide you with the access you've wanted but never had before, and some will remain aloof and distant to send the clear message that their acceptance is not automatic—that you must continue to earn your way in. Others may see you as a rival on the rise—someone to watch, measure, and occasionally manage to prevent your degree of influence from overshadowing their own. Among this new peer set you will likely feel isolated and wonder whom you can trust or confide in. As stated earlier, relationships with old confidants must reset, but new peer relationships have yet to form, leaving you in the murky middle for an uncomfortable period of time. Further distortions come when you make decisions about which of the existing executive norms you will adopt and which you will forgo—managing the pressure to become an insider, balanced with the broader impact on the organization, while also living true to your beliefs about effective leadership and the legacy you want to leave. How badly do you need acceptance? How do you want to be seen? Which of the executive prerogatives will you assume? Taking advantage of the valet car service and reserved parking space or eating exclusively in the executive dining room has one level of impact. Deciding not to relocate your office to the executive suite and instead choosing a location closer to the team has another. Of higher impact still will be the positions you take on colluding on pet projects and protection of budgets at the expense of higher-impact business opportunities, or sponsoring and promoting less deserving talent for political favor. Many respondents to our survey expressed common sentiments like, "I don't understand the politics of the organization," "I'm not a 'mover and shaker' by nature," "Decisions seem fairly straightforward, but then the merits aren't always what are important," "The importance of hallway conversations and after-hours lobbying is much greater than I anticipated." Perhaps the most sobering comment was, "The most helpful advice I got was not to assume that everyone wants you to succeed." Many new executives find such discoveries jarring and become discouraged or cynical. Being aware of these realities and deciding *well before* you face situations laden with such relational or political implications will help you to better navigate them once encountered. You will act with greater confidence when you are prepared with forethought, having answered for yourself: "How will I . . . ?" But also keep in mind that your answers will simply determine the type of alien you become and to whom.

Magnified versions of you, megaphone amplification of what you do and say, sifted data, and aliens: Withstanding these distortions is no easy task for even veteran executives. Navigating them effectively is best done with clear forethought and resolve before they are encountered. Here are the approaches we have seen guide successfully transitioning executives.

REFLECTIONS ON THE RISE

1. How do you assess how you are perceived in your organization? And how do you manage those perceptions and how they have changed as you've risen?

2. How do you calibrate the messages you send to ensure the least "alternate reality"?

3. How would you coach Jordan to better manage his own altitude distortions?

PREEMPTING DISTORTIONS: KNOW THE OPERATIVE NARRATIVES THAT SHAPE YOUR BEHAVIOR

One of the biggest challenges to clearing up altitudinal distortions is our own sense-making apparatus. Given all the stimuli entering our brains at any given time and the relatively small proportion we are actually able to process, most of what we say and do is on autopilot. Our emotional response to any given situation, and the counterproductive or even destructive behaviors we sometimes exhibit, originate from deep, formative moments in our past. We catalogue these moments and they become subconsciously recorded as the stories or *operative narratives* that help us make sense of the world, our role and relationships in it. Current events or situations simply trigger them. Unfortunately, most leaders fail to discover and address the origins of their ineffective behaviors before or during their ascent, putting both the organizations they lead and their own careers in peril. The higher you rise—the greater the visibility, influence, impact, and distortions of altitude—the greater the danger.

All of us have behavioral blind spots. Achieving greater fitness for the career climb ahead—more fully cultivating an asset, downplaying an overused strength, or eliminating unwanted consequences of a flat side—a leader's preparation must go deep to access and understand the origins of behavior.

Manfred Kets de Vries, world-renowned expert on leadership and a brilliant clinician who has studied the clinical paradigm in the context of organizations, says in his book *The Leader on the Couch: A Clinical Approach to Changing People and Organizations*, "Organizations the world over are full of people who are unable to recognize repetitive behavior patterns that have become dysfunctional. They're stuck in a vicious, self-destructive circle and don't even know it—much less how to escape."[18]

An individual's self-perceptions, skills, aspirations, insecurities, motivations, and pathologies (known and unknown) directly impact their effectiveness, and thus discovering, maturing, and refining these is one of a leader's most important mandates. You can readily spot the leaders who have done the necessary work to understand and manage their operative narratives and triggers. They are seasoned leaders with a career track record of successful organizational leadership, who have a following of loyal employees who say things like, "Best guy I ever worked for," or "I learned a ton from her," or "Sure, she's got high standards, but you'll never have a leader fight for you harder than she will." They are far from perfect, but they have consciously harnessed what makes them great, and have identified and quarantined what makes them dangerous. They have developed the ability to continually fine-tune and reinvent their leadership by reflecting on, and deconstructing and incorporating knowledge from, formative moments in a way that fuels their personal success and the success of the companies they work for. Before delving into your own operative narratives, consider the following:

CLARIFY WHAT YOU BELIEVE AND VALUE

The sum of your life experiences to this point has served to shape and reinforce a foundational structure of beliefs and values, which forms the ballast and the rudder that keep you aright and steer you through the vicissitudes of life. At its essence, this system of beliefs defines your individuality. In the past you have faced defining moments—challenging experiences that forced you to make hard choices and revealed much about what you most care about; the experiences served to shape your attitudes, biases, and assumptions about the way the world works, as well as who you are, how you fit, and how you can successfully navigate through. Now would be a great time to take an inventory and examine those beliefs and their impact on your behavior. Don't leave to chance any potential negative implications for their present impact on your personal and others' well being.

Begin by drawing a timeline of your life and identifying critical turning points—significant life experiences that shaped the way you see things. Ask yourself:

1. What was particularly impactful about the event?
2. What did it force me to decide or do differently as a result?
3. What did I learn about myself through that experience?
4. How has that experience impacted subsequent moments of decision?
5. What is the core value or belief I hold as a result of that experience?
6. How does that value or belief show up in how I lead today?

As you evaluate these emotionally significant events, your belief system will emerge. But don't stop there. Further assess how the value or belief shows up in how you lead today. Identify the positive, consistent aspects and any potential disconnects between your current behaviors and what you believe. For example, a leader who touts trust as a foundational value for how he leads but is driven by a narrative that says, "People here are really incompetent and for anything to get done right, I have to do it myself," tends to create a high degree of individual and organizational confusion and widespread reluctance of others to act. Such disparities compromise your ability to lead effectively.

OWN YOUR PATHOLOGIES, OR THEY WILL OWN YOU

No one arrives at adulthood unscathed by their formative years. Despite even the most positive intentions of those who shaped our early environments, they were still flawed, with impacts now on our individual attitudes and behavioral tendencies toward such things as achievement, ambition, confidence, control, esteem, patience, power, redemption, respect, risk, and trust. In their mildest form, attitudinal and behavioral dysfunctions manifest as irritating personality quirks, but in their more severe forms (and especially when magnified by the increased pressure at higher organizational altitudes) they potentially become weapons of mass destruction. At middle levels of the organization, narcissism can be annoying. At the executive level, it can tank billions of dollars of shareholder value. Depression can hinder progress when it grips a middle manager. A depressed executive can darken an entire culture. As you rise, do the deeper work necessary to confront what, to this point, you may have learned to merely contain. Push to discover potentially problematic thought patterns. Find the necessary safe environment to expose them, address their origins, and re-script any misguided narratives that drive unwanted behavior.

GIVE OTHERS PERMISSION TO NAME YOUR TRIGGERS WHEN THEY APPEAR

Most people are notoriously bad observers of their own reality, and this holds especially true for executives. Most aren't sufficiently self-aware to recognize when something has triggered them, and worse, once situations have devolved into unhealthy and damaging choices, they find themselves asking, "How did I get here?" Our reflexive actions, particularly under stressful circumstances, are so deeply ingrained that they happen far faster than our cognitive ability to recognize, arrest, and address them. Among trusted colleagues, it can be a powerful and redemptive experience to allow others to gently point out that we may be taking a situation down a regrettable path, saying or doing things we later wish we could take back. Courageously, one client gave her entire team permission to call her out when her drive for results turned into unrealistic expectations and harsh critique. Each time someone did, she thanked them profusely.

CLOSE THE GAP BETWEEN YOU AND THOSE DISTORTING YOU: CREATE AND ANCHOR YOURSELF TO POSITIVE PARTNERSHIPS

Being thoughtful and deliberate about focusing your best efforts on developing positive partnerships with key stakeholders is vital to success at any level; however, building effective working relationships with peers is increasingly critical the higher you move up the organization. In fact, it is our observation that the strength of your peer relationships will be the strongest predictor of your sustained success as you rise. Certainly you must be competent in your functional discipline, but if you struggle to get along with and relate to your peers, you will soon find yourself mired in and distracted by unhealthy rivalry and political posturing and eventually being marginalized.

With few exceptions, the issue of developing and maintaining effective relationships comes up in every organization diagnostic we do. We recently completed an assessment of an enterprise that was full of potential but struggling to grow. The new CEO had laid out a clear strategic path, but it was evident that little was being done to implement it. As we completed the interview process, a strong underlying theme had emerged. The quality of working relationships among the senior executives was poor, and that sad fact was amplified throughout the organization. One executive in particular was consistently described as "technically brilliant," but those statements were quickly qualified by pointing to his strained relationships with peers and others. Even though his function was central to the growth path, he became isolated and ineffective. His lack of collaborative behavior and the poor quality of his relationships had isolated him to the point of his being branded as one to work around, not with. As you work to establish positive partnerships, keep the following in mind:

KNOW AND UNDERSTAND YOUR COLLEAGUES

First, identify who are the key individuals with whom you must develop effective working relationships. Then, subordinate your own wants and needs and ask yourself: What motivates them? What critical goals and key milestones are they trying to achieve? By what standard will they judge success? What challenges might they be facing? How can I contribute to their success? Take notes of your hypothesis and be observant, and then meet with them individually to find out. When you meet, tell them that you want to be an effective partner to them, and focus the conversation on getting answers to your questions.

Throughout the conversation, also try to discover what they look for in an effective partner, how they prefer to communicate, and any "hot buttons" they might have that would trigger a negative reaction. Listen carefully to the questions they ask of you and consciously gauge whether they initiate any form of politicking. If so, you must risk the relationship by calling the question and establishing clear boundaries of expectation up front. Return the focus to your sincere desire to support their success, but not at any price.

Reserve judgment or making commitments until after you've met with all of your key partners. Give yourself the benefit of a little time to assess the full picture of need before jumping in. We know several executives who maintain a spreadsheet containing the names of their partners with answers to each of the questions above. They carry them together with their own objectives as a constant reminder of the priorities they should be working.

BE LOYAL WHILE AVOIDING EXCESSIVE ACCOMMODATION

Loyalty at its essence is about sticking together. In a corporate setting, it manifests as a genuine commitment to the success of your peers and the organization as a whole. In healthy relationships, its presence enables companions to become better people than they could be alone. Loyalty means that you value and care about the other's well-being. It means that you can envision and are committed to a common future and intend to actively maintain the relationship. This interdependence will impact your motives, preferences, behaviors, and outcomes, and it will sometimes require forgoing your immediate self-interest. Loyalty demands a measure of sacrifice. It means honoring others when they are not present, but also speaking tough truths to them when necessary in support of their success. You can't be loyal and play political or power games. Avoiding these will truly set you apart.

Loyalty is particularly important in the relationship with your boss. Ensure that you clearly understand and align with her vision and objectives. Advocate for her agenda where appropriate, but be an independent thinker. Spar supportively on ideas to make them better. Be transparent. Share any hard news early, and never surprise her. Don't be afraid to ask for help, but leverage her air cover judiciously. Give her no reason to doubt your motives and allegiance. At the same time, don't let your loyalty be confused with a level of accommodation that suggests you are buying favor. The conditions for your loyalty should be based on the worthiness and commitment to your partner's cause, not on what she returns for it. If you are seen as overly deferent, not only will your loyalty be questioned, but so too will your credibility as an executive able to stand on your own.

BE TRUSTWORTHY AND TRUSTING, BUT NOT NAÏVE

Trust is foundational to all human relationships. Building trust of an enduring nature requires effort as it is built and reinforced by consistent action and focused energy over a sustained period of time. Hard work, time, and energy, and some degree of risk taking, are required if people are to reap the full potential for satisfaction and productivity in their interpersonal relationships. Rising executives must particularly focus on building trust with peers and key partners.

The highest leverage effort you can make toward success in any endeavor involving interdependent relationships is to become trustworthy. It is a trait admired and sought after globally. For trust to grow, you must consciously work at earning the right to be trusted. Becoming a trustworthy executive depends on your competence and the consistent results you deliver, as well as the integrity of your character—the way you achieve those results. Your character is revealed in the way you communicate and stand up for what you believe in, honor your commitments, speak honestly and transparently without guile, admit mistakes, apologize when needed, keep confidences, be fair and show diplomacy when dealing with others, and forgive and move on. As you've likely experienced, the ability to deepen trust demands hard work, and yet destroying it can happen in one moment of lapsed judgment.

As trust grows, interpersonal dynamics will be positively transformed. Diverse skills and abilities become mutually acknowledged and valued as strengths. Positive attitudes and feelings toward each other increase. Communication becomes more efficient and clear. Candor increases as people more confidently offer differing opinions and disconfirming data absent any fear of offending or retribution. They risk conflict to push each other to deeper communication, involvement, and commitment because they believe the others' motives are pure.

Just as trust creates a positive multiplier effect by its mere presence, its absence has an equally debilitating impact. Always keep in mind the fragile nature of trust. It can be destroyed quickly. Just one misguided action can erase the bond that has taken years to build. Once trust is betrayed, a predictable and destructive pattern of suspicion and diminished confidence emerges. It is noteworthy that attempts to restore trust are more challenging than the effort required to initially gain it, and seldom is it restored to its previous state.

Your generous extension of trust to others is as important as being trust-worthy. Make certain people know what it takes to earn and keep your trust so they can work to meet those expectations. Assuming positive intent for executives is an important posture versus withholding trust until people jump through enough hoops to earn it. For many in the middle and lower ranks of organizations, earning the trust and regard of a respected executive is one of life's most satisfying experiences. The power you hold to make people feel sig-nificant and well regarded by how you offer them trust can't be underestimated. And so you should be generous, but discerning. With the trustworthiness you seek to earn, and the trust you offer, you must not be naïve about the fact that there may be times when the trust you are earning or offering is being exploited in destructive ways. Be circumspect as you monitor how the trust exchanged between you and key partners is forming to ensure that it is not being subver-sively misplaced.

DEVELOP SELF-AWARENESS, NOT SELF-INVOLVEMENT

Only when you know yourself and what you stand for with certainty can you truly and confidently act as a leader with any degree of credibility. Harry Kraemer Jr., former chairman and CEO of Baxter International, identifies self-reflection as the first principle of being an effective leader. He concludes,

> You must have the ability to identify and reflect on what you
> stand for, what your values are, and what matters most to you,
> [and] be willing to look within yourself through regular self-
> reflection and strive for greater self-awareness. After all, if you
> aren't self-reflective, how can you truly know yourself? If you
> don't know yourself, how can you lead yourself? If you can't
> lead yourself, how can you lead others?[19]

As you master internal reflection, shift your focus to observing the impact of your beliefs and behaviors on those around you. Acquire the discipline to regularly examine yourself through others' eyes. Develop a third eye that can stand apart and watch you and the dynamics you create in any given situa-tion. By learning to watch yourself you will develop deeper empathy and will come to understand what it must be like for others to have a relationship with you. Chances are that you probably already have a sense for how others must experience you. Still, there are many executives we've known who were completely oblivious to the effect of their words and actions on others and were the only people in their organizations who didn't know that they were failing miserably. Every organization has a few. A critical question you should answer is, "Am I one of them?"

One word of caution: Some executives take this too far. They work so hard at being "self-aware" that all they ever talk about is themselves. Every organization has "that leader" who reads a new self-help book every week and then spends exhaustive hours telling everyone else how it changed his life and pointing out reasons why others would benefit from it too. The communal benefits of your genuine self-awareness will be noticeable. No need for you to broadcast them.

REMAIN GENUINELY GRATEFUL AND GENEROUS TO RESIST ENTITLEMENT

There is no greater emotional force in an organization than gratitude. William James said, "The deepest craving of human nature is the need to be appreciated." Regardless of whether you agree, it is certain that we all desire to be seen as significant and to know our contributions matter; otherwise, we wouldn't strive so hard to win the veneration of those leaders we serve. Oddly, today's leaders seem to do one of two things that frustrate this craving. Some withhold their gratitude, feeling that people shouldn't be thanked for just doing their job. Others feel it's important to express thanks, but they use gratitude's cheaper counterfeit, the superficial compliment. "Way to go," "Nice job," "Kudos," and countless more platitudes fill office communication with empty calories that leave the soul undernourished.

Genuine gratitude is a social emotion that strengthens relationships because it requires us to see how we've been supported and affirmed by other people. By its nature, heartfelt gratitude acknowledges that the contribution is an extension of the contributor, whereas compliments can disregard them completely. To feel and express honest gratitude is to recognize that the source of goodness and accomplishment comes most often from outside yourself and not from anything you necessarily did yourself in which you might take pride. True gratitude is to readily acknowledge your deep dependence on others. As an executive, you will be surrounded by many who sincerely exert their best efforts to not only feel proud of their accomplishments, but to make you proud as well. Your gratitude will engender a chain reaction of emotions—generosity, delight, pride, and passion among them. It is one of the most generative expressions in any communal endeavor. Think about the times you have been genuinely appreciated for something. What did it make you feel? What did it provoke you toward? Gratitude is one of the most underutilized postures of an executive's leadership. It takes into account the bone-deep understanding that the position you occupy is a privilege; therefore, the opportunities you enjoy are to be cherished. The influence you extend should cause you to pause and feel humbled.

Of course, gratitude is a difficult posture to sustain. It requires constant effort in the face of grinding demands and draining responsibilities that leave us feeling depleted and resentful. As a general rule, humans focus on the negative— what is wrong or lacking. This natural preoccupation begins to dominate our mind and too soon becomes our expectation, and as we come to expect it, we seek it out and create even more negativity in our life. The ultimate result is a lifetime of disappointing outcomes, or worse, a sense of entitlement—keeping an inventory of what the world owes us for our sacrifice rather than an inventory of what we have been blessed to experience and contribute. Entitlement is one of the most dangerous precipices on which executives can find themselves and leads to a host of bad choices that we'll explore later.

Living with gratitude requires that you consciously and daily affirm the goodness in your life. This doesn't mean that life is perfect; it doesn't ignore complaints and burdens. But firmly embracing and expressing thanks for what you should be genuinely thankful for lightens the load for yourself and those with whom you work. Staying focused on the abundance of our lives and in our world will revolutionize your impact and the experience others have of your leadership.

DETECT PATTERNS TO CLEAR UP ORGANIZATIONAL DISTORTIONS

One of the biggest hurdles many executives face as they rise to the rank of executive is shifting from seeing themselves as *problem-solvers* to *pattern recognizers*. In the Strategic system you need to see patterns in the marketplace, patterns in how your organization responds, patterns in how groups operate, and patterns in how people behave. You need to evaluate and respond to patterns at a systemic level instead of responding to a particular instance outside of the greater context. Like the images hiding in stereograms, organizational patterns sometimes don't appear until you squint enough and seemingly unrelated dots suddenly connect.

Effective leaders have great pattern-recognition skills, and, over time, build pattern libraries in their minds that enable them to easily spot trends, detect shifts in the organization early, and look at issues and opportunities from a much higher altitude. There are many types of patterns one could watch for, but we have seen four that can be of great benefit to leaders looking to lead big change.

Historical patterns

Appropriately considering the history of an organization—its successes and failures, its struggles and growth, its evolving reputation—is critical in predicting how well an organization may perform in the future. Stepping back and looking at patterns instead of isolated events helps inform decisions about future direction. This doesn't mean using the past as an excuse—"We've tried that before and it didn't work;" it means using the past as a reference point for choices about future change. In one organization in which we worked, the history of failed change efforts was so pervasive that the mere mention of the word *change* was received with rolled eyes and cynicism. The credibility of any change—no matter how brilliant—was so low because of their poor track record that the organization had become immobile. Executives mistakenly determined the problem was too many people "from the past" who couldn't "get" the vision. They decided what was needed was fresh thinking from people less steeped in the past. They did need fresh ideas to an extent, but because nobody was offering any from within the organization, the dangerous fallacy in their diagnosis was that people from the past couldn't get it. A careful study of nine years of change efforts revealed that at every major intersection—new competitive entrants, changing technologies, new geographic opportunities— the organization responded (fourteen times over nine years) with a massive "campaign" approach to change. The campaigns had great fanfare and sizzle: posters, logos, big kickoff events, and lots of glitzy communication from the

CEO. Unfortunately, the implications of the proposed changes were very often operational and technological, and employees in those roles didn't respond well to mandates and that kind of communication. Worse, those being impacted generally had some of the best potential ideas and knew how to bring them to life, but were never engaged or listened to. Instead, ideas were consistently pushed down from the top to the operations and technical experts who couldn't take them seriously because they were, for the most part, not implementable in the form in which they arrived. Had the organization recognized that pattern sooner, it could have grown by billions of dollars over the period we analyzed.

Horizontal patterns

There are patterns across the enterprise indicative of emerging norms that may or may not be desirable. Unfortunately, rather than digging in, assessing and really understanding what these true patterns are, many leaders pick up on anecdotal comments—generally those that align with their preconceptions—and then use hyperbole to bolster the case for their views. "Everybody" is feeling this way. "I've heard from all over the organization that . . ." "It's not that big a deal, we don't need to worry about . . ." Whether to heighten a sense of urgency or to minimize it, leaders often make fairly weak attempts to spot patterns that cross the enterprise. In one commercial real estate company, forecasting had become dangerously erratic and unreliable. In a booming real estate market, there is room for messy forecasts because cash is pouring in. However, when the real estate market turned, it revealed a number of substantial deficiencies in the company, including a weak sales force that, for fear of losing its jobs, embellished forecast data with vague terms and irrelevant numbers. The misuse of scant data was an evolving pattern across the entire company. The issue was twofold. People feared the loss of their jobs in the face of recent RIFs, and the systems and capabilities needed to produce data that would enable more reliable forecasts, budget projections, and market trends had never been built. The more pressure that was put on the system to perform in an increasingly challenged market and the less useful or accurate the data, the more people felt compelled to make things up. Had the senior leaders spotted this pattern early in the market decline, they could have accelerated the work to build the data sets needed for better decision making. They would have allayed a lot of anxiety and improved the organization's performance a lot sooner.

Economic patterns

Economic patterns are revealed only by looking *across* an array of data sets—sales trends, costs, margins, ROIC, cash reserves, industry or geographic buying patterns, or commodity costs—to see what of significance emerges. Even in the era of great enterprise resource planning technology, many organizations still lack the analytic capability to spot early economic shifts, both in their marketplaces as well as their organizations. However, having the necessary analytic capability—both technological and intellectual—to see the patterns and translate them into insights and actions is what creates competitive differentiation. Making well-informed moves before competitors do, stemming unwanted tides of cost increases, or accelerating sales volume in the face of unforeseen demand is what sets truly successful companies apart.

Cultural patterns

A host of surveys available today can reveal a veritable gold mine of patterns that, if detected and acted upon, could unleash unimaginable levels of commitment and engagement. The use of employee engagement surveys, organizational health surveys, and online employee feedback tools, as well as communication devices such as newsletters, town halls, intranet sites, and mass email distributions, are all very common in organizations today. What is striking is the small degree to which the data collected are leveraged to increase the overall health of the organization or the engagement of employees. Nearly 75 percent of all large companies in the United States now use some form of employee engagement survey. In one organization that conducts an employee engagement survey every two years, a close look at the data from the last four surveys (eight years of data) quickly revealed the number of tenured employees (more than ten years) who would leave the company for a better opportunity was increasing with each successive survey. It had increased from 38 percent (already an alarming number) to 64 percent over eight years. HR leadership had concluded that since actual attrition hadn't risen at the same rate, there was no cause for alarm. They failed to realize that quitting and leaving weren't the problem they needed to worry about. The real issue was many long-tenured employees—those with the greatest levels of institutional knowledge and experience—were actually quitting and staying! The struggles of newer and younger employees to advance or get their ideas heard was causing huge turnover at less-tenured levels—not because that population was the most dissatisfied, but because those who led them were. Had someone recognized and acted on the pattern revealed by the data, efforts could have been made to reengage tenured professionals, reactivate their commitment, and leverage their great wisdom and experience. Their performance would have improved, as would have the engagement and retention of those below them. The same way market insights about cultural patterns help drive understanding of consumer behavior and inform choices about product portfolios and features, so too should insights about cultural patterns enable leaders to make strategic choices about how to shape or shift the organization's behavior to ensure that employees from top to bottom are fully participating in optimizing performance.

REFLECTIONS ON THE RISE

1. How have you built relationships differently to reflect your leadership role?

2. Are there systematic ways in which you detect patterns and distortions in the information you are receiving?

3. In Jordan's place, how would you run the Newrizon team meeting before they leave?

SURVIVING AND THRIVING AT HIGHER ALTITUDES

To be sure, your personal reactions to higher organizational altitudes cannot be completely known in advance. But, whether you are rapidly ascending, newly arrived, or currently suffering from symptoms of altitude distortions, you can reorient, manage, and recover. Pattern recognition and managing perceptions of how you are seen and heard are part—but not all—of it. We've talked in this chapter about the distortions inherent at higher altitudes and how to combat them intellectually. You also need to consider the strain they put on your body. You are an integrated organism, and the things that happen to you intellectually and emotionally impact you physically as well. They can have strong repercussions on your mood and outlook and how sharp your perceptive and cognitive skills are at a given moment. We never cease to be amazed at how many of the leaders we work with ignore their physical being as they grapple with their organizations' concerns. You can learn to acclimatize effectively— but not taking care of yourself throughout the process is not an option. Make a point of incorporating the following positive steps as you work to get oriented to your new altitude:

- **Rest.** Overexerting yourself physically can be deadly, especially during transition. Maintain or define a healthy routine of diet, exercise, and sleep. Avoid the temptation to overwork to prove yourself early. Pushing yourself too far physically is a sure way to crash. Force yourself to maintain a reasonable work schedule both at the office and at home. Purposefully schedule time into your day for the things that replenish your energy and enthusiasm. Steer clear of unhealthy coping mechanisms that "get you through." Watch your alcohol and food intake, and know your vulnerabilities. Predictably, substance abuse problems among newly appointed executives who'd never struggled previously is a lethal but all too common trap.

- **Make time for intentional reflection.** Become acutely aware of your reactions by keeping a journal and taking note of what you are experiencing. Using journaling tools like the one suggested in chapter 1, reflecting on what is happening to you can be cathartic and serve as a sanity check. Study what you write. Consider what a reasonable, rational person might expect or do, given the situation. Take special note of emerging elements in your thought patterns that require adjustment.

- **Have climbing partners.** More than one-third of our respondents reported feeling lonely and isolated, an executive danger that can have astounding consequences. From loss of objective perspective to relational failure, the damage from being disconnected from colleagues should be avoided. Nurture peer relationships. Find someone you trust who can help you detect symptoms you might not otherwise see in yourself. Skydivers take their first jumps with an experienced diver, frequently no more than a bungee cord away. Mountain climbers use partners to help them identify signs of mental fuzziness or irrational thinking by repeatedly quizzing each other about simple things. You too will benefit from a trusted partner—preferably one already accustomed to the altitude—who can be another pair of eyes and ears and offer you counsel. You cannot avoid the altitudinal distortions of rising to power.

You can, however, calibrate how they affect you, and you can lean into them with maturity and humility to ensure that you adapt productively and sustainably.

- **Take the time to think before you say or do**—even push for additional time if needed—to gain a proper perspective before taking action on issues apparently demanding immediate attention. Actions taken too quickly with the intent to make an impact often come back to haunt you. Resist the temptation to prove yourself or show what you're made of until you have thoughtfully considered the issues from the new altitude. What further insights does the expanded view afford? What other variables must you now consider that weren't within your previous purview? Measured, deliberate action is best. Be wise, even in the face of rash commitments or comments you may have made during your ascent when you didn't yet have a complete picture.

- **Help others adjust their distortions.** When you know others are misperceiving you, call the question. Don't let misunderstandings or others' myopia about you—especially if you helped create them—linger too long. Have the courage to confront outright, deliberate fabrications of you that serve some political agenda or avoidance of accountability. And have the humility to take responsibility for perceptions your actions may have inadvertently provoked, and do so *before* others have the chance to broadcast their distorted views to wider audiences.

In the face of intense pressures to make an impact, or to "earn your stripes" and the regard of those watching your rise, many of these points may feel futile given the magnitude of the journey. That is exactly what makes them imperative. These are the transition factors that have the potential to define your leadership, set the trajectory for your long-term success, or put your demise into play. It won't be any one spectacular event that secures your rise to power. It will be the way you transact your business and relationships—one consistent interaction, trade-off, apology, challenge, and high-five after another. Executive credibility is built on the day-to-day experiences of your leadership. Legitimate reputations are formed and ruined by track records of results, not single feats of heroism or failure. True, catastrophes can sometimes be career-fatal. But for the most part, a steady reorienting of your view of the world and others' views of you is a winning formula. Indeed the choices you make in response to the inevitable distortions you will face have far-reaching consequences. Take it slow and choose wisely.

HUNTINGTON
Industrials
durable. reliable. affordable.

IN FLIGHT

THE SWARM OF SEC INVESTIGATORS dampened the otherwise upbeat mood Huntington had enjoyed in the week since their visit to Newrizon. By all accounts, the presentation had gone spectacularly well, and everyone had thought they would have gotten the final green light by now. Carolyn had thought about putting a sign on her desk simply stating "nothing yet" to keep people away. She told people, "I promise we'll send up a puff of white smoke when we've heard."

Kyle Morgan wasn't celebrating. He had been shut behind conference room doors for several days along with Huntington's legal team, four members of his finance staff, and two vice presidents from Operations. Jordan was summoned in occasionally for a few questions and then dismissed. By now, Jordan had informed the executive team of the charges being filed against Kyle and other Huntington executives. He'd had to explain Mac's attempt to inflate earnings in order to drive up share price before he died, how he'd been caught, and how that was a likely contributing factor to his suicide.

Andy Farber, Huntington's chief counsel, knocked on Jordan's door and stepped in.

"We're settling. Kyle and the others are pleading no contest to four counts of falsified earnings, six counts of under-accrual of reserves and improper use of reserves to reduce current period expenses, one count of improper capitalization policies, one count non-GAAP capitalized interest methodology, and eleven counts of falsified depreciation estimates. They must all relinquish officer-level voting rights at Huntington, and each will pay pretty hefty fines. Huntington will be fined $17.6 million. Unfortunately we couldn't get the settlement sealed, so it will be public. They will give us two weeks to prepare analyst statements and get our PR machine ready for the onslaught. They know you were not involved and it was pretty clear from the forensic email examinations that, though Mac was complicit and ultimately responsible as CEO, Kyle was the driver behind the scheme, and Mac felt it was his best option given the death march he was on, and wanted to keep you in the dark to protect you."

"Gee, wasn't that awfully sweet of him. Why the hell didn't he think about the mess he was leaving me in before he offed himself?" Jordan spat out bitterly.

Andy closed with, "All in all, it could have been much worse. We can salvage this and we can move on. The Newrizon deal could help soften the blow."

"Are you completely out of your mind? We haven't inked that deal yet, and once this goes public, do you think Newrizon is just going to look the other way? Do you think they are going to enter into one of the biggest J/Vs they've ever done with a company accused of fraudulent practices?"

Andy was silent.

"Fire them all," Jordan said with his head in his hands.

"Are you sure?" Andy asked in a cautionary tone.

"YES I AM SURE!" Jordan barked. "If we let them stay, what are we saying about our values? That they're sacrosanct *except* when committing SEC fraud?"

"What about Kyle?"

A sick feeling of nausea overcame Jordan. Kyle knew his secret habit. And by the knowing look on Andy's face and the tone of the question, he'd told Andy too. Jordan wondered who else he had told.

"Send him in. I want to talk to him," Jordan said looking down.

About ten minutes later, Kyle entered Jordan's office. He was hardly contrite, but it was without his usual pompous flair. Jordan was facing out the window.

"Andy said you wanted to see me?"

"Why? Why did you do it?" Jordan didn't turn to face him.

"Please tell me this isn't the part where you try and get me to be remorseful, where I look out over the Huntington grounds and tell you that I lost my way, that I can't believe the darkness I've brought on our otherwise noble company, and how I hope you can forgive me and give me another chance. Because that's not gonna happen."

Jordan turned around. In a slow, tight voice, he said, "You . . . arrogant . . . piece . . . of . . . shit. You help a man destroy his legacy, help drive him to suicide, bring tens of thousands of people to the potential brink of bankruptcy and unemployment, and you have the audacity to mock? You are more of a psychopath than I thought."

"Is that what you summoned me here to say, Jordan? Because if that's all you've got, I've got a mountain of papers to sign."

"You think I won't fire you, don't you?"

"Of course you won't. Because you know if you do, I'll turn over all the evidence I've been collecting about your little recreational pharmaceutical hobby and hot on the heels of all of Huntington's financial fraud headlines will be the wonderful story of you as a drug addict. Is that really what you want, Jordan?" Kyle asked smugly.

"You are such a. . . ."

"I'm a what, Jordan? A vile bastard? A demon? You think you're better than me, Jordan? You think you're less unscrupulous? Don't kid yourself, my friend. You're every bit as self-serving as I am, so don't think for a minute your nice-guy routine has anyone in this building fooled. And once Newrizon learns that the mastermind behind this brilliant J/V they've signed up for is actually a barbiturate-ingesting machine presiding over a mountain of financial fraud, they'll have no choice but to pull out of this deal no matter how great the opportunity. Then what? Welcome to Wal-Mart—may I get you a cart? You'd look awesome in that blue vest, buddy."

"Get out. Just get out," Jordan said, deflated.

"I knew you wouldn't have the balls," Kyle left snickering.

Jordan sat in his chair and turned back to face the window in utter disbelief at the place he found himself. He hated Mac for what he'd done, he hated Kyle for who he was, and he hated himself for not having the courage to find a way forward that wouldn't destroy his integrity. Did it have to be that black and white? Either compromise everything he believed or lose what he and Huntington had worked for?

Jordan picked up the phone, and a few minutes later, Andy Farber returned. They spoke for a while. Kyle had indeed told Andy about Jordan's drug use and had provided copies of the evidence. It was damning. But Andy knew that there was a wide chasm between Jordan's character and Kyle's. He clearly knew Jordan, despite his unfortunate choices, still had a conscience and a moral compass. He'd already begun working on a strategy.

"Hang tight, Jordan. I don't think all is lost. Give me until the morning. Try and get some sleep."

After Andy left, Jordan opened the desk drawer and, ironically, next to one of his pill bottles was the employee assistance information Kyle had jammed at him weeks prior.

SECTION III

ASSERT

CHAPTER FIVE

EXECUTIVE POWER

PERVERSIONS, ABUSES, AND THE GREATER GOOD

THE CONUNDRUM OF POWER

THE EXERTION OF OUR WILL UPON OTHERS, regardless of the source of that influence, is one of the most mysterious social forces in human existence. It calls into question our motives, our character, and our constructs of social reality. It pits our sense of basic human kindness against whatever predisposition we have toward self-interest. It both defines and reveals how we participate in relationship. And that conditioning starts in the earliest periods of our social development. Playground bullying teaches us the painful consequences of misusing power over others—whether we're the bully or the bullied. Having our parents give away our Halloween candy to late trick-or-treaters teaches us the unfairness of resource allocation decisions. A teacher's mistaken accusation and punishment of cheating on a test teaches us the capricious nature of decisions made by those in power and the injustice of having the guilty go free without accountability. The soccer coach who puts in his own child to kick the winning goal instead of the most talented player reveals the disempowering experience of favoritism and the scarcity of true meritocracy. Being asked to captain recess kickball and pick teams haunts us with the consequences of decisions that reject friends whose estrangement must then be lived with. These formative moments of power shape our predispositions early in life and accompany us right into the corner office.

Literature is replete with every possible perspective on this topic. On one extreme, Thich Nhat Hanh's *New York Times* bestseller *The Art of Power* attests that power is something most pursue to find freedom and happiness. He goes on to suggest that while pursuing financial and political power are not in themselves bad things,

> Our society is founded on a very limited definition of power, namely wealth, professional success, fame, physical strength, military might, and political control. . . . There is only one kind of success [power] that really matters: the success of transforming ourselves, transforming our afflictions, fear and anger . . . the kind of power that will benefit us and others without causing any damage.

Hanh's altruistic view of power is rooted in the belief that true power is founded in things like faith, diligence, and insight.[20]

By contrast, Jeffrey Pfeffer's book *Power: Why Some People Have It—and Others Don't* provides a view of organizational power as a ruthless and cutthroat contest to the top. He makes organizations out to be matter-of-fact, dog-eat-dog battles of the fittest. He warns,

> The higher you rise and the more powerful the position you occupy, the greater the number of people who will want your job. . . . Some people will be looking to create opportunity for themselves through your downfall. . . . When you are in power, you should probably trust no single person in your organization too much. . . . Some of the individuals competing for advancement bend the rules of fair play or ignore them completely. Don't complain about this or wish the world were different. You can compete and even triumph . . . if you understand the principles of power and are willing to use them. Your task is to know how to prevail in the political battles you will face.[21]

We believe neither of these extreme views of power is helpful or complete. Power holds the capacity to both corrupt and transform, and understanding how to live within the tensions of both is the executive's challenge of rising to power. Whether you are head of a corporation, a head of state, or head of your local Little League team, how you use your power will reveal itself in both ways. By abandoning power, erring too far to its altruistic side, you abuse it to the same degree as erring too far toward self-indulgent dominance. Indeed, self-protective cowardice is as much a failure as avid self-interest. Paul Tillich, German philosopher and theologian, notes that we all are striving to discover who we are and what we are purposed to do. Tillich refers to this as the "power to" and contrasts it to "power over"—the stealing or suppression of the self-realization of another." Here Tillich is drawing close attention to the contrast of power's two complexions. "Power actualizes itself through force and compulsion. But power is neither the one nor the other." Many great thinkers have doubted whether both sides can coexist. Robert Johnson, student of Carl Jung, said, "Probably the most troublesome pair of opposites that we can try to reconcile is love and power. Our modern world is torn to shreds by this dichotomy, and one finds many more failures than successes in the attempt to reconcile them."[22]

But reconcile them we must. The tensions between power for self-interest, or *power over*, and power for greater good, or *power to*, will never be quelled. Learning to exert our will to advance our own *and* others' agendas is the perpetual dilemma of the rise to power. Indeed they are the very polarities that have long thrwarted maintaining one's "balance of power." Let's explore both.

For the purposes of this book, we are looking to better understand the power that accompanies the rise to roles of significant influence within organizations. Be it broad budgetary control, the hundreds, even thousands of people over whose careers and lives you have direct influence, or the range of stakeholders you must serve—all of whom have high, often competing expectations for the impact you will make—such roles come with extraordinary power to wield. In a 2007 study on the role of power in effective leadership, the Center for Creative Leadership surveyed approximately 260 executives on their perceptions and experiences of power. Interestingly, over half (55 percent agreement) stated that power is concentrated among a few select individuals in their organization. Twenty-eight percent of survey participants agreed that power is misused by top leaders within their organizations. Only 29 percent believed that their organizations teach their leaders how to effectively leverage their full power. Further, respondents cited the two most leveraged sources of power as relationships (89 percent) and information (57 percent). Given the changing landscape of social media and information access, these two top cited sources of power are not surprising. However, when asked for examples of how participants used these forms of influence:

- 52 percent described situations in which they were promoting their own agenda,

- while only 23 percent described situations in which they were promoting someone else's agenda,

- and only 19 percent described situations in which they were promoting the organization's agenda.

These data certainly reinforce the fact that very few organizations teach their leaders how to use power effectively.[23]

AVOIDING POWER FAILURE

The perversions and abuses of power that we most commonly see are those born of self-interest and self-protection. Leaders, mesmerized—in fear or in lust—by the positional authority accompanying their new role, as well as influence over key relationships and access to privileged information, are often confounded by how challenging it is to be responsible with the extent of such power. (Jordan has found this out quickly in his power struggle with Kyle.) The great irony here is that, once into their tenure as an executive, they lament over how powerless to make an impact they feel. "How is it I have this budget, and all these resources, and I still struggle to make anything happen?" We even frequently hear this from CEOs, who many misperceive as having ultimate power. Nearly two-thirds of our respondents indicated that others ascribed more power to them than they actually believe they have. The paradox of having so much power yet feeling powerless to act leads many executives down pathways of power failure.

Robert Greenleaf wrote the manifesto on power and leadership more than thirty-five years ago, and it remains to this day one of the most widely read texts on leadership. The story of its origin is less well known, but fascinating. Greenleaf was a career executive at AT&T and he had conceived of the idea of a corporate personnel assessment center in 1948, when no one had ever heard of such a thing. Instead of setting it up right away, Greenleaf took time to lay the groundwork. He read widely on the topics of leadership and management, worked to understand the common challenges, had conversations with a wide variety of people, and slowly developed a concept of an assessment that took the whole person into account. During graduate school, one of his professors urged his class to "help these big companies figure out how to serve the greater good. I don't see anyone running them interested in serving society in the ways they should." This lecture set in motion a movement that Greenleaf would champion for decades. What Greenleaf posits is that the only legitimate application of power within organizations is *in the service of others*. Regardless of the source of that power, whether positional, relational, or informational, when power is abused for self-interest and not used to serve the broader organizational good, then it is corrupted power. Greenleaf himself was revered as a mentor at AT&T for years but was also well known for his honest, unassuming humility. Three hundred years earlier, in 1647, Spanish Jesuit priest and poet Batassar Gracian said, "The sole advantage of power is that you can do more good." The struggles to harness power for a greater good are as old as time itself.

If executives are to effectively wield the power that accompanies their roles, they must come to terms with the many ways *they* would be prone to abuse or pervert it. Too often executives enter higher altitudes telling themselves, "I would never do that." A failure to recognize their own arrogance, denial, or naïveté can be tantamount to failure. No leader is immune to the pitfalls of power. Leaders can mitigate the negative aspects of power's effects, however, by knowing themselves deeply and attending to the vulnerabilities that may entice them to abuse or pervert the power available to them. More than one-third of our respondents view executives as misusing the power that comes with their role, and 40 percent have changed their views of the degree to which executives misuse their power since becoming executives themselves. A full 50 percent of our respondents indicate that executive politics undermines their ability to trust their peers. Our respondents note, "Politics come into play to a greater extent than I would ever imagine, even to the point of superseding the actual work. What isn't said can be as important as what is said. Those nuances and undercurrents are hard to understand, much less navigate. The one persistent challenge I find is the uneven level of power in the executive ranks. When objectives are misaligned, the politics of working across the organization outside your own unit make getting anything done very difficult. The orientation of many is to promote their own interests before the company's." The implications of these observations can't be overstated. When those with the greatest degree of influence over an organization's life struggle with their own or others' use of power, the degree of enterprise risk surges.

To be clear, we believe the power that accompanies executive roles to be neither inherently good nor bad. What surprised us, however, was the pervasive underlying belief among our respondents that positional power is something "to be used only when necessary," apparently confusing "authority" with "power." Clearly conditioned to believe that power is defined as the extent to which an executive uses his or her position to "tell others what to do," our respondents made many cautionary comments indicating power should be used "infrequently," "sparingly," "invisibly," and "responsibly."[24]

While the opportunities for, and forms of, perverted or abused power within organizations may be extensive, we will narrow our focus to those we have seen to be the most recurrent, and, ironically, which we believe to be the most avoidable. We will explore the most common abuse of power: *indulgence* for the purpose of self-interest. And we will explore what we believe to be the most common perversion of power: *abdication for self-protection*.

Figure 5.1 summarizes the sources of power and the corresponding perversions and abuses we will discuss ahead.

While it may be tempting to ignore the abuses in the left-hand column, believing you're above such temptations—"I know leaders who have done that but I would *never* stoop so low"—the truth is they can emerge in such subtle forms and be so easily justified that even the most upstanding people can find themselves toying with them in ways they might not recognize as abuse. We've all heard rationalizations like, "Well, if I don't toot my own horn, who will?" or "I just wanted to provide her a little incentive, that's all," or "Hey, I work hard in this thankless job and they don't pay me nearly enough, so I deserve what few perks I get," or "There's no reason to burden her with endless details—she just needed to know the key parts of the data enough to make a decision [i.e. the one he wanted her to make]." At first glance, there is an implied innocence about these justifications, a sense of harmlessness to them. We hear them so often and employ them so effectively that we become immune to the toxic truths beneath them. The moment you believe you are above reproach and immune to temptation is the moment you become susceptible to power failure.

Fig. 5.1

Power Source	Abuse: Indulgent Self-Interest *Takes the form of:*	Perversion: Abdication for Self-Protection *Takes the form of:*
Positional Power	**Egoism** • Self-aggrandizement • Berating/belittling of others	**Indecision** • Paralysis • Over-inclusion • Fear of mistakes or disappointing others
	Self-service • Extravagance • Immorality	**Accommodation** • Individuals' agendas trumping enterprise agenda • Tolerance of mediocre or poor performance
Relational Power	**Exploitation** • Using people to advance your own cause	**Counter-dependence/ Co-dependence** • Behaving as if others don't matter to you and you don't need them, or as if others are indispensable to you and you can't do anything without them
	Bribery • Promising or providing others reward in return for loyalty, political support, or compromising actions	**Stakeholder blindness** • Failure to recognize or sufficiently include key players whose support/input/advocacy you need
Informational Power	**Spin/Hoard** • Twisting or withholding information to manipulate circumstances	**Havoc/Confusion** • Failure to listen and control flow and messaging that leads to confusion and uncertainty
	Blackmail • Threatening to use information to harm another	**Indiscretion** • Divulging confidences or ignoring sensitivity of information; disregard for consequences of "executive gossip"

Sources of Executive Power Failure:
Abuses & Perversions of Organizational Power

On the right-hand side of the table, you might be surprised to see some of those power perversions included in such an inventory. We're sure you've seen the behaviors plenty of times. In contrast to the abuses, it might be easy to dismiss them as benign idiosyncrasies or common leadership deficits found in even the most effective leaders. Please hear us well: *They are every bit as egregious and destructive as their abuse counterparts, and just as much a failure of power.* That they are more commonplace does not make them more excusable. That they don't overtly violate some inherent code of ethics or morality doesn't make them any less offensive or damaging. We've just learned to accept them more as status quo. We believe we should be just as outraged and intolerant of the perversions of abdication as we are of the abuses of indulgence. And frankly, by the frequency with which we read about the abuses in headlines, it's probably fair to say we aren't intolerant enough of those either. Let's look at each of the abuses and perversions more closely.

REFLECTIONS ON THE RISE

1. What are the worst abuses of power you've witnessed or been subjected to? How did those abuses impact the organization?

2. When have you been tempted to abuse or pervert your own power? What would those you lead say about how you exercise your authority?

3. While Kyle is clearly abusing his informational power by threatening blackmail, how would you coach Jordan to best respond without abusing his own power?

POSITIONAL POWER

Abuses of positional power

Egoism: *Self-aggrandizing, or berating others*

We once worked with a leader whom we struggled to help see the need to acknowledge and appreciate the team he led instead of always trumping them with his own brilliant ideas. Once, when a member of his team generated a truly breakthrough idea, believing he was responding to our feedback, he declared, "That idea was so good . . . it could have been mine!" We have all been around pompous, egotistical leaders and questioned how they rose to positions of great power. There are more subtle forms of self-importance—taking credit for others' work, ensuring you get invited to important meetings or making sure you sit next to the important people in them, speaking in self-deprecating ways to provoke others to counter you with showers of affirmation—that are just as abusive. The deep-seated insecurities that become inflamed in positions of power where we feel exposed, threatened, or unsure can lead us to behave in very irrational, immature ways. When leaders feel off balance or when their sense of significance feels diminished, it is not surprising that they look for ways to replenish it. Pay attention to the level of acknowledgment you need, and find healthy ways of getting it. And expect that at higher organizational altitudes, you tend to get less of it, not more. So if you've been the organization's "rock star" who has been showered in accolades on the way up, don't expect that to continue upon arrival into the executive ranks. To everyone around you, your arrival is the ultimate accolade.

Egoism can also take the form of berating or belittling others. It's scary to think, as we move into the second decade of the twenty-first century, after the countless lawsuits and mandatory learning around respect, employee engagement, and valuing differences, we still have leaders whose unfettered anger and perfectionism remain a license to degrade those around them. But we do. Overt abuses include sarcasm, shouting, offensive language, and condescending criticism, but perhaps more insidious is the covert belittling that can sometimes occur. The simple withholding of any regard for the contributions of others, the hyperbolic and dramatic expressions of exasperation that sound like, "Geesh—do I have to do *everyone's* job around here? Why can't anyone deliver what's expected in this place?"—these abuses are no less venomous than the leader who rages in profane language at the administrative assistant in front of the entire department. If you have any proclivity toward holding others accountable to unrealistic standards or if you've ever heard the words from anyone in your life, "Why isn't anything I do good enough for you?" then take heed and get it under control. If you have the proverbial short fuse that you have excused with, "I'm just passionate," or "I just have high standards," you must accept that, at a higher altitude, imposing those high standards becomes a proverbial caning ritual to flog the very people you most need to help you succeed.

Self-service: *extravagance or immorality*

Many executives struggle to know how to enjoy the material privileges that accompany their role. So they overcompensate by either denying themselves the enjoyment or flaunting it for others to notice. The vicious cycle of flaunting or denying yourself can set in motion ugly choices. And once you cross that dangerous line where you have confused your means with your meaning, it is hard to turn back. Suddenly you can easily justify your entitlement and feel compelled to greater excesses to keep the cycle of deprivation or indulgence in motion. Dennis Kozlowski of Tyco became a byword for unjustified excess when he used $1 million of corporate funds for a "shareholder meeting" that was actually a Roman-themed birthday party for his second wife. Kozlowski said in a video released after said party that viewers were seeing Tyco's core competency: the ability to party hard.[25] Tyco was not a troubled company—in fact they were performing well under Kozlowski's leadership and they survived the scandal of his fall. But once you start justifying more than your share as a perk of your high office, the road to Kozlowski territory is surprisingly short.

The other form of self-service power abuse is immorality. While Title VII and sexual harassment laws have created some boundaries to guard against this, the fact remains that executives still feel impervious to the rules when it comes to the power they hold and the adulation that power attracts. From Bill Clinton and Monica Lewinsky to the allegations of improprieties involving Congressional pages and the long list of allegations against Catholic priests, power over others seems to invite a feeling of immunity and amorality in some people. You may be telling yourself, "I love my spouse and I would never cheat." Ironically, however, millions of married Internet users engage in online flirting that sometimes leads to extramarital affairs. Smartphones and Internet logs on computers often lead to these activities being revealed, which is terribly embarrassing and damaging to everyone involved.[26]

The impact of extramarital affairs on workplace productivity presents some interesting paradoxes. A survey of three thousand HR professionals by the Society for Human Resource Management found that office romances caused complaints of favoritism from coworkers (28 percent), claims of sexual harassment (24 percent), decreased productivity of the participants (24 percent), decreased morale of coworkers (16 percent), and decreased productivity of coworkers (11 percent). The study also noted that "although workplace romances can benefit their participants with respect to factors such as job satisfaction, they can also result in punitive managerial actions such as a denied promotion, job relocation, or employment termination."[27] In one recent client engagement, the CEO, in the midst of planning his succession, had to call in two of the lead internal candidates and actually tell them to stop having an affair with each other because it was affecting the credibility of them both as possible successors. Ultimately neither of them got the job.

Perversions of positional power

Indecision: *paralysis, over-inclusion, fear of making a mistake or disappointing others.*

Paralysis is one of the most widespread forms of power failure and, at the highest levels of organizations, can have crippling effects. One executive we worked with bore the nickname "The Waffle" because of his painful inability to make and stick to a decision. He was known to be highly susceptible to the "last one in" phenomenon—the last person in his office was able to sway him toward their view on a particular issue. Regardless of the amount of data he amassed or support he garnered for a particular direction, this leader never declared a final choice, leaving the organization confused about what they should do and conflicted about whether a decision had actually been made. The team quickly learned that this lack of clarity worked to their advantage. Absent any concrete evidence or documentation that a particular decision had actually been made, they could interpret outcomes of any meeting in alignment with their views, and then act accordingly. The risk was minimal because they could always claim it was what they understood his decision to be. Eventually, we helped him surface and address the operative narrative underneath his behavior—his fear of having one of his decisions go wrong and the potential backlash rendered him immobile. "If this blows up it will be my fault . . ." was the tape in his head when it came to big, complex decisions, paralyzing him in fear and inaction.

The next form of indecision is *over-inclusion*. Leaders overly fearful of taking decisive risk often delude themselves into thinking the way to disperse that risk is to get lots of people involved in the decision. The "empowerment" movement of the '80s and '90s has overcorrected the command-and-control managerial mind-set by creating a false belief that the more people involved in a given decision, the more ownership there will be for that decision once executed. Not always true. We're not advocating a return to a more autocratic form of managerial decision making; including those who must execute a decision and live with its consequences is certainly important. We do mean to debunk the myth of false consensus that comes with over-including people at the expense of action. Many of our respondents pointed with exasperation to the challenges of this problem among executive ranks. "The number of people who expect to have a say in decisions is ridiculous. I spend more time building false consensus as a protocol rather than increasing the quality of the decision. I thought I would have more authority than I actually do."

One indication that this is happening is that you may hear people in your organization saying things like, "Everybody's accountable so nobody's accountable." Dispersing decision risk provides a convenient place to hide the accountability for that decision. Once the decision plays out differently than hoped you are apt to have a case of "scarecrow arms" where people are pointing in multiple directions to assign responsibility for the failed decision. Once people have weighed in and been heard, an executive ultimately has to make the final call, name the potential good and bad consequences, and unburden people from diffused accountability so they can execute with confidence. If a leader's need to avoid mistakes or fear of disappointing others is too great, he won't be able to do this. Ron Heifetz, author of *Leadership on the Line* and *No Easy Answers*, defines leadership as "the ability to disappoint people at a rate they can absorb." Newly appointed executives must have sufficiently thick skin to withstand the inevitable disappointment and emotional residue that comes with unpopular decisions. It is a significant portion of the job, and to avoid it under the illusion of getting everyone "on board" and dispersing accountability only serves to heighten risk.

Accommodation: *Individuals' agendas trumping the enterprise agenda; tolerance of mediocre or poor performance*

The second perversion of positional power is *accommodation*, abdicating leadership by pandering to the agendas of others at the expense of a greater good. Another backlash of the empowerment literature has been the notion that people need to feel deep ownership for their work, and the way to achieve that is by letting them feel greater control over the direction they are helping drive. Of course, there is partial truth to this—people will feel greater ownership for what they believe they helped create—but that doesn't mean at the expense of a larger agenda set in motion by the executive. Your job as an executive is to shape the vision and strategic direction of the organization you lead. This will leave plenty of room for others to make their mark by shaping the choices that translate the vision into action. Doling out lots of yeses to requests for resources to drive initiatives on individuals' agendas is not empowerment, it's abandonment—however good it might feel. Not every great idea—no matter how strategically relevant—is meant to be pursued. Narrowing the priorities and focus of an organization to strengthen its execution is one of your greatest contributions as an executive. Almost always, enabling the greater enterprise to succeed must remain your primary concern. When your need to say yes overpowers your courage to say no, it can often lead to the final form of accommodation: *tolerance of mediocre or poor performance.* The morass of confusion that results from a fragmented organization, with too many competing priorities and poorly allocated resources kills performance. Once leaders conclude that the stated plan can't be taken seriously because the priorities aren't clear or change by the day and/or that resource allocation trade-offs are made in backroom meetings among a random few instead of transparently in the open, they revert to autopilot. Their commitment to drive the strategy is diluted. The ultimate peril of accommodation—doling out too many yeses—is that it will serve to exterminate the very ownership and commitment an executive sought to strengthen and will lead the organization directly into the performance pitfall they so desperately believed they were avoiding.

REDEEMING POSITIONAL POWER: HOW JUSTICE AND MERITOCRACY BUILD CONFIDENCE AND TRUST IN AN ORGANIZATION

"It's not fair" is probably one of the greatest laments of organizational life. People see advancement and compensation decisions, performance ratings, organizational configurations, and resource allocations and scratch their heads, unable to reconcile those choices with the principles and policies the organization claims to live by. Here is the risk for you as an executive: When people participating in any communal activity (like an organization, a school, or a nation) believe that their contribution matters and they will be rewarded accordingly, they commit differentiated effort to the cause. However, when they have been conditioned to expect capricious leadership and rewards distributed to a privileged group despite their lack of contribution, they withdraw their trust and minimize their contribution—doing the least amount to get by safely without being singled out. The longer these norms are reinforced, the more difficult they become to reverse. Sustained decisions in the direction of justice and meritocracy will, over time, result in an organization reengaging and recommitting. It's unlikely that we'll ever hear executives in the coming generation of management say, "I'm fine with the bare minimum contribution. Our products are so distinctive, our customers so loyal, our margins so large, our processes so efficient, and our competitive position so unassailable that it really doesn't matter whether my people participate fully or not." So it behooves executives to shape their leadership around justice and meritocracy to the fullest extent possible, even if that means unseating long-standing mediocre performers and asymmetrically shifting resources to those leaders and businesses with the greatest promise of success.

A few years back we had the privilege of working with the nation of Slovakia to help them with the initiative "Next Generation Leaders of Slovakia." The goal was to engage young leaders inclined to leave the country and help them find careers and establish lives they believed could be more rewarding and lucrative in their home country. Although most of the young leaders we encountered loved their homeland and culture, their government was doing little to incentivize younger entrepreneurs and businesses, or to build an education system and social structure that would lead these leaders to believe they could find the life and career they dreamed of in their own country. Interestingly, twenty years after the fall of communism and the arrival of consumerism, socialism, and a middle class, the vestiges of ambivalence and apathy from the communist regime still lingered. We worked with the private sector and government and volunteer leaders to build a movement designed to captivate the imagination of this generation and encourage them to stay and help drive the future of their country. After three years, the movement continues, but the upward push against decades of conditioning will not be easy to overcome. It will require the will and resolve of leaders in positions of political and corporate power to take demonstrable actions in public policy, education reform, and economic development to convince emerging leaders that their nation is one to which they can entrust their future.

Similarly, if a company has been run by an ogre for many years, the arrival of an inclusive, empowering, respectful leader will not suddenly unleash a powerhouse of committed and engaged performance. It takes years to turn a culture around. As you don the mantle of executive leadership, somewhere in the organization you've inherited will be stories of injustice: poor performance that has been over-rewarded and great performance that has been undervalued. You will uncover incidents in which the hypocrisy of double standards has been explained away with well-developed rationalizations. See your positional power as a resource that, while unable to right all of the wrongs of the past, can resolve not to perpetuate them and can shift the organization to one people can trust and participate in confidently. Organizational injustice may always be a harsh reality of communal life and "fairness" an arbitrary criterion applied subjectively. Instances of organizational injustices are perpetrated systemically deserve executives' unmitigated application of power to identify and right them. Your legacy as an executive, and your credibility to effect far-reaching change, will be garnered by your intolerance for injustices perpetrated by processes you do have control over. And you will be amazed by the performance you will unleash, the passionate sense of significance you will set free by establishing a culture that values equitable treatment of people instead of the superficial appearance of "equal treatment." Consistently, our respondents noted that the most important exercise of positional power was to "do what is right for the company, never for yourself or individuals." One put it nobly, "If I can consistently make choices that put the best interests of the greater good ahead of any individual agendas, I will be setting the trustworthy example I ought to set."

We saw this exemplified by an executive in a vivid display of executive courage. She was newly appointed to the organization, its only female executive, to run their global product commercialization organization. As one of the world's leading biotech companies, the organization had a small number of products on the market, but they were mega blockbusters. The number in the pipeline was troubling—there were many struggling to find their way to market. Their average time to market needed to be reduced by multiple years in order to push their products, and patents, to market faster in order to hit their growth commitments. She quickly deduced that the therapeutic silos in which products were developed and commercialized was preventing the organization from managing an enterprise portfolio with the ability to prioritize the most promising drugs regardless of their class or indication. Historically, the "fiefdoms," as she came to name them, had earned lots of political clout, and each managed its own portfolio despite pulling from the same enterprise pool of resources. The strain this put on the scientists and development teams was enormous as the "lords of the fiefdoms" vied for priority focus, exaggerating the merits and market potential of their projects. Newer "lords" leading the most promising therapeutic areas had little chance of garnering the needed resources to get their products to market, while the established lords had the political clout to get their products over stage gate hurdles barely meeting the criteria for being advanced. She declared, "This is just lunacy!" She called all of the lords together into a very contentious session, knowing she risked substantial political retribution by them and her peers, whose P&Ls were built around their own markets and products. She said, "Look, I may be new here, but this is the most Darwinian approach to running a pipeline I've ever seen. I can't even detect what criteria, scientific, financial, or competitive, we're using to accelerate or kill these projects. It's grossly unfair to the teams working on these projects that are getting whiplashed as the priority du jour changes on them, and it's dishonest to our shareholders whose money we are spending on projects that clearly have no shot at making it in the market. As of tomorrow, we will have one pipeline, with one set of criteria, and we will manage it as one portfolio. The following projects are to stop work immediately, and their teams will be redeployed onto these top five projects whose development we will accelerate." She finished with her prioritization assessment and concluded, "I understand this is radically different from what the organization has known before, and that perhaps this is abrupt, but I just don't see any reason to keep this in place a moment longer." Of course she'd secured the support of the CEO and the board for making this radical move, acknowledging it could mean the loss of key leaders who couldn't tolerate the exposure or loss of power. As expected, the anger, pushback, dismissal, and even sabotage that ensued for the following months was monumental. But the cheers from the broader development community were equally as loud. Messages of "Thank God, we now have clarity and focus, and the right projects are getting the money and focus they need!" flooded her inbox. Eventually she prevailed, and two of the lords ended up departing the organization and one therapeutic area was completely discontinued. Some might conclude that what she did just made good common business sense—do what will make the company most efficient and profitable. But she saw it as much bigger than that. To her, the horrible inequity in how the organization operated that meant that the most talented people, the medicines with the greatest promise, and the patients with acute needs were all getting compromised. Her courage to use her positional power exemplifies the type of justice that can be brought to organizations where dynasties of ineffectiveness and politics have successfully opposed leaders attempting to bring about change.

RELATIONAL POWER
Abuses of relational power

Exploitation: *Using people to advance your own cause*

The biggest fallacy of empowerment is that power is something a leader can give away. Power is something that leaders choose to exercise of their own volition, not at the behest of other leaders. The notion that power cascades down from above is wrong, contradicting the very premise itself. If a leader's power must come from someone else, it's merely borrowed power. The difference here is not small, especially when the executive giving the power is really just using others to drive his agenda. Exploitation can still begin with good intentions.

Many leaders today are torn between wanting to direct and wanting to include. The result is a muddled form of leadership that is little more than benevolent manipulation. In our book *Leadership Divided* we refer to this as faux inclusion. You invite leaders into a room under the ruse of participating in a decision you've already made, engage them in what appears to be open discussion, subtly (or so you think) steer the conversation in the direction you want, and the moment anyone hints at an option mirroring the direction you've privately selected, you pile on with grand reinforcement, sealing the deal. People see right through it now, and this form of exploitation can be damaging to trust and engagement. Some leaders accustomed to this form of inclusion stop showing up for meetings.

During a routine check-in with Barry, the CEO of a large consumer electronics organization we worked with, his assistant buzzed to say that Chad, their young CIO, was there to see him. The CEO instructed us to wait, that it would be brief. Chad entered saying, "You asked to see me?" His numerous tattoos and piercings publicized his generational difference. Barry pulled out a file from his drawer and said, "Yeah, Chad, I just wanted to get your final input on the IT capital plan going to the board. I wanted to make sure you were OK with it and felt it could be executed in the upcoming fiscal year." At first there was silence, and then Chad's face began to contort. Finally he spoke. "Barry, I'm not quite sure what you're asking me. I know you already sent that plan to the board last week—one of them called me already. So if you're asking if I'll get it done, fine—I'll get it done. But please don't waste my time making it look like you're asking me for input on something you've already committed to." With that he exited. Barry's face turned red and, turning to us, he started to vent, "Do you see the kind of disrespect I have to take around here—?" We interrupted him and said, "Barry, what do you think just happened? You may think you were disrespected, but we think he gave you a great gift. He trusted your relationship enough to be honest with you. You got caught. Now you feel embarrassed. But the truth is your anger is misplaced. Rather than feeling insulted by Chad, you need to feel indebted to him, and head right down to his office, thank him, and apologize." Barry did. And in the coming year, Chad became a reliable and trusted confidant of Barry's. Would that many more leaders had the courage to call the question with their leaders the way Chad did instead of enduring wasteful exploitation. The relational power available to both of them increased as a result.

Bribery: *Promising others reward in exchange for loyalty, support, or compromising actions*

The other form of relational power abuse is bribery. Perhaps not in the overt sense of "If you do this, I'll give you this," but executives who curry favor with other executives by exchanging political support or assistance weaken the fabric of an organization's integrity more than they might understand. One of the common anomalies of organizational governance is the "meeting before the meeting." That's where executives travel around to certain other executives in advance of a team meeting to garner support for the decision or position they will be advocating. This has become acculturated as normal practice, and some even view it as a change-management competency. We're not suggesting that good change-management practices aimed at building commitment and understanding are all corrupted by manipulative technique. But when relationships between executives become little more than scoreboards of who's got whose back, or who owes who what, the integrity of the organization's governance becomes untrustworthy. When soliciting the support of others, whether peers or direct reports, the request must stand on its own merit. The moment you drop the line, "If you'll back me on this supply chain integration, I'll support your request for the increased marketing dollars I know you need to boost advertising," the request for support becomes a bribe. Such exchanges and compromises may seem innocuous on the surface. And perhaps it's unrealistic to think an organization would be entirely free of decisions rooted in such politicized exchanges. However, when they become standard practice, the extraordinary power of relationships and the transformative results that power can bring become dangerously compromised.

Perversions of relational power

Counter-dependence/Co-dependence: *Behaving as if others don't matter or you don't need them or as if you can't live without them, or they without you*

Staunchly self-reliant executives tend to plow their way to the top of organizations, sometimes leaving bodies in their wake. For some, the root of counter-dependence lies in the fundamental inability to trust others. It's perhaps caused by an early life trauma, or a general fear of being vulnerable and a belief that letting others help you will make you appear weak or give them the opportunity to take advantage of you. Regardless of the origin, counter-dependence eventually results in others keeping their distance because the challenge of trying to build a relationship is too great, and seemingly futile. Counter-dependence can ruin more than professional relationships and many a marriage and family has fallen prey to this perversion. If you have any predilection for keeping others at arm's length, avoiding being vulnerable, or if you work hard to sustain an image of self-reliance at the expense of others' desire to participate in your success, you should address it before taking on an executive role. The challenges inherent at higher organizational altitudes will inflame this impulse, not quell it. And once there, your ability to trust and invite others in will prove even more difficult.

On the other end of the continuum, executive co-dependence can be equally pernicious. This perversion is generally demonstrated in a leader's inflating the importance of others and living vicariously through those they feel have more courage, more presence, more intelligence, more . . . something. Because of the co-dependent nature of the relationship, the "something more" individual is treated as indispensable. They can do no wrong. Their mistakes and shortfalls are discounted and their strengths and contributions inflated. Of the many tragic outcomes in such cases, the worst is the loss of credibility among the rest of the organization the over-worshipped executive suffers. They are often viewed as intentionally manipulating the "dependent executive," and others tend to withdraw their support and trust. The other version of co-dependence is when executives make *themselves* indispensable to those they perceive to be weaker, luring them to feel deeply reliant on them for even basic choices and direction. Regardless of which end of the co-dependent continuum you may find yourself, the unhealthy parasitic attachments usually crumble under the weight of any kind of pressure. You can avoid the extremities of unhealthy dependency, whether counter- or co-dependence, with an honest assessment of your own proclivities for attachment in relationships, and where you have inclinations that are potentially detrimental, pay attention and make needed adjustments.

Stakeholder Blindness: *Failure to recognize or sufficiently include those whose support, input, and advocacy you need*

Some newly appointed executives—either as a by-product of counter-dependence, or just relational tone deafness—disregard or fail to recognize stakeholders who are critical to their success. Part of the reason for this is that as a leader in the Coordinating system, you rely on many people who are within your functional, geographic, or business organization. At the executive level, major components of the organization must come together and work across the enterprise. Many of those who now help determine your success are peer leaders in adjacent parts of the organization. Executives often underestimate the degree of influence they have over the success of their peers, and vice versa. A recently arrived SVP of Global Sales in a large consumer products organization set out to build his entry plan with us. Eager to be effective and avoid the many pitfalls we'd warned against, he put the chief marketing officer on the top of his stakeholder list. Given the organization's history of classic sales-marketing tensions, he was determined to build a bridge and improve the relationship between the two organizations. Naturally we applauded his zeal. When we asked, "What about the folks in Supply Chain, specifically demand planning—do you need to consider them in your stakeholder inventory?" he said, "No, not really, they don't really have much direct impact on my work." We knew differently. We said, "Really? What about your organization's impact on them? Haven't there been tensions between your field sales organization, your customer marketing group, and the demand planning function over forecasting and go-to-market processes?" We knew there had been, and that tensions were intensifying *precisely* because Marketing's promotional efforts were focusing on specific categories. We knew that if his relationship with Marketing were to get better, it could actually further deteriorate the relationship with Demand Planning. He said, "I hadn't heard that. So, no, I guess they wouldn't make my top priority stakeholder list. But I can get to them in the next round." This is classic stakeholder blindness. He was looking at his relationship with Marketing through the eyes of his *former position*, and the frustration he experienced there. He was failing to see the relationship with Supply Chain through the enterprise lens of his current role because he'd never experienced the pain there. As a new executive, step back and take a systemic look at the stakeholders who will be part of your success, as you will be of theirs. There will inevitably be relationships outside your field of vision that you need to consider, and before prematurely deciding who's important and who's not, be sure you have complete information. At the executive level, relational strength, or the lack of it, has far-reaching implications.

REDEEMING RELATIONAL POWER: HOW POSITIVE REGARD AND PERSONAL INVESTMENT SHAPE RELATIONSHIPS OF COMMITMENT AND SACRIFICE

People have been studying organizational climate for years. In the 1980s these surveys were called "employee opinion surveys." In the 1990s they were often referred to as "organizational health" surveys. In the early 2000s the genre shifted to "employee engagement." According to one study, Gallup's State of the Global Workplace report, "only 13% of employees worldwide are engaged at work. New Zealand has one of the highest levels of engaged employees among the countries surveyed, at 23%. Australia's engagement rate is similar, at 24%. But both countries fall short of the United States, where 30% of employed residents are engaged at work. Engaged workers stand apart from their not-engaged and actively disengaged counterparts because of the discretionary effort they consistently bring to their roles. These employees willingly go the extra mile, work with passion, and feel a profound connection to their company. They are the people who will drive innovation and move your business forward. . . . Not-engaged employees . . . sleepwalk through their day, uninspired and lacking motivation. They have little or no concern about customers, productivity, profitability, safety, or quality. They are thinking about lunch or their next break and have essentially 'checked out.'"[28] Executives rising to power today are entering an unprecedented crisis of ambivalence and boredom in organizations that will only be counteracted with the most meaningful relationships of personal impact they can possibly form.

At the core of this body of research, including Gallup's, is the premise that you can correlate the performance of the organization with the satisfaction and engagement of employees. Not particularly earth shattering. The notion behind the surveys is that you can provide executives feedback on their particular part of the organization and then hold them accountable to improve results in areas that are unacceptable and putting performance and retention at risk. In some places it has worked; in others the research remains cosmetic at best. The latest wave of research has suggested that even engagement and commitment aren't sufficient factors to predict performance and retention. The metric that will most predict the degree of contribution of employees is "sacrifice." So the million-dollar question for all companies becomes, "What would lead employees to willingly make sacrifices for their organization?" The answer isn't that profound: their boss. We all know the cliché that people don't quit companies, they quit bosses, and we also know that the primary determinant of employee satisfaction is the person to whom you directly report. As we discussed earlier, two of the three most common causes of executive failure are relational—with peers and direct reports. So, what kinds of relationships with peers and directs would result in their wanting to return sacrificial contributions? The answer: relationships in which you make genuine personal investments and show them positive regard. Just think about the leader in your career who made you want to give your best no matter what it required of you.

It doesn't matter if you like them or "feel chemistry" with them. It's not about you. But offering them genuine regard for and opportunities to grow the talents they bring, being curious about their lives and interests, and delighting in who they are as people as well as the contributions they make can dramatically shift the posture they bring to work. This attitude will spread throughout your organization, affecting even employees outside your direct reach. The same holds true with your peers. Rather than seeing them as people with whom you must transact business (at best) or enemies to be kept at bay (at worst), what if you saw them as people with whom it was an honor to work? Yes, even if you also think they are jerks. When people feel treated with honor, they are more likely to behave with honor. Step back and take inventory of your existing relationships with peers and directs. How well established are they? How meaningful? How would they say you treat them? With positive regard? That you've made personal investments in their success? If you aren't sure what they would say, you should be concerned. Start now and build one relationship at a time. You will be amazed in six months at the difference in how you experience one another and in the performance shift you see.

At the heart of relational power is trust—how you choose to extend or withhold it. As discussed in chapter 4, extending trust is not absolute; rather, it is given and received in degrees. At some point in their careers, most executives fear that everyone who comes to them wants something and will say whatever the leader wants to hear to get it. While there are people who will try to exploit your power for their own gain, *not everyone* will do this. Be cautious about making blanket statements regarding the commodity of trust. You must not yield to the altruistic, and often naïve, view of trust, that everyone deserves it no matter what. If you've been burned, you must not succumb to the cynic's view that you cannot trust anyone once in power because they will inevitably betray you. Treat trust as a currency that you trade in on clear terms and with clear conditions—extend it, withhold it, withdraw it, and deepen it—all with clear evidence to support your choice.

Family businesses are notoriously vulnerable when passing generational hands. We recently had the privilege of working with a family-owned business run by three siblings who inherited the company from their father. Wildly successful in the media industry, sometimes despite themselves, they inherently knew things weren't working. As siblings, they had great relationships with deep love and regard for each other. As co-owners and runners of a business, however, things were tense. They privately questioned one another's competence, nobody was really "in charge" of anything, and while revenue was coming in the door because of the great customer relationships they had, no one had any idea whether the company was even profitable or not. Our intense diagnostics revealed the lack of a clear strategy, organizational governance that had most of the nearly three hundred employees confused about "who was doing what," a passionate "familial" culture where people loved their jobs but hated the pressures of feeling like things were always coming off the rails, and no organizational clarity about how all of the work fit together. One of the siblings needed to assume the role of CEO, which meant the other two siblings would become direct reports. And there was a clear front-runner, most qualified for the role but deeply ambivalent about taking it. But for the greater good, he did. Two years later, he has grown into a well-regarded and beloved CEO. He had tremendous relational equity prior to the role, but more as "one of the guys" than "the boss." In fact, some employees who'd been at the company for decades remembered babysitting him as a toddler. Now he was their leader. No one questioned his ownership of the company, but his amazingly humble posture never showed any status differences. He knew that to be a strong CEO he would have to change. He had to dramatically shift how he led others and how he spent his time. He had a lot to learn about running an organization and building a profitable, strategically focused business. He has built a strong team of leaders around him, eager to have a shot at broader careers, and has continued to personally coach them. He has redefined the relationships in the organization with healthy boundaries and has garnered the respect of his siblings he now leads. He fiercely guards the company's culture—a secret weapon of their success—by ensuring relationships remain open, honest, and service oriented. He takes time to teach others how to embrace the company values, and isn't hesitant about removing people who violate them. He parlayed his wonderful character traits of humility, integrity, deep care for his people (vividly modeled for him by his parents), and passionate vision for the company's future into a reconstituted set of relationships with the organization that has now set it on a new course for success, wildly beating the odds normally against family businesses changing generational hands.

INFORMATIONAL POWER
Abuses of informational power

Spin/hoarding: *Twisting or withholding information to manipulate circumstances*

One of the major shifts in informational power in the last decade has been the widespread availability of information. The shelf life of any piece of good information has been reduced to seconds, and the power struggle is shifting from "who has the information" to "whose interpretation of the information will prevail." Executives who provide balanced interpretations of information, including analyses that contradict or compete with the position they are taking, are far more credible than executives who position the information to serve only their point of view. Build your fact bases from reliable sources and paint a compelling picture of your position, being careful to offer alternative views. There is nothing wrong with passionately advocating for your position, but when you leave out critical information that might weaken your case, you risk having others raise it with the inference that you intentionally left it out—a double hit on your credibility.

The other common form of information spin and hoarding is the "I know a secret" game executives tend to be so fond of. To prove they are in the know, they carefully drop names, facts, and quotes. This generally causes colleagues to wonder what else they might be out of the loop on and to become envious or anxious. Beyond childish, this abuse of information power is often short-lived. Each time you play this card, you further dilute your credibility and believability. Be wary of nurturing palace intrigue. When it comes back to bite you, you will inevitably be at the center of the story in a very unflattering way.

Blackmail: *Threatening to use information to harm another*

Just seeing the word in print raises one's bile. Take note, Kyle, these abuses often backfire. Once again, as with all the other abuses and perversions, the more pernicious forms of this abuse are subtle and can be accompanied by compelling justification. Executives who blatantly confront colleagues in private settings with threats like "If you don't want to be humiliated by people knowing about your little side hobby, I strongly suggest you . . ." may be rare, but sadly they are still alive, well, and leading in our corporations. Let's look at the more common forms of this perversion in everyday executive life. How many times have you heard the expression "Oh, well, he knows where all the bodies are buried, that's why he hasn't been fired." Regardless of the degree of exaggeration, the implication is that a leader has very damaging information that if made public could be highly inflammatory, even career ending, for those in power. Individuals who appear to have career safety despite obviously poor performance leave the rest of the organization with the impression that there is an unspoken agreement that the "secret files" they possess will remain secret as long as they remain employed. Sadly, it appears organizations find themselves in this situation quite often. Blackmail does happen among high-profile, professional people. Recently a *48 Hours* producer demanded $2 million from David Letterman in order not to reveal Letterman's sexual improprieties with members of his own staff. Letterman elected to go to the district attorney, but he admitted his own misconduct on national television. This was deeply embarrassing—but had the man merely asked for career advancement, we likely would never have become aware of this scandal. Indeed, those that accept the bribes are as complicit as those who offer them.

With the proliferation of litigation in today's organizations, "lawsuit avoidance" has tragically become one of the most important roles the Human Resource organization plays. Here's a critical word of advice from Aunt May, portrayed by Sally Field in the movie *The Amazing Spider-Man*. "Peter, there are no secrets. They will always find you out." Know that potentially fatal information you have about someone, or information you guard from public view, will not serve you well. Information like that is a house of cards that will eventually come crashing down. How many more corporations, from AIG to Enron, must collapse before we take this lesson to heart? Those organizations were full of leaders who believed they were impervious to the effects of the information they withheld or leveraged for gain. Now many of them sit behind bars wondering where it all went wrong. Determine now you will never use information as a weapon or source of self-protection.

Perversions of informational power

Havoc/Confusion: *Failure to listen and control flow and messaging leading to confusion and uncertainty*

One of the most dangerous mistakes new executives make is their failure to appreciate the organization's capacity to misinterpret key messages despite how well crafted and conveyed they are. The chief human resource officer and the CEO of a large financial services organization were playing central roles in their global transformation. The result of a substantial merger, the integration of three lines of business, retail brokerage, institutional investing, and retail banking were coming under one brand organized in three global divisions. Extensive communication campaigns were built to unify the organization quickly and create a sense of shared mission around the power of this newly formed organization. The usual town hall tours, talking-head videos, webcasts, and written communiqués were launched with impressive velocity and volume. Despite all of the effort, a pulse check survey assessing the transformation's progress just six months after the announcement revealed people were still confused about how the new organization was intended to work, unclear about the market benefits it was intended to achieve, and uncertain if it was worth all the chaos and mayhem. Angry, the CEO exclaimed to the transition team, "How is this possible? We've bent over backwards to make sure the organization was well informed and up to date on every inch of progress. How could they possibly still be so confused?" Clearly, accelerating the change would be a disaster given what the data reported. Invited in to help get the alignment of the organization back on track, we asked a simple question: "How much have you listened to them?" Defensive, the CHRO said, "We've given them everything they asked for and then some!" We said, "That's not our question. How much have you *listened to them*? How much have *they* been allowed to talk versus you doing the talking?" Information management, particularly during times of major upheaval, is not purely a function of the amount, quality, or method with which you dispense content. The successful impact of information and communication on an organization is directly predicated on the amount and quality of information you *hear*, balanced with what you distribute.

There isn't an organizational survey in the world that doesn't return low marks for "communication." It is the catchall bucket for every organizational ailment from too much email, bad newsletters, no access to important data, and insufficient engagement to how much I dislike my boss. At the heart of all "communication problems" in an organization is most often people's unmet need to be heard. As an executive, understand that people are processing, metabolizing, and embracing your messages when *they are talking*, not when *you* are talking. It may seem counterintuitive, but executives must curb their natural impulse to make speeches, send memos, explain, justify, and defend the messages they want to convey. Organizational havoc and confusion ensue when, in the absence of any place to productively process what they are hearing, people turn to one another in pockets to grapple with what they heard. The typical outcome of this is that they generate hundreds if not thousands of potential translations. Many executives react to this by simply pushing more content at people in hopes of reducing the noise. As was the case in the financial services organization, the cycle continued for six months before anyone realized it was only getting worse. At the outset of your executive tenure, condition yourself to put *listening* to how people are metabolizing your messages at the top of your communication priorities.

Indiscretion: *Divulging confidences; ignoring sensitivity of information; disregarding the consequences of executive gossip*

Let's be honest—who doesn't love a juicy bit of office gossip? Whether or not you indulged in gossip in previous roles, as an executive you must avoid it at all costs. The forms of this are many. "Hey, Bill, do you have a minute? I'd like to get some coaching on how I might work better with Deana. I'm finding her really hard to collaborate with." Bill's response to the request is critical and will set the stage for how indiscretion is encouraged or discouraged among his colleagues. If he takes the bait and responds with anything like, "Oh, please, are you kidding? Trust me, it's not you . . . we all struggle . . . ," then he has formally institutionalized collusive indiscretion as a legitimate form of informational power. If, on the other hand, he takes the conversation in the direction of, "I'm sorry to hear that. When you've raised this with Deana directly, how has it gone?" he begins to shift the responsibility back to those involved, avoiding collusion.

As an executive, you will be privy to surprising amounts of sensitive information about those with whom you lead—their personal lives, their compensation, their performance struggles, their reputations, their personality quirks, their ethical practices, and their career ambitions. The discretion with which you hold this information sacred will play a significant role in establishing and keeping your credibility. The moment someone discovers that disclosing information to you is a liability, everyone you work with will know it. Treat all sensitive information you get from others as sacrosanct.

As with relationships, you must know your own proclivity for being "in the know." What does having access to privileged information trigger in you? What experiences have formed the degree of discretion and confidentiality with which you have treated vital information? Knowing these things in advance of facing them will go a long way to enabling you to be responsible with the informational power of your executive role.

REDEEMING INFORMATIONAL POWER: HOW KNOWLEDGE AND TRANSPARENCY ENHANCE COLLABORATION AND DECISION MAKING

When people feel that they have access to the information they need to do their jobs and that they understand the rationale behind decisions made, two things happen. First, they learn. They feel more connected to the larger enterprise agenda and better understand how their contribution fits within it, which enables them to more confidently repeat that contribution next time. Second, they feel more inclined to work across organizational boundaries with others whose contribution joins theirs in the service of that enterprise agenda. Shared knowledge acts as glue that binds an organization together. When people learn together, they inherently trust one another more because the shared knowledge levels the playing field. And when trust increases, so does collaboration. That, in turn, accelerates effective decision making and requires fewer do-overs. In an environment of trust, collaboration, and transparency, decisions are more likely to be executed successfully the first time because a broader group of informed leaders shares ownership for their success.

In one organization we worked with for several years on a complex global transformation, the previous management regime sequestered nearly all of the information and decision power in two people—the CEO and the CFO. All data flowed to them; all decisions flowed from them. People were guarded, and information had to be pried out of anyone who had it. When the new regime came to power, the CEO had a radically different approach to information and decision making, pushing it down to those who were closest to the work. He changed out almost his entire senior team in hopes of impacting the culture of secrecy and information hoarding. Despite his calling for executives to be responsible for decision making in their respective parts of the business, they didn't know how and they didn't have access to the information they needed. For the first year, governance was clumsy as critical decisions continued to flow back up to the CEO. He spent endless hours with business unit general managers as well as functional heads to design the right information flow, clarify and define decision rights for each of them, charter the work of the executive team and the decisions they would own together, and engage the leaders below the executive level to begin owning decisions they should be making. Two years into the transformation, the organization runs radically differently. Yes, there are still information-vacuum hangovers in some pockets. But for the most part, information flows far more freely up and down the hierarchy and across organizational boundaries. Not every leader made the journey—some had to be turned over when it became apparent they couldn't operate in the new model. In their employee engagement survey during the first year, on the dimensions of information and decision making, only 28 percent of leaders said they had access to the information needed to do their jobs, and only 36 percent of leaders said they felt ownership of decisions in which they participated. Fully 78 percent of leaders said they felt like decision making was not transparent and that they didn't trust it. Two years later, they saw dramatic improvement, with 68 percent of leaders saying they had access to the information they needed to do their jobs, 82 percent of leaders saying they felt ownership for the decisions they participated in, and only 35 percent of leaders saying decision making was not transparent. Impressive results in such a short period of time when you consider where they'd come from.

Resolve now to ensure that transparency in information and decision making is how you will govern your organization. If you understand the deep connections between transparency, trust, and collaborative decision making, you can dramatically change performance.

REFLECTIONS ON THE RISE

1. What adjustments will you make to your leadership to ensure you are effectively managing the power you have?

2. Which form of power failure across the three sources of power represents the greatest threat to your leadership? How will you mitigate the threat?

3. How could Jordan better steward his power to strengthen his effectiveness as CEO?

REDEEMING EXECUTIVE POWER: THE ULTIMATE PRIVILEGE

We trust that the exploration of these abuses and perversions has been eye-opening for you. If it provoked some stark reactions within you, hit a few nerves, or challenged a few assumptions, note those and pay close attention to them. Those are likely places where you may be at risk of succumbing to an abuse or perversion you don't see coming.

Although these abuses and perversions are common, they are not inevitable. While you will undoubtedly have your own power failures, you can redeem those failures and achieve far greater success than the short-lived gains those abuses and perversions promise. What's more, the lasting impact you desire to make on the world, the legacy you hope to leave through your leadership, depends largely on how you deploy the power that comes with your position. Self-interest and self-protection must be duly suppressed by the interests of a greater good and the courage to act in the face of opposition and criticism.

Understanding the dynamics of executive power demands a lifetime of study and experience. You may never fully grasp the importance of the power you hold. Understand the pitfalls of its abuses and perversions, and place your effort on harnessing the great good that power can do. You can beat the odds of executive failure by becoming an honest, humble, diligent steward of your positional, relational, and informational power. The time to decide what you hope to see when you look back on your career is now. With courage you have the potential to positively impact hundreds, if not thousands, of lives. It will require sacrifice and exposure. It will mean disappointing people with unpopular actions, and being disappointed by the forfeiture of perks you might easily have taken. Keep the faces of the employees, customers, consumers, constituents, students, parishioners, neighbors, friends, and family members—the list of stakeholders touched by the power of your role—in mind with each decision you make. They are the ones who will bear the benefits and disappointments of those decisions. They are the ones whose lives you will change forever based on how you choose to exercise your power. Your power will transform others. You must choose how. And know that for generations to come, they will be forever marked by the choices you make. You get to decide if that mark is one of grief or one of gratitude.

"I JUST THINK THEY ALL hate me, Jordan," Jacinta sighed. "This place is impossible to enter and be welcomed. And it's twice as bad for a woman. I've done everything you coached me to do since we spoke a few weeks ago. I can see now I may have been pushing too much too fast. I circled back and reset with Helen, and got that fixed. I engaged the Supply Chain folks more collaboratively and positioned HR in a more supporting role related to their cost-cutting efforts. I'm working as hard as I can to not ruffle everyone's feathers while still trying to do what you brought me here for—to develop and implement the HR agenda Huntington needs to be successful. I don't seem to be making anyone happy now! No sooner do I feel like I'm getting traction on one front when someone else has a beef with me on something else. Honestly, Jordan, I'm starting to question if this may just be a no-win situation . . . at least for me."

Jordan tried to hold back a grin of understanding, but with some empathy said, "Welcome to my world, Jacinta. We are the new cadre of leaders at Huntington and most are still pining for the last regime. I appreciate your frustration. I know you are eager to succeed at Huntington, and see how great the opportunity is to build HR into a key strategic muscle for us. I also know you feel a real sense of urgency because we're about a decade behind on this."

"But do you actually think people want change, Jordan? Or do you think they just *say they want it* without really meaning it? Because every step I feel we take toward the very things they say they want brings out all of their excuses for why we can't or shouldn't. 'We've tried that before and here's why it didn't work.' Or 'That might have worked at your last company, but at Huntington, we're unique. We need to take things a little slower.'" Donning a condescending tone, she was more intense now: "Or, my favorite, 'Jacinta, you obviously are a very smart woman and you know a lot about HR. We all really want to learn from you. I am just a little worried that, well, we're not as sophisticated as you are. You may be, well, more than we need right now. It's not you, it's us.' This is their passive-aggressive code for 'Back off Jacinta, you're exposing how behind the times we are and we don't like it.'"

Now Jordan was laughing. "Those were some great impersonations. And I've had those same things said to me. So you're not alone, Jacinta. Initiating change in a place that has enjoyed the level of success we've had for so long is far more difficult than if everything was falling down around your ears. Right now, the organization doesn't know what it doesn't know, and there's no real pain motivating change. Sure, we know we are woefully lacking talent structures to help grow, but in their minds, we've gotten by for so long without them and done well, so how bad could it really be? What they aren't yet able to do is *anticipate* the pain we'll be in if we don't fix this now."

"Exactly, Jordan. How do I help them do that? Right now I get dinged if I can't read their minds. I get dinged if I don't know what one of our gazillion acronyms stands for. I get dinged if it looks like I have favorites I go to for information or input. I get dinged for not being on email twenty-four seven. And I get dinged if it looks like I AM on email twenty-four seven. How did people come to expect such ridiculous things here?"

Jordan stepped out from behind his desk and sat in the chair next to Jacinta. "Well, Jacinta, I think it's because they don't know *what* to expect, so they're making it up as they go along. Part of the sense-making role you have to play now is helping to inform their expectations. Never forget that the person you replaced was like their grandfather. Walt was beloved. He didn't ask much of them and did everything for them. He threw a mean Christmas party, welcomed every baby born to a Huntington family like royalty, and could write a heartfelt and moving retirement announcement. He didn't know what 'OD' stood for, was tolerant when the training people wanted to do a two-hour webcast, but that's about as far as he dabbled in anything resembling talent development. He is the architect of the HR function that we have now and it bears no resemblance to what you came here to build. So, most people are terrified of you and what you represent. Put yourself in their shoes. What if everything you did suddenly went from being just fine to irrelevant overnight? You've shaken their senses of competence and confidence. In return, every flaw of yours they discover, rational or not, is fodder to help them feel better about themselves and excuse them from changing."

"So what do I do? How do I win? Can I even win?" Jordan could hear the exasperation in Jacinta's voice.

"Of course you can," Jordan reassured her with a big grin. Beneath his assurances, though, he was haunted by the same question. "To win with them you first have to get to really know them. Don't make them look for your humanity—just show it to them. Let them see who you really are. Underneath their irrational expectations are genuine needs they've never expressed before. Help them find a safe way to tell you what they need rather than you telling them what they need. You are a driven leader, Jacinta. It's clear you want to make a difference, and I'm confident you will. But you have to be clear about what they can count on you for before you start holding them accountable for changes they will struggle with and some may never be able to make. They need to understand how you think and know what is nonnegotiable and where you are flexible. I've got your back, Jacinta. I know this is going to take a lot of time. Don't feel like it has to be done in a year or even two. You have some very hard decisions ahead of you, and if folks aren't fully 'on your bus,' it will be very hard to get traction when you start making the hard calls. Once they come to see you as a reliable and consistent leader, their expectations will start to feel less utopian."

Jordan and Jacinta spoke for another hour or so, and Jordan coached her through how to handle specific players, and suggested places where he might be able to help directly with long-time Huntington people. For Jordan, the chance to set aside the raging fires of his own story and be of genuine help to someone else was a welcome relief. He wondered if she knew anything of his problems at this point. The thought of disappointing her was painful. He wondered if she would show him the same grace he was trying to show her now.

"How do you cope with all this, Jordan? I mean, does this stuff ever get to you? Do we ask herculean levels of leadership from you that we shouldn't? You seem so even-keeled and measured. I'm sure there must be days you just lose it, no? With all of this SEC drama still winding down, the Newrizon deal pending, and goodness knows what else, how are you holding up?"

Jordan tried not to be paranoid about why she was asking these questions, and just assume beneficial intent—that she was simply genuinely concerned. The dilemma was how to respond.

"Well, funny you ask that question, Jacinta. . . ."

CHAPTER SIX

MANAGING EXPECTATIONS

TRANSLATING CHRONIC FAILURE AND UNREALISTIC DEMANDS INTO KEPT PROMISES

Up until the last couple of decades, people in positions of authority were venerated simply *because* they were in those positions. Executives of companies were esteemed for their long, loyal careers and for rising up through the ranks of their organizations. And leaders were inherently trusted. Unrealistically seen as superhuman, they received reverence that was overextended and misguided. Leaders were no less fallible then than they are today. The spate of executive failures over the past decade has led us to consider whether or not the executives of past generations were as corrupt as those of today; however, this is something that may never be known. What we can be sure of is that the residual impact of widespread ethical and moral failure has caused most of us to believe leaders are to be *distrusted* until proven trustworthy. And proving oneself trustworthy is becoming increasingly difficult.

The inverse correlation between decreased trust and increased expectations leaves new executives with the implied requirement of walking on water. Followers have grown intolerant of substandard executive leadership over the last decade and have responded by raising the bar much higher. Our research suggests that the unforgiving nature of followers and the harsh standards to which executives are now subject can make leading others one of the most unpleasant aspects of executive leadership. Public scrutiny from so many directions imposes an intense and unrelenting pressure on leaders to contort themselves into godlike creatures that can do no wrong. Of course no follower would ever admit to having these expectations, but their behavior and responses to their leaders' shortcomings tell a different story. Two-thirds of our respondents lament they spend too much time dealing with the performance shortfalls of others while more than half feel they are held accountable for problems outside their control. And as previously mentioned, the demands on executive time far exceed its availability.

While unrealistic expectations can come from all sides—your boss, your peers, and your direct reports—direct reports is the relationship we find most compelling, since it is failure here that can often derail executive careers. We have routinely observed six unreasonable expectations of executives from followers that, while rooted in reasonable desires, actually manifest themselves in no-win outcomes for both followers and their leaders. You may certainly broaden their application to your relationships with your boss and peers where relevant. Figure 6.1 on page 162 summarizes these expectations: the unrealistic demands formed by failed leadership, the underlying legitimate needs and expectations most followers have of their executive leaders, and the reasonable promises executives should make with their words and actions to those they lead. Let's look at each more closely, along with effective strategies for managing these expectations. By exploring what followers *really want*, our hope is that you will be better equipped to proactively make and keep appropriate promises and set healthy expectations with those you lead from the outset of your relationship.

REFLECTIONS ON THE RISE

1. Consider how you have responded to unrealistic expectations in the past. Do you play at the level people expect and need? How have you adjusted to instances where someone comes to you too often, or too little?

2. When you've taken the time to familiarize yourself with people's backgrounds, how has this changed your interaction?

3. How would you coach Jordan to respond to Jacinta?

4. And how would you coach Jacinta to continue to shape realistic expectations within the HR organization, without compromising the direction she needs to take?

PERFECTION

Many driven executives' struggle to accept their own humanity further establishes and reinforces others' expectation of perfection from them. When you act is if you *are*, or *should be*, perfect, eventually you convince others to require it from you. Perfectionism is a painful affliction for overachieving executives who won't tolerate anything less than greatness from themselves and others. One of the consequences of this behavior is that followers, on whom those standards are imposed, typically revolt and withdraw support from the leader. Waiting to pounce on the slightest hint of deficiency, abused followers, starved of any acknowledgment of their own contribution and giftedness, leave no room for their executives to misstep. This becomes a downward spiral. Executives, fearing criticism or exposure of their imperfections, work to hide their humanity, perpetuating the illusion of infallibility. To quell their sense of inadequacy and exposed imperfection, executives become more harsh on themselves and those they lead. Followers, weary of the unscrupulous behaviors they have seen and come to expect of leaders, and bitter over the punitive critique of even the most minor errors, see the inherent hypocrisy in their executives, and allow them no margin of error.

We believe it is appropriate for followers to expect their leaders to perform to high standards. Their integrity should be above reproach, and they should have achieved some degree of technical mastery in whatever discipline they've chosen. That doesn't mean people they lead should never be smarter or more proficient in any given area of expertise. In fact most effective executives have discovered the wisdom in hiring people *more talented* than they are in key areas over which they have responsibility. If you take on an executive-level role without having achieved reasonable mastery and demonstrated a track record of results, or if you possess questionable principles, you open yourself up to intense scrutiny. The people you lead will question your appointment and believe there are others who would have been better suited for the role, including themselves.

Fig. 6.1

Expectation	Unrealistic demands formed by decades of leadership failure	Underlying legitimate need and expectation	The promise you should make and keep
Perfection	You hold the top position; you make the big bucks and you have no right to or room for failure—morally, technically, or relationally.	I do expect you to perform to higher standards of competence and principles.	I will not hold you accountable to standards I myself am not willing to live up to, and I will take responsibility when I fall short of those standards.
Equity and Fairness	There should be parity in every choice you make and I should never be made to feel I got a raw deal.	Organizational injustice IS something you should work against; there should be solid rationale behind how rewards are distributed, careers progress, accountability is levied, and resources are allocated.	I will strive to lead an equitable organization, which doesn't mean everyone is treated "equally," and where there is injustice, I promise to use my power to right it.
Transparency and Justification	I'm entitled to know the reason and thinking behind all of your decisions, especially those that impact me.	Secrecy, self-interest, cowardice, and political influences should not corrupt your decision making, and the fact-based, sound information and judgment that informs your choices should be detectable over time.	I will be clear and transparent in my decision making; I will weigh the merits of fact bases and contradictory data, and share the criteria I use when complex decisions create inevitable disappointment.

Unrealistic expectation structure of executive leaders

Expectation	Unrealistic demands formed by decades of leadership failure	Underlying legitimate need and expectation	The promise you should make and keep
Clairvoyance	You should read my mind and know what I want or need before I have to ask.	Having gotten to know me, you should reasonably demonstrate some anticipation of my needs and likely reactions; you should have some forethought about our interactions based on patterns you have seen— even if I've not yet recognized them myself. You should be a "student" of me.	I will get to know you as a human being and make it safe for you to share your aspirations with me, and I will do what I reasonably can to enable you to reach those aspirations. I will do my best to understand your unexpressed needs, and invite you to ask me questions when you are concerned I am missing something or are uncertain of my views.
Accessibility	You should be available whenever I want access—24/7.	I shouldn't have to jump through hoops to get time with you or input from you; I shouldn't feel like there are layers of security to get to you.	I will be as responsive as I can within the demands of my role and my desires to balance my life outside of work. I will make it clear how to reach me and the process of how to get time with me/input from me.

(continued on next page)

Fig. 6.1

Expectation	Unrealistic demands formed by decades of leadership failure	Underlying legitimate need and expectation	The promise you should make and keep
Inspiration	Keep my emotional fuel tank full at all times—make sure I feel safe, energized, and encouraged.	My emotional well-being should be something you help steward; you should provide inspiration and an honest view of how things are—grim or otherwise; I trust you are seeing a bigger picture than I and can help me see perspectives that I might be missing.	I will freely share why I am passionate about where we are going and be honest about any setbacks we might face. I will do my best to enable you to be fully engaged and feel deep ownership over the work you have been assigned. I will keep the bigger picture in view for our organization when the immediacy of our daily challenges may obscure it.

What they really want

Deep down, followers need to know that *you know you are flawed.* Your best offense against unrealistic expectations is to be up front with your followers about what they can expect from you—where you have strengths, and what your flat sides are. Tell them you welcome their feedback and encourage them to come to you directly when one of your weaknesses is problematic for them, or is getting in the way of their work or relationship with you. Before they come to expect perfection, assure them they will more regularly experience your imperfection. Apologize early and often when you make a mistake, and show your followers grace when they slip up. Establishing an environment of mutual support when things don't go well actually raises the bar on performance and accountability. When people know they have the freedom to fail, they are far more likely to avoid it. Conversely, when they fear failure, they are more likely to run headlong into it and resent you for any of your shortcomings.

EQUITY AND FAIRNESS

When it comes to any processes for allocating resources over which you preside—from compensation and promotions to strategic priority setting—you will be scrutinized for "fairness" in very unfair ways. Many people in organizations today simply expect to get screwed when it comes to an evaluation of their contribution and decisions about their careers, compensation, and access to resources and opportunities. A recent article in the British newspaper the *Daily Mail* quotes Sir Roger Carr, chairman of the consortium that owns British Gas, as stating: "As businesses and individuals, standards have been variable, greed occasionally prevalent and fairness forgotten in a number of sectors. Banking and media [are] at the forefront, but others from all walks of life sometimes also show signs of bad behavior."[29] Of course, as Sir Roger uttered these words, his company was being criticized for raising British gas prices immediately ahead of cold weather.

In his recent book, *The New Few, or A Very British Oligarchy*, Ferdinand Mount notes that the collapse of the world banking industry has left a legacy of persistent high unemployment in Europe, the UK, and the United States—and a credit crunch in all of those regions—yet the financial services industry executives who perpetrated the collapse have been immune to the disastrous effects of their own management. Mount notes that between 2000 and 2008 the FTSE All-Share Index fell by 30 percent, yet cash payments to executives increased 80 percent. Some chief executives are paid hundreds—and even a thousand times—more than the average pay of their workers.[30] Mount is speaking mostly of the UK, but an American reader can easily transpose to the US economy—the story is the same. Fairness is in short supply.

But just because *some* companies are unfair and there are numerous examples of executives who have acted badly while holding on to staggering compensation packages does not mean *all* companies are bad and all leaders are inequitable. As discussed in chapter 5, organizational injustice is in the eye of the beholder, and frequently those that play the "that's not fair" card lack all the facts. Part of your challenge is that there will often be times when you can't share all the facts, or when subjective factors must also be weighed in your decision making. For those you lead, you must distinguish the difference between *equity* and *equality* at the very outset of your assignment.

When people say they want *equality*, quite often what they are really looking for is *equity*. In truth, though, people are not all equal—not every contribution holds the same value—and it is better to be very clear from the beginning that disproportionate effort, performance, and results will get disproportionate rewards, resources, and opportunities. When executives try to neutralize these differences by creating the appearance of "treating everyone the same," or "equally," they often provoke the very anxieties they were trying to allay because people instinctively know such equality to be untrue. Being treated "equitably," by contrast, means rewards and resources are distributed commensurate with value and contribution.

What they really want

Followers want to *know the rules*, and to know you care when the rules are *being broken*. If they understand at the outset what the standards are and how rewards will be distributed, they will recognize there is no capriciousness beneath your decision making. They also want to know that you understand the realities of organizational injustices and will advocate for them—have their back—within the broader system. One executive we worked with, thinking he was showing empathy, said to a direct report, "I know our bonus structure is messed up, but there's nothing I can do about it. Let's work to make the best of it." Unfortunately, making himself a victim of the process just reduced his credibility with his direct report because he advertised the fact that he felt powerless to advocate for something better. Let those you lead know when you become aware of systemic injustices as well as episodic ones. When someone in the organization is behaving in ways that disrespect or disadvantage those you lead, be very clear and swift in stopping it, *no matter who it is*. Yes, even if it's your boss. Resist the impulse to lower your standards of behavior to match the unjust behavior. Your advocacy on behalf of those feeling its effects sends a powerful message about your standards of organizational justice. Even if you don't prevail, those you lead will know you defended their dignity.

TRANSPARENCY AND JUSTIFICATION

Executives who retain, or relinquish, too much control over decision making—or, worse, do neither and stifle it altogether—create chaos in their organizations. Followers end up vying for decisions they feel they should make, pushing decisions they feel are too complex back up to executives, or tearing their hair out because no one will make a decision that is vital to something they are working on. Unrealistic expectations for complete transparency have some executives perpetually on the defense. Basic questions like, "Why did you do it that way?" or "How did you land on that as a way forward," or "I just need to understand what was behind your decision so I can explain it when I have to implement it" can put executives back on their heels, scrambling to justify their choices.

In organizations where it is not safe to openly question or push back on decisions, followers may feign support publicly while mocking, venting, scrutinizing, and resisting the decision behind the leader's back. Scratching their heads, we commonly hear executives lament, "But I thought we were all aligned!"

Leaders who fail to provide sufficient transparency into their decision-making criteria and approaches known *in advance of actually making decisions* are at risk for owning those decisions alone. Letting people know on the front end what criteria you intend to use and how you intend to make the decision will go a long way to building support. While many executives often fear being overly declarative in their decision making, the fact is followers find it liberating when leaders simply say, "I'm making the call and here's how I'm going to make it." Contrary to popular organizational mythology, followers *do not* expect to be involved in every single decision that touches them. And it would be cruel to expect them to participate in decisions they are neither equipped nor experienced enough to make. Be clear when you are asking for input for a decision that *you* will ultimately make. When you intend for a decision to be reached by consensus, make that clear. When you are delegating the authority for making a decision to others, and do or don't want to offer any input, make that clear. And when you are just making the call, be clear about that as well.

What they really want

What followers want is a sense of *predictability*. They want to be able to decode your analytical process, your moral compass, and your trade-off criteria when making tough decisions. They want to be able to predict, with a reasonable sense of accuracy, how you will behave in a given situation. When they can't predict, it is too easy to assume that you are hiding something. This leads them to fear your political motives, question who may have curried favor with you, wonder about the disaster you are working privately to stem, or speculate what plot you are devising against them or another organizational nemesis. Head such "Kremlin watching" off at the pass by providing a consistent and clear approach to decision making that sustains followers' confidence by allowing them to reasonably forecast how your leadership is going to show up at critical decision junctures.

CLAIRVOYANCE

Very little is more frustrating to an executive than a follower who is clearly "stewing" about something but won't say what it is. The classic "No, everything's fine" to inquiries from genuinely concerned executives leads to everyone walking on eggshells and nobody talking about why. Such manipulative behavior is one of many forms the expectation of clairvoyance takes. There may be a sudden burst of surprised disappointment when a follower expresses displeasure over not being given a plum assignment she never conveyed any interest in until it went to a colleague who stepped forward and asked for it. "*You should have just known that I wanted it—I've been here for five years, for crying out loud*" is another common form of clairvoyance, and was actually a statement made to one of our clients. He was stunned by the insinuation that he had deliberately withheld the opportunity from one of his direct reports in favor of giving it to someone else. As we probed a bit with our client, we discovered that he had little knowledge of this direct report at all. "She's quiet, doesn't say much in meetings, but she's a solid performer and gets her work done." He knew she was married but didn't know her husband's name or if she had any children. He vaguely remembered her having a graduate degree, but didn't recall in what. Turns out she'd spent years going to school at night to get her master's in advanced financial analytics and was dying to use what she'd learned. With increasing technology and a subsequent need to do something with the mountain of information appearing on everyone's desks, she was hopeful she could dive into the data and help create processes for analyzing it and applying gained insights to key opportunities. Of course she'd never told anyone that was her desire. She failed to let her aspirations be known, and the executive failed to have sufficient knowledge of a key resource on his team whose contribution was being suboptimized and who was feeling marginalized as a result.

What they really want

What followers really want is to be *seen and known*, which is what we saw Jordan begin to say to Jacinta. Of course they don't truly expect you to read their minds. But most people's experience of the workplace is not of being understood, but of being *watched* and *judged*. They too often feel labeled and pigeonholed. As obvious as it may sound, knowing those you lead, and letting them know you, allows for a relationship of mutual regard that brings out the best contributions of both of you. Absent the need to keep up a front or hide, followers feel free to express ideas, volunteer for assignments, push back on assumptions, challenge common practices, and trust that you will see them for who they are, not judge or misperceive them. While you don't have to read your followers' minds, you do need to read them, gaining insights into them and applying what you learn to how you lead them.

ACCESSIBILITY

Followers with overdependence on executives in the Strategic system burden the Coordinating system with sluggish responsiveness and an inability to execute the strategy they've been charged with. On the other hand, the Strategic system can handicap the Coordinating system if your people can't get their questions answered, get appointments on your calendar, or get responses to, or feedback on, work you've asked to see. While there is no formula to determine exactly how much time should be made available to others, recognize you'll never feel you have enough of it to give, and they'll likely never feel they get enough of it from you. So, setting that dilemma aside, the challenge is how to negotiate with each of your followers what exactly they need and how best to provide it. Don't let militant gatekeepers prevent access to you, and don't offer unlimited access either. Set clear boundaries and enforce with followers the need to work within them. And maximize the impact of your time with the creative use of governance that gets teams of people access to you versus a series of one-on-one conversations. We'll touch on how to leverage governance a bit more in chapter 8.

What they really want

What followers really want from their executives is *reliability*. They need to know that if they have problems, you'll be there to help them find solutions. If there's something they can't make sense of, you'll offer helpful perspective. If they can't get someone in an adjacent department to cooperate, you'll run interference. While the amount of *time* you spend doing these things will obviously vary from person to person, when followers conclude that you *aren't* reliable, the amount of time you *don't* spend with them becomes the issue. While you can't—and don't want to—become everyone's answer ATM, and you need to build self-sufficiency among those you lead, knowing you are there as a resource to guide, support, challenge, admonish, and just plain help bolsters their trust in your leadership and helps them more effectively decide when and how to engage you most effectively.

INSPIRATION

Inspired performance is not routine. It comes from a much deeper place within, a sacred part of followers where they *choose* to offer their best. It is the contribution that exceeds expectations, goes beyond what is good enough, takes ideas to unprecedented heights, and sets personal records. At one time or another, we all have a need for the source of that inspiration to come from outside of ourselves. We need to know that we matter and that there is reason to remain committed to the mission, especially when circumstances are less than ideal. Leaders need to be able to provide such inspiration, so long as it is genuine and not rooted in Pollyannaish platitudes.

Organizations are too often draining places. While passion, engagement, and vision are common vernacular, what is less common is the energizing impact they are intended to have. Followers, bereft of a sense of meaning and purpose, yearn to know their work matters to a larger context. They want to feel part of and contribute to something greater than themselves. While it is unreasonable for followers to expect their executives to be personal cheerleaders, therapists, or vessels from which to quench their insatiable needs for emotional support (and we've seen many executives get lured into becoming these things), it is reasonable to expect that some portion of a follower's emotional gauge is directly impacted by her executive's choices. We ask people to take pride in their work, to see their contributions as a personal expression of themselves, and to discover those things about which they have the most passion. So when they actually do, executives need to be prepared with the emotional reinforcement required for followers to sustain such contribution. Many executives are uncomfortable with the expression of emotions, especially strong emotions like anger, sadness, panic, or even sheer delight. Fearful of their own emotional range, they often unintentionally squelch such expressions from others by withholding their own. Peter Bregman[31] goes so far as to say that "people who suppress their emotions aren't safe in an organization."

Further research goes on to suggest that spending energy suppressing emotions only brings them back twofold. People who "never get angry" actually spend twice as much energy trying to suppress their anger as those who regularly exercise it. When expressing a range of emotions is signaled as unacceptable, such suppression becomes a widespread norm. The sad result is that it arrests the individual and collective capacity of an organization to rally when needed, to celebrate when great success is achieved, and to productively channel discontent, even outrage, into double-down recovery efforts when major setbacks occur.

What they really want

Followers need a reason to maintain hope. They need to know that what lies beyond the horizon of their perspective is a reason to keep going, and they need to know you sense what that reason is. In a truthful and balanced way, they need to hear from you the realism of what is, and the optimism of what could be. Peterson and Byron[32] point out that high-hope individuals are more goal oriented and more motivated to achieve their goals than those with low hope. It doesn't matter where in the organization people are. Peterson and Byron found that regardless of whether they were talking about sales employees, mortgage brokers, or management executives, high-hope individuals had higher overall job performance. They also found that higher-hope executives produced more and better quality solutions to work-related problems, suggesting that hopefulness may help employees when they encounter obstacles at work. Hope, then, is also a fundamental choice. Hope would not be the powerful force that it is if it were chosen only when a reason to do so was obvious. The true power of hope lies in choosing to have it when the presenting data would suggest otherwise. Hope invites the leap of faith to place one's confidence behind an initiative or a dream without necessarily having the tangible evidence to back it up. Your conviction about, and expression of, hope in the future underpins your credibility in asking your followers for their hope.

The executive stage is a high-wire act without a net. For sure, your performance will be judged against leadership standards you've not seen before. Some may give you a standing ovation when you feel like you deserve to be booed off the stage, and others will throw tomatoes when you think they should throw roses. You will have to contend with the reality that executive leadership through the experience of followers doesn't always feel rational, and the more you resist this, the more you will struggle. Anchoring yourself with a set of values that aren't vulnerable to the sometimes fickle, unpredictable needs of followers; knowing yourself well—your character, your strengths, your flat sides, your passions; and possessing a genuine desire to make a difference, not just for yourself but for the organization in which you lead, will help you weather the sometimes overly harsh blows dealt by followers through stringent and unrealistic expectations.

In our final section, *Affect*, we will turn our energy toward the unique dimensions that shape the exceptional executive, along with extraordinary opportunities of the executive role, and the efforts of organizations needed to multiply exceptional executives.

IN FLIGHT

Provisional acceptance.

The words hit Jordan like a ton of bricks as he reread New-rizon's contingencies related to accepting the terms of the deal. Most of what Jordan found within the forty-plus-page contract was predictable. But not this. Newrizon's due diligence was so thorough they'd dug up and were raising the one risk he'd hoped he'd be able to address over time as the partnership unfolded. The majority of contingencies in Newrizon's response were easily addressable. This one would require seismic choices Jordan wasn't sure Huntington was ready to make. The one risk he'd hoped Newrizon would miss is the one he should have been most prepared for.

And the real kicker . . . they had seventy-two hours to respond.

"They were waaaay more exhaustive in their digging than I ever expected," he opined to himself.

During Newrizon's visits to several of Huntington's plants, their manufacturing experts uncovered a long-known, but well-disguised, weakness in Huntington's manufacturing operation—inconsistent capacity management. Jordan had known about this since he started at Huntington more than a decade ago, having spent two years working in the supply chain organization. They had tried every demand-planning and forecasting approach known to man, streamlined production processes, and even gone to three shifts in several plants. Unfortunately, all of these adjustments produced only moderate and temporary improvements. At the core, the problem was Huntington's two outmoded plants, which could produce only products with standard plastics and in longer runs. The two newer plants had state-of-the-art production facilities, enabling them to produce with multiple materials, including the new composite materials required in Newrizon's deal. They could also produce in both short and long runs, a degree of flexibility the older plants would never have. These new plants had been built with expansion and the eventual consolidation of the older plants in mind. Mac had resisted the consolidation because it would mean letting go of some of Huntington's original employees and the first production facility he'd built. This hit him too close to home. So they'd lived with the imperfections of an imbalanced supply chain and manufacturing footprint, as well as their associated costs and limitations, because the needed hard decisions were too emotionally charged for, and therefore eluded, the company's leader. But they didn't elude Newrizon.

Newrizon was not convinced that Huntington's existing supply chain could manufacture, inventory, and ship the agreed-upon packaging solutions specified in the accepted designs. In order to realize the cost savings promised in the deal, and the consolidation from eleven suppliers to just Huntington, Newrizon needed more confidence that Huntington could deliver. Jordan always knew there was some risk, but deal fever shrouded his angst over it. Now he had seventy-two hours to produce a plan that committed to rapid expansion of the production capacity of the two newer plants, half of whose eventual total capacity would have to be dedicated "exclusively" to Newrizon. Newrizon's terms required this be accomplished within the first six months of the deal.

And in order to agree to those terms, and not completely tank Huntington's earnings, Jordan would have to shut down the older plants.

"How the HELL did they ever dig up this issue?" Elise barked as she bounded into Jordan's office waving the agreement. "Obviously we were naïve about how deep they would go."

"Last thing I expected," Jordan replied, still stunned by it all.

"So now what?" Elise looked at Jordan in hopes he had some brilliant plan for how to respond.

"I assume you realize the implications if we accept these terms?" he queried her.

"Uhhh, hell, YEAH—like shutting down our plants, laying off a bunch of people, and pissing off the whole company, not to mention impacting those two towns across the valley. I can hear the old timers now . . . 'Mac would have never done this to us. He would have stood by us. This guy is just out for the money. He doesn't care about us the way Mac did.' Yup, I see the picture pretty clearly, Jordan. Are you ready for that kind of popularity?"

If Jordan could have stopped time to absorb the magnitude of her question, he would have. Given his personal struggles, all that had happened with the SEC, his crisis of confidence entering the CEO role, and the profound risks associated with what he knew he had to do, running the other way was an alluring choice. He knew that win, lose, or draw, he had to play the hand he was dealt. He knew that Mac would have urged him to "go big, or go home." He knew this crossroads represented the opportunity to define the leader he would be for Huntington, and the organization Huntington would be in the future. However painful, doing what was right for Huntington had to prevail over what felt comfortable and safe for him. He knew he could not approach this like a victim. He needed to embrace it as a privilege. He didn't have the luxury of obsessing over what to do as he might normally have done. Despite the temptation, there was no time to yield to self-pity or the urge to resent Mac. Jordan had to mobilize his team and develop a response for Newrizon. If he failed, it wasn't going to be because he froze. If he went down, he was going down swinging.

"Carolyn, can you get me Wayne, please?"

"Wow, you're going for it, aren't you?" Elise was impressed.

"No use avoiding this any longer. It's now officially bitten us in the butt. And there's no way through this without Wayne."

Wayne Tanner had led Huntington's supply chain for about four years. Included in his responsibilities were manufacturing operations as well as logistics and distribution. He'd been at Huntington for more than thirty years, had grown up in the plants, and had done a three-year stint in Sales along the way. Having kept abreast of manufacturing trends, and seen the expert's reports about Huntington's outdated footprint, Wayne was well aware of the dilemma. He had been working on a gradual plan to eventually expand the capacity of the new plants and phase out the older ones. Jordan had worked for Wayne back when he was a plant manager, and Jordan was on the line. They'd stayed close over the years. Wayne was a great source of insight for Jordan as he took on the marketing role, and when he needed something "out of the ordinary" from the supply chain, Wayne could always broker the deal.

Jordan knew that if they could phase the capacity migration just right to coincide with both Newrizon's requirements and the pace of change Huntington could absorb, they just might be able to pull this off. He also knew that the level of care and diplomacy needed to close plants and let longtime employees go would exceed anything in Huntington's experience.

After the exchange of pleasantries and family recaps, Jordan got right to the point.

"Wayne, not gonna beat around the bush. We got the response from Newrizon and they're in, but they're calling the question on our capacity issues. If we don't agree to fix them, it's a deal breaker. You know what a phenomenal opportunity this represents for Huntington. And I know we've been marching to a more phased, gradual plan to consolidate capacity. I don't think that approach is an option anymore if we want to capitalize on this opportunity, and if we don't, I'm not sure when we'll get it again. I really need your help."

At first, Wayne withdrew and stayed silent. Then he dug his heels in and fought. It was an intense conversation. Together, eventually, they sketched out a plan they believed could work. Wayne would have to get key leaders in Supply Chain on board, which wouldn't be easy, but he had the credibility and relational equity to do it. Given he'd been thinking about it for a while, he also had determined that, with more disciplined planning and some creative maneuvering, they could retool one of the older plants to take on all of their traditional manufacturing, leaving the new plants to focus exclusively on new deals like Newrizon's. Their plan might even enable them to accelerate reaching the deal terms. Jordan realized that would, in turn, require some shifts from Sales and Marketing so that forecasting was integrally linked to demand planning—which would require key process changes he'd need Elise to start making immediately.

Jordan had Carolyn summon Elise, Jacinta, and Brandon, Huntington's head of Sales. Fortunately, Jacinta had actively worked to repair her relationships with Wayne and Brandon after the unfortunate emails she'd sent early on, so they didn't wince when she walked in.

For the next two hours, Jordan was a masterful quarterback. He insightfully orchestrated where to build the needed linkages between forecasting and demand planning, and asked Elise, Brandon, and Wayne to hammer out the plan by the next morning, including the required technology upgrades. He asked Jacinta to work with Wayne on a communication and RIF plan for the plant closure and dictated the honest, compassionate core messages he wanted them to incorporate. He wanted it kept completely confidential until the Newrizon deal was secured, but asked that a town hall be scheduled within two weeks. He told Wayne that while he didn't want to undermine his leadership, he wanted the plant to hear the news directly from himself. He knew that the town in which the plant resided would take an economic hit until jobs were found for those affected. Because Jordan sat on the city council, he could work with the mayor to make finding jobs a citywide priority for that town. And finally, he asked Elise to work directly with him to craft the response to Newrizon that outlined the overarching plan agreeing to their terms. Given how forensic they were in their due diligence, he wasn't taking any chances— their response would be bulletproof. When they were done, he thanked the four of them profusely for helping to secure Huntington's future, a future that without the Newrizon deal would never be realized.

Elise hung back as the others left to go work on their various assignments. She stared at Jordan with a bit of a grin.

"What?" he asked awkwardly.

"That was impressive," she said with genuine admiration.

"What was?"

"What you just did. You may have just pulled off the single greatest moment in Huntington's history."

Embarrassed, and dismissive, he began to respond, "Naaahh-hhh, it was just a good meeting. When you've got the right people around you, you can get seemingly impossible things done."

She walked over to the desk, leaned over, and with a bit of an edge said, "Don't ever correct me when I'm in the middle of complimenting you. Is that clear?"

He retaliated, "Just who do you think you are, talking that way to the CEO?"

With a short laugh from them both, she persisted, "Seriously, Jordan, what did that feel like?"

He put his head down. It was a more salient question than she realized.

"Truthfully, Elise, it wasn't easy. There have been moments since taking this job I've felt like an absolute imposter, and knew I was acting like one too. I feel like I've had more days failing than doing any good. And personally . . ." Jordan stopped to compose himself. "Well, let's just say I haven't been at my best through all of this. But I'm working on getting it all back on track. Today was just evidence of a little progress . . ."

"I don't know who the hell would be at their best with what you've had to deal with this year. The fact that you're still here standing is a testament to why Mac picked you in the first place."

"Thanks, Elise. If we can get through these next six months, and I can face those people over in the valley who've served us well for so many years, make sure they are treated well and with dignity and not have them stone me, then maybe, just maybe, I'll have a shot at making something of this job. Right now let's just get this plan done! . . . Carolyn, can you bring in the take-out menus? We're gonna be here pretty late . . ."

"Jimmy John's or Domino's?"

SECTION IV
AFFECT

CHAPTER SEVEN

THE EXCEPTIONAL EXECUTIVE

POWERFUL LEADERSHIP IN ACTION

SETTING THE STAGE: HOW WE EXCAVATED WHAT'S ON THE PAGES AHEAD

As PART OF OUR CONSULTING PRACTICE, WE regularly conduct in-depth qualitative interviews to identify and understand the context, patterns, and current results of an organization as the starting point for our work. When working with individual executives, our diagnosis typically includes twenty to thirty interviews with superiors, peers, and direct reports using a consistent interview protocol focused on an exploration of their strengths and weaknesses, and the strategic imperatives for their role. For this study, we chose eighty-four high-performing executives from the hundreds we have worked with over the past ten years. They represent various industries and over 1,600 separate interviews. We rated and ranked each executive based on their impact and business results. We then studied the consistency and effectiveness of behaviors used to achieve the results as part of an in-depth quantitative assessment to understand the defining characteristics and patterns of behavior between the top twenty-five "best of the best" and bottom twenty-five "worst of the best" performers of the total population. In the appendix you will find a detailed description of the statistical analysis conducted on the data.

We started from the premise that strong moral character is foundational to effective leadership; however, it is worth noting that our executive study revealed only a strong positive correlation with the absence of integrity of character, but no significant positive correlation with its presence. In other words, you get no extra credit for being honest. But, absent strong moral character, the results conclude that a leader is *73 percent more likely* to undermine business performance. Put another way, if you intend on doing something corrupt or immoral, you only have a 27 percent chance of *not getting caught*. Our study reinforced flawless integrity and ethics as the *expected standard*. Those we interviewed expect the existence of moral character as a *prerequisite* for occupying an executive role and, therefore, only highlighted its absence. Decades of excessive ethical failures have likely contributed to these heightened expectations while reducing the level of "credit" for having irreproachable integrity and character. Barbara Kellerman, in her scathing, but justified, critique of leadership and the leadership industry, says,

> Whether justified or not, attacks [on executives] signal a time in which business leaders, like political leaders, are considered fair game. This applies in spades to bad leaders, to failed, flawed CEOs who are by now thought to be so many in number there is occasionally the impression they are not the exception but rather the rule. . . . Many who were too greedy have managed to escape unscathed. Add to this the media's voracious appetite for bad news about bad people, and our own insatiable curiosity about the high and mighty who fall far fast, and you have explained our fixation on those who did wrong. Small wonder so many think the problem is not just a few rotten apples, but in fact whole bushels of them.[33]

Competencies define leaders' ability to do something, desire defines their focus of attention, but character ultimately defines what they will do in a given circumstance. It is not something that you have or don't have: We all have character. The key lies in demonstrating behaviors anchored to a set of virtues that others consistently experience in your interactions with them. Your challenge is to constantly remind yourself that, although you may judge your actions by the intentions that precede them, others can rely only on demonstrated behaviors, and it is on those they will judge whether or not you are worthy to follow.

THE BEST AND WORST OF THE BEST COMPARATIVE BEHAVIORAL PATTERNS

Keep in mind the fifty executives being compared were *all* considered to be "top performers." We didn't compare "great leaders" to "crappy leaders." By rating leaders based on relative business performance and the effectiveness of their behavioral approach as reported by hundreds of interviewees, we isolated the top twenty-five best leaders from twenty-five otherwise solid leaders in our "best of the best" study to see what distinguished them from one another. (You will find a detailed description of the study design parameters in the appendix.) The statistical analysis of interview comments for the top and bottom among our set of rising executives reveals the following:

- The most effective leaders were described as having mastery of the "big picture" in two distinct ways: First, they have a current, intimate understanding of the economic and competitive marketplace dynamics. They understand the direction of its movement; they can generate probable future scenarios, and they can identify and anticipate causal forces. Second, they clearly understand how the business works. They show extensive knowledge of how an organization is purposefully put together—how the pieces and parts must effectively work together—to deliver the chosen business strategy. And, importantly, their knowledge of where value is created and destroyed enables them to make effective trade-off decisions. The most effective of the executives in our study generate power and influence from their demonstrated proficiency of both types of "big picture" behaviors.

- Top executives are overwhelmingly described as having exceptionally strong knowledge of the business, especially of the role and contributions of the organization they lead; however, it is rarely limited to technical knowledge alone. Most often it is defined in much broader terms and context. Lower performers' knowledge of the business was also strong, with the main difference being that it is described in a way that is more functionally isolated or limited to technical understanding. Executives in the bottom twenty-five were described more often as anchoring their leadership influence more in their passion for the business and less to the strategic context.

- Top executives generate power from highly developed networks of cross-functional relationships. Networks of both internal and external relationships are a vital underpinning of their success. Through these relationships they develop the deep influence and skills necessary to successfully execute enterprise-wide initiatives for business impact. Conversely, executives in the bottom twenty-five are often reported as overtly focused on managing upward relationships and to a much lesser extent those with their peers. This inherently diminishes their ability to exercise influence and have broader impact. They are also described as having weaker relationships with their direct reports. This apparent pattern of actively managing upward in an attempt to position themselves for greater responsibility while largely ignoring horizontal and downward relationships from which they can draw legitimate influence diminishes their power. While they may believe it is not obvious, others clearly note the behavior and withdraw their support.

- Top executives are distinguished by the consistency with which they listen to others. They actively seek out ideas and opinions from across their networks and incorporate them into their plans to solve organizational problems. This skill enables them to generate influence in their relationships upward, laterally, and downward. Executives in the bottom twenty-five are also reported as listening, especially by subordinates; however, they lack the follow-through to do much, if anything, with what they hear.

- Top executives' decision making is frequently described as making their opinions known but relying on their analytical skills and methodical process, along with the opinions and knowledge of others, to guide the ultimate decision. The bottom twenty-five also made their opinions known but were less interested in listening to or incorporating others' ideas and opinions. And although the study revealed that they generally exercised good judgment, they more frequently made decisions in isolation and developed a clear reputation as the primary or sole decision maker.

- The best executives are described as paying attention to or having appropriate tactical abilities, whereas their bottom twenty-five counterparts are consistently qualified as being "non-tactical." Descriptions of the bottom twenty-five have significantly less to do with delivering business results and much more to do with actions focused on planning work. In contrast to the descriptions for top performers, it is as if those describing the bottom twenty-five were seeking a nice way to say, "All hat, no cowboy!"

- Top executives are consistently transparent and balanced in their communication. They effectively translate their view of business potential and challenges, as well as expectations for action, using succinct, direct, and readily understandable language in doses that are easily digestible. They consistently stay connected to those they lead through a variety of communication mechanisms. The bottom twenty-five are seen as extremely passionate but not necessarily adept at communicating, transferring that passion, or effectively conveying expectations.

These findings are by no means the definitive and exhaustive list of the attributes of effective executives; however, the patterns among the top and bottom performers in our sample are clear, consistent, and worthy of careful consideration. They present a compelling focus for rising executives who aspire to acquire and effectively wield power and influence within their organizations toward the achievement of exceptional results.

We incorporated the behaviors observed into a highly integrated set of dimensions based on the statistical ranking of which most correlated to impact on business performance. The illustration below depicts what we believe defines an exceptional executive. They are *not* offered as "the answer." While our confidence in their efficacy is high, they are by no means definitive. As you read through each dimension you will recognize that threads of these concepts are woven through the first six chapters. We intentionally did not label them as these dimensions until now because we wanted you to discover them in their various forms as you would on a "rising" journey. In the appendix, you will find a table that organizes the content from chapters 1–6 around these dimensions to enable you to return to previous sections to gain deeper understanding of how they appear in action.

As we stated in the introduction, our intent was also to build toward an understanding of their collective, inherent power. So as we explore the power in each individual dimension, keep in mind that ultimately exceptional leadership comes from exercising them in concert. Our greatest hope is that they will cause you to think more deeply and holistically about your own choices and uses of the power available to you, and then make needed adjustments to increase your positive impact on others and your organization. Figure 7.1 illustrates the four dimensions in an interconnected way.

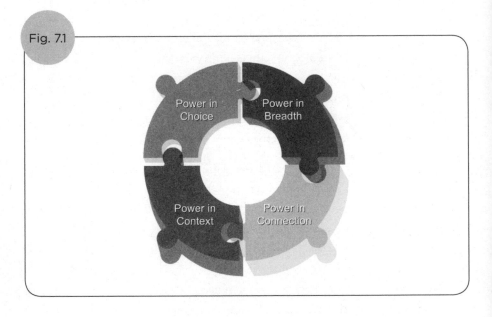

Fig. 7.1

Power Sources of Exceptional Executives

Power in Breadth

In December of 2007, David West was promoted to president and chief executive officer of the Hershey Company. Prior to joining Hershey, he had a successful finance career, rising through the ranks at Kraft Foods, Inc. and Nabisco, Inc. to ultimately assume positions as vice president and chief financial officer for large divisions of those companies. He joined the Hershey Company in 2001 as the senior vice president of Business Planning and Development and from that role broadened his exposure and understanding of the business by leading, and eventually redesigning, the sales organization, and then serving as chief customer officer, chief financial officer, and chief operating officer.[34]

When he assumed the top position, Hershey's stock price hovered around $39, and the business was not in great shape. He quickly focused attention on the historic starvation of Hershey's iconic brands. Earlier in his career, Dave had conceived the "Circle of Doom" (see figure 7.2 below) to explain a perpetually vicious cycle he saw prevalent in consumer packaged goods organizations: Setting unrealistic objectives leads to: missing top-line goals, which drives spending cuts, infuses trade spending to incentivize promotional purchase behavior and drive volume, which ultimately reinforces an undisciplined approach to business; and starves a company's brands of their ability to drive growth. This was his assessment of the Hershey Company as he assumed the top job. The cycle had been perpetuated for years, and Hershey's brands languished with results far below their potential as he took charge of the company. He quickly beefed up advertising to remind consumers of, and reengage them in, the pleasures of confectionary products. He reestablished his brands as iconic household staples, reviving the power of Hershey's brands to drive growth for the company and for retail partners.

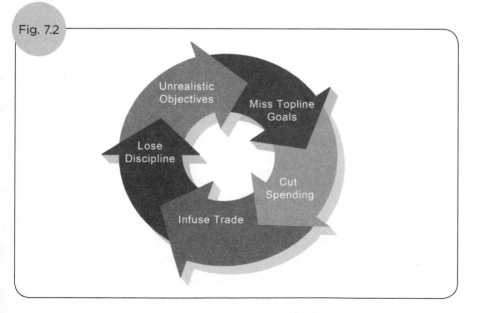

Fig. 7.2

Circle of Doom

Two years into his tenure as CEO, having reestablished their competitive positioning, he turned his attention to market expansion. He realized that for Hershey to grow beyond the United States and beyond the confection category, the enterprise configuration had to be transformed to one able to accommodate new categories and new markets. His end-to-end understanding of the business and the culture enabled him to design an organization radically different from the functional organization he had inherited. His new emphasis was to establish an innovation capability able to fuel growth outside of Hershey's traditional business by building and accelerating a pipeline of new offerings. He accomplished them by integrating product development and marketing, and establishing scalable categories with their own P&Ls. This reconfiguration of the business could tolerate asymmetrical investments in more promising opportunities, expand into priority geographies and find nontraditional trade routes to market, and better link the talent processes associated with selecting and promoting leaders with the growth needs of each business. What Dave set in motion powered Hershey's stock to climb to $53 per share by the time he left the company in 2011 and continue its upward climb to $97 per share at the close of 2013. Dave's understanding of how to build and optimize investments in brands, how to reconfigure routes to market in a variety of settings, and how to design and link new configurations of an organization—all while honoring a deep and unique culture—afforded him the Breadth he needed to credibly, and effectively, lead Hershey and reinvigorate the brand to attain new levels of achievement.

WHY CHRONIC PROBLEMS PERSIST

Now, think about the various problems that you've dealt with recently in your organization. Of that mental list, how many of those problems had you addressed previously, and when it came up again thought to yourself, "Seriously, we're dealing with this again?" Our guess is that your list contains more than a few. Most organizations contend with a revolving door of repeat-offending issues that are frequently addressed but never fully resolved. Consider problems such as the lack of the right talent to fill unexpected voids, cost overruns, or missed monthly forecasts—ongoing challenges for many businesses. When they happen, the appropriate divisional leaders, together with their supporting cast, gather for the download of details and hypothesized causes. These discussions often start out tense, but generally hypotheses for the causes ultimately surface, appropriate blame is levied, and the meeting then breaks with each leader having received marching orders to go "fix" the problem.

Issues persist because leaders tend to lack the skill or discipline of systemic problem solving. They typically define the problem through the lens of their own experience and expertise, as well as the confines of their function or business. And it is within these confines that they attempt to make adjustments without full appreciation or regard for the potential difficulties and added complexity they may create across the broader system. Their insular view and lack of peripheral vision largely ignores the critical seams of the organization. One client of ours struggled for years to consistently satisfy its customers. In fact, in comparative rankings of customer satisfaction, it consistently ranked at or near the bottom of the list. Sales had long been an impenetrable fortress that traded on the strength of personal relationships with key individuals. Customer Marketing was a newer and less understood function that reported up separately from Sales and the brand businesses. When monthly results were reviewed and forecasts were missed again, Sales retrenched to fix a pricing issue and Customer Marketing focused their attention on better content, while Supply Chain did their best to stay flexible to meet last-minute shifts in priorities. However, when their well-intentioned solutions showed up at retail, they did little to improve customer satisfaction or results. Absent a shared, holistic picture of the issues and agreement on a systemic solution, employees scrambled while the company's valuable, limited resources were wasted on well-intended but often disjointed or competing solutions that served only to heighten everyone's frustration. Ultimately, miscues and failed results became such a problem that the leaders finally felt compelled to work together to redesign their entire go-to-market approach.

In contrast to the compulsion that drives such leaders, a defining characteristic of our exemplar executives is that they consciously seek to understand the organization as a whole and actively exploit their knowledge of how the various parts work in concert to manage complexity and create value. Instead of working out solutions in isolation, exceptional executives are drawn to explore opportunity and solutions at the points of divisional intersections where there is tremendous potential for value to be created or destroyed. Although the complexity they must manage remains fairly constant, their ability to rise above it with sufficient purview to see more opportunities and options enables them to conceive and execute solutions that ultimately benefit everyone through the results they deliver.

A challenge in developing Breadth lies in the reinforcing messages received while at the Operating and Coordinating system levels. Peripheral vision is limited and individualism is more often rewarded simply by the defined focus of these roles. Consequently, when you ascend quickly to the Strategic system your ability to see and act broadly is nascent or nonexistent.

Increasing complexity is a compounding factor that you must contend with as you assume roles of greater responsibility: complexity in the form of an overwhelming barrage of information, an increased number of opportunities to explore and exploit, and the demanding speed of change, all while simultaneously recognizing that the consequences associated with the dilemmas you must resolve have increasingly greater impact. No pressure! But when you persist in seeing and engaging the organization as separate, fragmented pieces, you only amplify the issue. Unfortunately, the antidote is not to simplify things, because you really can't. The world is complex. The business environment is complex. Complexity is a constant factor of organizational life best managed by consistently rising up to achieve an elevated viewpoint from which the whole picture is clearly revealed. From this bird's-eye vantage point, you can more easily assess and manage the interplay of organizational divisions in service of enterprise objectives.

Strength will emanate from your clear, detailed understanding of how the broader organizational configuration works in concert to deliver your defined market strategy, and from your ability to facilitate the same understanding for those you lead. In the absence of Breadth you will become constrained by narrowed views of issues and opportunities. Greater power and impact result from an increased facility to more readily sort through the barrage of information and opportunities that come your way, separating the relevant from non-relevant and determining with greater confidence if and how your organization must evolve. Leaders who maintain an intimate understanding of the dynamic interplay of the various parts of the organization understand where and how value is created or destroyed, and know how to optimally configure—or reconfigure—the organization's assets to support seamless execution and achieve greater returns for shareholders. Patterns of behavior among our exemplar population highlighted key warning signs of underdeveloped Breadth, including difficulty with execution, remaining overly tactical with a short-term perspective, and a dominant reliance on previous functional technical depth.

REFLECTIONS ON THE RISE: MASTERING BREADTH

In my approach to leading with Breadth, I . . .

1. Have a clear understanding of the charter and contribution of each function and business line of the company.

2. Have a clear and holistic picture of how the various components work together to deliver value to the market.

3. Effectively use my understanding of the big picture to sort and lead others through the complexity inherent in organization life.

4. Effectively use my understanding of the big picture to clarify actions and decisions for those I lead.

5. Have clearly identified and prioritized the organization's capabilities that generate value for the company.

6. Invest in critical capabilities above others to ensure their sustained ability to generate value.

7. Have detailed knowledge of the value that is created or potentially destroyed at the seams of my organization.

8. Hold leaders accountable for ensuring that the critical linkages between their functions and businesses are established and effective.

9. Periodically gather firsthand information from across the organization to stay abreast of emerging issues challenging individual divisions.

10. Consistently seek for ways to improve the integration of the organization to remain competitive over the long term.

POWER IN CONTEXT

Many articles have been written in business journals over the last decade about Reed Hastings and Netflix, and with clear reason. Ten years ago few could have projected that cable television subscriptions would be challenged by the current growing consumer trend of streaming TV and movie entertainment online. But consumer demand for a "my way, my time, my place" lifestyle has moved most entertainment and cable companies to provide on-demand services and recorded television online streaming: Netflix is most notable among the businesses that have anticipated and actively capitalized on the confluence of enabling technologies and changing consumer expectations.

Netflix was founded by entrepreneur Reed Hastings, then 38, and his partner Marc Randolph originally as an alternative to the video rental store and the insufferable late fees that irritated all of us when we forgot or just didn't feel like driving to the store late at night to return the video before the imposed deadline. Reed said,

> The genesis of Netflix came in 1997 when I got this late fee, about $40, for *Apollo 13*. I remember the fee because I was embarrassed about it. That was back in the VHS days, and it got me thinking that there's a big market out there. So I started to investigate the idea of how to create a movie-rental business by mail. I didn't know about DVDs, and then a friend of mine told me they were coming. I ran out to Tower Records . . . and mailed CDs to myself, just a disc in an envelope. It was a long 24 hours until the mail arrived back at my house, and I ripped them open and they were all in great shape. That was the big excitement point.[35]

Since solving for his original dilemma, Hastings has used his innate curiosity and career experience as a US Marine, a Peace Corp volunteer, a high school math teacher abroad, a computer programmer, and an entrepreneur CEO of Pure Software to consistently push the status quo, always looking ahead to what is possible. Of his experience in the military, Hastings said, "I found myself questioning how we packed our backpacks and how we made our beds. My questioning wasn't particularly encouraged, and I realized I might be better off in the Peace Corps. I petitioned the recruiting office and left the Marines."[36]

Through Netflix he initially challenged the movie rental industry simply by using an existing delivery source in combination with the emerging media format to create an unprecedented DVD-by-mail business and eliminated late fees, putting the industry-leading Blockbuster on notice. He then combined his personal experience and understanding of the consumer appeal for convenience with an "all you can consume" model—offering as many movies as consumers wanted to watch for a flat monthly rate. This model increased demand and required added emphasis on developing strong partnering relationships with major studios to acquire latest releases faster and at a lower cost, as well as with independents to take advantage of a growing niche trend. And it required heavy reliance on the US Postal Service to successfully manage the efficient logistical exchange of millions of DVDs each week.

Former powerhouse businesses, like Kodak or Blockbuster, have become merely historical references because of their leaders' inability to envision and move ahead of trends and radical new business models. Hastings was determined to not let that happen to his company. He recognized early the power of streaming video and in 2007 launched a subscription-based, video-on-demand model via the Internet—a marked shift away from their relationship with and reliance on the US Postal Service. They strove to build and manage an online streaming capability sufficient to satisfy their increasing base of subscribers. As both technological capability and consumer demand for computing mobility increases, he expects to take full advantage of it.

Hastings' leadership of the company—his ability to anticipate, envision, and move deliberately toward radically new models and to take advantage of opportunities in a sea of shifting market dynamics—isn't without risk. Anxious to shift the focus of Netflix's future, in July of 2011 Hastings split the DVD subscription and online streaming businesses, which effectively doubled prices. Handling the price hike poorly sparked outrage among consumers. The media and investors concluded that he'd never be able to win back consumers' trust. In May of 2012, Forbes contributor James Marshall Crotty reported:

> Netflix cofounder Reed Hastings is known for making the biggest business blunder of 2011. In July, he announced that subscribers to both the Netflix streaming and DVD service now had to pay for each separately, a sudden 60% increase

that took the Netflix subscription from an $8 a month charge you barely noticed on your statement to a $16 a month charge you definitely noticed. To make matters worse, in September, Netflix spun off its popular DVD-by-mail service into a new entity called Qwikster.

These rare missteps caused Netflix's stock price to crater from a high above $304 a share in July to a low of around $62 a share by late November; a market cap loss of around $12 billion.[37]

From Hastings' perspective:

We had to figure out what we would be doing with our declining DVD business, and we know the future is in streaming. So we simply went too fast and didn't anticipate how devoted some people still were to that part of our business. We learned from it, corrected it and moved on.

. . . [The fact] that . . . we were able to make the shift from DVDs to streaming, is the bigger story. It is really hard moving forward. [Leaders] at Blockbuster . . . were smart, and they worked hard, but still didn't manage to do that. Looking back you could say we tried to spin off the DVD business too fast. But it is so much easier to cling to the past than to make that leap into the future that I still would rather be too soon than too late.[38]

The forecast looks bright. His mastery of the Context of his business and competitive landscape to transform his streaming service to a Web-based television network is paying off. And early indicators are also positive for the next-generation Netflix plans to grow through the development of proprietary content. Recent launches of series such as *House of Cards* and *Orange Is the New Black* have the critics' endorsement. More importantly, current results demonstrate their ability to generate customer loyalty and to stand out from competitors such as Amazon Prime, Hulu, and Redbox Instant with Netflix generating over 31 million paid subscribers in the United States by September 2013, rivaling even HBO.[39] And, most critical to shareholders, the stock price plummet of 2011 has recovered as share price moved from just under $90 per share at the end of 2012 with a market cap of $5.28 billion to end 2013 at $367.50 and $19.68 billion, respectively.[40] Who needs a TV, DVR, or cable subscription when Netflix offers it all for the low price of $7.99 a month? And the more intriguing question, What confluence of emerging technological, logistical, demographic, economic, and consumer trends will he take advantage of next?

Value and loyalty will continue to shift from one business model to another precipitated by ever-evolving consumer preferences, as well as the broader economic, geopolitical, technological, and demographic dynamics. A business model is the sum total of the choices a business makes about (1) the targeted customers it aspires to serve and the need they are aiming to meet, (2) the solution it will offer and how its utility is differentiated from available and emerging alternatives, (3) the capabilities required to deliver the strategy—those that it will offer and those that require outsourced partnership, (4) how its physical, financial, and human assets are best configured to optimally deliver value to its target markets, and (5) where and how profit will be extracted. This set of choices must uniquely position the business and create a defensible advantage against competitors if leaders expect to succeed.

Where Breadth is focused on how the pieces of an organization fit together, Context primarily focuses on *depth*—how key elements of the business work in concert to take advantage of evolving possibilities to sustain viability and profitability within a defined competitive set and landscape. The ability to apply intricate knowledge of one's business to emerging competitive threats requires constant scanning and the ability to see trends, patterns, and emerging possibilities on a multiyear horizon. It demands that leaders maintain cutting-edge knowledge about their business and how it fits into the broader industry and economic story—a complete 360-degree perspective of the market and competitive dynamics in play. Where HBO may have once seen Hastings as a potential distributor for their content, they must now contend with his business as a direct competitor and clear disruptive threat to their success. Hastings has made it clear that he doesn't necessarily want to replace HBO but does intend to compete on the same plane.

Much has been written in recent years about the importance of anticipating what is coming next. Our study confirmed its criticality to success. While perhaps not as aggressive in their deconstruction and reconstruction of their respective businesses, like Hastings, our exemplars were consistently described as having an innate curiosity about and a deep knowledge of their business context, which they are able to translate, articulate, and apply to the wider economic, technological, and consumer trends within their industry sector. They are also able to extend this knowledge and pattern recognition to adjacent sectors with comparable dynamics or required capabilities. Armed with a clear point of view, our exemplars more readily prioritized and addressed threats and took earlier advantage of opportunities. This is the very definition of the work of the Strategic system we outlined in chapter 2. Too often leaders are stymied by competing investment proposals or are caught flat-footed in the face of profit shortfalls. Lacking an understanding of how and where value is created and delivered to the market, they make suboptimal investments that have only marginal impact on success. Even more typical, they reflexively make across-the-board cost cuts that ultimately restrict their ability to maneuver effectively in a shifting competitive arena. In chapter 1, we looked closely at failures of Context—executives who arrived with misguided mandates and who attempt to stubbornly impose past successes on new contexts. They employed maladaptive approaches while failing to study their surroundings, which in turn led to forfeiting the power in their context.

Exceptional executives maintain a solid grasp on the relevant and ever-changing context within which their business competes. Power in Context lies at the intersection of their insights into how their organization uniquely competes and makes money, and what is most relevant to the markets and customers they serve—even when customers may not know themselves. Mastering their context fuels the power that comes from increased degrees of freedom and confidence to actively influence how current and future success will be realized. The dominant indicators of underdeveloped Context and the watch-outs for executives on the rise include adherence to a strategy dominantly driven by a short-term financial view, as well as isolationism, ignorance of or lack of curiosity about broader marketplace dynamics, and being too far removed from day-to-day business to recognize and act on possibilities.

REFLECTIONS ON THE RISE:
MASTERING CONTEXT

In my approach to leading with Context, I . . .

1. Understand the deepest picture of where and how value is created and destroyed within my industry.

2. Am confident of my ability to ask the questions that will uncover whatever is next.

3. Have identified and am actively tracking potentially disruptive industry and broader market trends.

4. Have a deep understanding of my organization's business model and can clearly articulate its strengths and weaknesses.

5. Have a clear understanding of all relevant competitive business models, their strengths and weaknesses, and the critical capabilities they rely on for success.

6. Have identified and assessed my business model's vulnerabilities in contrast to direct and emerging competitors.

7. Am exploring potential alternatives to address threats and take advantage of opportunities.

8. Present options that are appropriately informed but not overly constrained by near-term financial results.

9. Maintain proper balance of attention between current and potential business needs.

10. Regularly seek perspective from a broad network of colleagues and experts within relevant industries.

POWER IN CHOICE

Most sectors in the nonprofit world suffer the dilemma of being fragmented. Countless relief and development organizations bringing various forms of aid to impoverished regions struggle to make a sustainable difference despite the extensive resources being expended. The water sector is no exception. There are estimated to be more than forty organizations, either exclusively or in part, dedicated to bringing clean water to poor areas of the world currently lacking access to water and sanitation. The realities of an existence without ready access to clean water are unthinkable to most of us. Children die daily from water-related illnesses. Women spend upwards of seven hours each day walking miles just to carry unclean water in large vessels back to their villages. Access to clean water and sanitation literally changes everything for a community without it. Unfortunately, the failure rates of installed hand-pump wells and other water systems around the world by well-intended organizations are disappointing. Between 35 and 50 percent of all water projects fail within the first three to five years of completion, and the knowledge and capability to fix them doesn't exist in the community where they are installed.

Marla Smith-Nilson, selected in 2013 by *Self* magazine as one of three "Women Who Change Lives and Make a Difference," founded Water 1st International in 2005 after more than a decade of watching a proliferation of water projects fail. Since that time, Water 1st International has completed over 950 water projects, *all of which are 100 percent operational.* They have had *no failures,* and more than 100,000 people's lives have been changed forever. The impressive success she has achieved in the face of industry norms lies in the power of Choice.

Marla and her team built Water 1st International to approach the design, installation, and maintenance of water systems in ways dramatically different from conventional approaches. Defying established norms and accepted practices, Water 1st starts with a set of fundamental guiding principles focused on the dignity and ownership by the communities who will benefit from the water system and are also targeted at the local partners who will construct them:

1. She has limited the scope of her organization's presence to just four countries.

2. She works only with local partners with a proven track record of installing sustainable water projects and holds them accountable to sustained results. She commits to long-term relationships with them.

3. Unlike most other organizations, Water 1st visits its installations at least yearly to inspect the work, ensure quality standards are met, and

to honor the benefactors with transparency about how their donations are being spent.

4. When partners fail to uphold standards, funds are withheld until corrections and repairs are made.

5. Whenever a community is not committed to participating in the creation of their water source, funds are not provided and other projects are selected.

Beyond the stringent quality standards, rigorous project selection, and sustainable engineering designs, the greatest departure from conventional approaches Marla has established is how she views the very constituents she serves.

> We start from a true place of respect for the people we want to assist. Poor people are their own best resource in escaping poverty, and we support solutions based on the priorities and perspectives of the poor people themselves. The key is asking the poor person what *he or she* thinks their problems are, listening, and involving them in the solution. Every poor community is rich in the most valuable resources—human intelligence and strength of spirit. We are successful because we invest in those resources and provide the poorest people in the world with an opportunity to accomplish something they see as critical to their own well-being.[41]

By making hard choices, knowing the ramifications of her trade-offs, being willing to buck the status quo—including the forfeit of dollars she would otherwise have access to if she were willing to compromise her beliefs—and helping orchestrate the construction of important choices across an array of constituents, including donors, local partners, and NGOs as well as poor communities with a vested interest in their own futures, Marla has focused an organization that is realizing unprecedented results.

THE OPPRESSION AND LIBERATION OF CHOICE

Fewer aspects of organizational leadership are more perplexing, even oppressive, than the processes for making decisions. The laments are endless. "I don't have the power to make my own decisions." "We walk out of meetings not knowing if a decision was made or not." "I have all the accountability but none of the authority." "We have too much data." "We don't have enough data." "My interpretation of the data is right and yours is wrong." "We don't include people enough in decisions." "We're too consensus driven." No doubt you can add dozens more from your own experience. In chapter 5, we discussed the perversions and abuses of power and how they infect decision making, largely with self-interest or abdication. In this section, we highlight where our exemplar executives excelled, specifically in how they constructed choices to resolve a major dilemma or chose from among various opportunities and trade-offs to align their organizations around focused priorities—an increasingly rare phenomenon in organizations. Ironically, the freedom to make choices should be liberating. It should unleash an executive's best ideas, harness a team's greatest talent, and distinguish an organization's most competitive features.

Volition is what separated our exemplar executives from their second-best counterparts. Their ability to unapologetically declare their views, generously engage others' ideas, analyze the available data for sufficient insights, weigh the consequences among a set of alternatives, and own the final call inspired a markedly higher degree of confidence and focus among those they led than was true for the less effective executives.

At the heart of great decision making lies a balance between instinct and analytics. On one end of the continuum are leaders who "trust their guts." Ideally this approach combines well-developed intuition over time based on experience with the presence of emotion—conviction, anger, fear, excitement—which all play a role (sometimes destructively) in the construction of Choice. The other end of the continuum is distinguished by the presence of data—often in great abundance—and the need to mine data for insights to address the decision or problem before you. Executives often have at their disposal teams of analysts comparing and contrasting fact bases to create the wisdom upon which they can act. Across the continuum you have the voices of others, and the voices within your own head (our discussion about Operative Narratives in chapter 4).

Great choice makers are able to function across the continuum with agility. In their book *Decisive: How to Make Better Choices in Life and Work*,[42]

Chip and Dan Heath describe "four villains of decision making." As we have observed, we see these villains as living along a continuum. Two of the villains, binaryism and confirmation bias, are corruptions of the analytics end of the continuum. The other two villains, short-term emotion and overconfidence, are corruptions of the instinct end of the continuum. Binaryism happens when executives get stuck between the tyranny of only two choices and then must debate the either/or factors of the two options. Once a decision has been reduced to only two options, the likelihood of failure is much higher. Confirmation bias happens when leaders go looking for the answer they want in the available data. Exceptional executives can resist the temptation to impose the answer they want and can avoid being backed into binary corners. They widen the menu of available options and listen closely to multiple, intentionally contradicting interpretations of the data.

On the instinct end of the continuum, exceptional executives know when to trust their emotions, and they also know when their own fears, prejudices, ambitions, and confidence may be clouding their judgment. While emotion and conviction are important aspects of constructing a choice that can actually be implemented, the exemplar executives knew how and when to detach and distance themselves when needed objectivity was becoming obscured by strong emotions.

Marla Smith-Nilson is passionate and convicted about the need for the poor of the world to have access to clean water and sanitation, but never at the expense of constructing quality, sustainable water projects that are owned and maintained by the communities for whom they are built. She readily dismisses the "fads of the day." She is not impressed by the data that highlight solutions like filtered water straws or "Peepoo bags" (yup, that's what they were called)—superficial solutions that do not address the underlying problems the poor are trying to solve. By harnessing the power of Choice, Marla and her organization are changing the lives of hundreds of thousands of people around the world.

Exceptional executives have well-defined processes for constructing the choices needed for their organizations to advance. They use a healthy balance of instinct and analysis and blend their own ideas with the voices of others into focused choices that align their organizations in a common direction around chosen priorities. They work to avoid the common predicament of too many organizations: an overwhelming set of unfocused priorities, misalignment among leaders about criteria for alloting resources, lack of clarity about who has the authority to make a call and under what conditions, and a proliferation of competing, slanted fact bases that drive individual agendas at the expense of enterprise solutions. By avoiding these pitfalls, they focus their limited set of resources against choices that will give them the highest probability of success in their markets. Pronounced patterns among exemplars reveal the key warning signals of underdeveloped Choice to be less developed analytical abilities and inattention to detail or, conversely, an overreliance on numbers—the classic analysis paralysis—and the lack of demonstrated courage to make a call. Another noteworthy alarm is an unprioritized pipeline of innovation—pushing too much too fast and overtaxing the organization.

REFLECTIONS ON THE RISE: MASTERING CHOICE

In my approach to constructing choices, I . . .

1. Assemble data sets that allow sufficient analysis from multiple vantage points.

2. Don't get stuck in "analysis paralysis" and avoid becoming confined by excessive volumes of data.

3. Know when to trust my instincts, and when not to.

4. Allow my emotions to fuel my conviction about a choice, but not at the expense of needed objectivity.

5. Appropriately engage the voices and ideas of others.

6. Declare the rationale behind my choices.

7. Am not afraid to disappoint people whose views or preferences don't prevail.

8. Regularly say no even to great ideas and opportunities in order to keep the organization focused and on track.

9. Foster open dissent and disagreement in the exploration of options for choices I am making or problems I am solving.

10. Forfeit popularity, approval, and self-interest in the service of the right decision for the organization and those we serve.

POWER IN CONNECTION

In 2011, Mike Smith was appointed general manager of a retail business in a category that sat within a larger foodservice organization at ConAgra Foods. Only in his mid-thirties, he was clearly the youngest and least experienced of his general manager peers. But with a track record of impressive results achieved within the marketing and sales functions, as well as the experience he brought from previous companies, he was up for the challenge.

Foodservice solutions, not consumer-branded retail products, were the dominant focus of the business division within which he worked. As such, the supply chain organization was oriented to long runs and configured to produce and satisfy Foodservice's customers with similar product requirements efficiently. Mike's retail customers, however, expected custom solutions to differentiate them from their competitors. To support Mike's expectations, his Manufacturing and Operations counterparts were challenged to disrupt their efficient operations flow to meet his need for customized product and packaging solutions.

On Mike's first day as GM of the business, he received a call informing him that one of their largest retail customers was about to put its business out for competitive bid. The timing could not have been worse, as his business was in the process of implementing a major new organization redesign, with a steep learning curve on managing the business differently. Establishing credibility with his new peers, winning the respect and support from former peers who were now his direct reports, and working with a new boss, as well as securing the stability of the business and raising its priority and visibility within a foodservice-dominant portfolio, were on the list of challenges facing this newly minted GM.

Mike has a stellar reputation as an upstanding, down-to-earth, and approachable guy. His influence comes from a deep and genuine concern for others. Mike approaches each role with the expectation that he will take the necessary time and make a sincere effort to connect with those within his circle of influence. He says, "I see other leaders fail because it is little more than an exercise to check a box: they do it because it was assigned. Your intent matters, it shows through." The primacy he places on authentic Connection with others is a cornerstone of his success. Building credibility with his seasoned peers whose businesses contributed disproportionately to top- and bottom-line success in the shared portfolio required that he balance treating them with respect and acknowledgment of what he could learn from them, while also finding his voice as their peer and asserting the needs of his business with clarity and conviction. Mike acknowledges that positive competition among peers is healthy to the degree that it makes the organization stronger, but he believes what is most critical is getting alignment and then acting in concert. Referring to the initial customer challenge and working with his peers toward a solution, Mike said, "I knew I had to win their trust with the tough and risky decisions I was going to have to make with one of our largest customers. I sought them out for advice. I talked to them and shared my thinking, and I showed them respect by asking for the benefit of their experience and thinking. At the same time, I was clear that I would do what I believed was right for my business and would ask for their support."

Observing those peer interactions was also critical in strengthening Mike's Connection with his boss: Watching Mike negotiate such a sensitive and weighty business matter while winning the support of his peers won greater confidence from, and reinforced for, his boss that he had chosen the right man for the job.

With the customer crisis in motion, Mike was forced to establish himself in his new leadership role immediately while simultaneously building credibility with his new direct reports. Some had been Mike's peers for a while, but now their relationship had to shift because Mike was now responsible for the business to which they each contributed. Under such pressure conditions, quick action was needed, but Mike knew it was equally vital to position himself as a trusted leader of his team for the long term. Over the course of his career he had been a thoughtful observer of the leaders he reported to, taking deliberate note of the things he admired, as well as of their less effective traits. Now he was confronted with asking himself the question he had long thought about: "If I were in their shoes, what kind of leader would I want to be? What kind of leader would I want leading me?" The immediate crisis would reveal to his team a great deal about his leadership philosophy.

As we discussed back in chapter 3, any executive who must reformulate former peer relationships into reporting relationships has an artful challenge. Mike manages it this way: "I start from my belief that the right people make a difference. You need others to succeed in business. I certainly needed and was counting on their support, but first each of them had to know that I saw them as individually important and valuable contributors to our success. Without that connection and belief, people won't sacrifice for your benefit." So, in the same direct but respectful way that he initially approached his peers, he also engaged his team. He rallied them around the collective challenge at hand. He gave them his honest and direct assessment of the situation and shared his initial thoughts and ideas. He then invited them to do the same. Ultimately, Mike's courage to take some calculated risks and the ability to coalesce his team enabled them to keep the vast majority of the business with their large customer.

With the initial crisis successfully averted, Mike reverted to his normal course of investing in the connections on which he would depend for his long-term success. Consistent, informal interaction is one of the critical keys Mike highlights. He says, "I try to get out of my office regularly. It's through informal drive-bys that I have the most influence and impact in shaping and moving the business forward. Every conversation—boss, peer, or direct report—begins with a personal connection, a sincere interaction to check in and get to know them better, but it must always end with business. Every conversation is an opportunity to positively influence the business and the people. The questions you ask provoke thinking and you influence them by sharing your own experience. That adds to their ability to succeed. I also learn a lot, so there is mutual benefit."

Mike insists that when you ask a question, you must sincerely want their response; otherwise, don't ask. "There should be no questioning for its own sake. Every interaction counts: you either strengthen or diminish your connection." He further believes that people want to be dealt with honestly. While at times it is difficult, people respond most positively to candid, direct communication spoken respectfully. Speaking truth can be uncomfortable and most leaders aren't highly skilled at doing it effectively, but it is ultimately vital to holding people accountable in service to their own as well as the business's success. Finally, Mike shares the source of power that he finds in giving sincere praise. Verbal praise is important, but he finds the greatest influence results from an occasional handwritten note. He says, "Acknowledging good work in written form is particularly meaningful and will have lasting, positive impact on whoever receives it. It is something they can refer back to over time." Ultimately, people want to have confidence in the leaders they work for; they want to enjoy them, not fear them.

The impact of his leadership is found in the following representative comments made by others across the business to describe their experience of Mike:

- "I wish Mike could clone himself. He has the leadership style and ability to cut through the BS, see the bigger picture, and move things in the right direction. He absolutely has all of the credibility to make this transformation work. People are willing to follow him and get behind his vision."

- "I think Mike is a very energizing leader. People get engaged with him and his presence and that was missing before he arrived. I think people will listen to him. I think the great thing is that he has a bigger voice. He is a real diplomat."

- "Mike is great at asking follow-up questions and following up with work that's in progress. If I see him in the hall, he'll ask about the new products that we're launching in other divisions that don't even affect his business. It shows that he's aware of and interested in what we're doing and that he has a finger on the pulse of the organization. That's really effective."

- "Mike has received a level of respect for his position that provides him with a solid starting place for his current role. Mike's reputation with senior leadership is awesome and that will benefit us all. He has a lot of relational capital and he can spend it."

- "Mike is open and a good communicator; he doesn't get defensive. He wants to release people to do their work, and he's helping to communicate new expectations to the broader organization."

- "I like Mike's style. He epitomizes what leadership on our SLT should be. Mike is affable and charismatic and knows how to effectively negotiate the politics. I trust that Mike has my back."

- "Mike is awesome. He is a great motivator of people and I love the way he thinks. I always learn a lot from him."

There is great power in the influence you will generate as you put your best efforts toward cultivating positive connections with stakeholders at all levels. As we highlighted in chapter 4, you will increase the reach of your influence tremendously by getting to know your constituents personally. Meet with them regularly and listen deeply with a goal to discover what motivates them and what their priorities are, as well as understand the challenges they may be facing—especially at key points of intersection with your areas of responsibility. Meet with the purpose of clearly communicating your needs and aligning on mutual direction and expectations. Then, follow through on any commitments you make. Expend conscious effort to be widely known as trustworthy, and to wisely extend trust to others, as it is a highly valuable currency of exchange in every business. Finally, be grateful for and acknowledge the contributions of others. Indeed, no man is an island and our successes are usually made possible by the efforts of others. Powerful connections are made by the exceptional executives who communicate in compelling ways and reach well beyond superficial transactions to form deep, trust-based relationships of mutuality, vulnerability, and clarity. Their legacy becomes a positive reputation within the organization for consistently delivering business results and for genuinely respecting and caring for those who deliver them. The key watch-outs to highlight include ignoring or lacking interest in stakeholder needs and developing only a narrow, exclusive set of relationships and with the wrong people. Less effective executives communicated on an irregular frequency and lacked an appreciation for the audience and their needs. These leaders also lacked assertiveness in their approach.

REFLECTIONS ON THE RISE:
MASTERING CONNECTION

In my approach to leading with Connection, I . . .

1. Have clearly identified and established a healthy, trust-based relationship with all connections vital to me in effectively performing in my role.

2. Have a healthy, trust-based working relationship with my boss.

3. Have a healthy, trust-based working relationship with each of my peers.

4. Have a healthy, trust-based working relationship with each of my direct reports.

5. Regularly meet to listen and have a clear understanding of my partners' expectations and needs.

6. Clearly and passionately articulate my vision for my organization and how those I lead fit into that vision.

7. Clearly articulate needs and required support for success within my areas of responsibility and within the broader context of the enterprise.

8. Effectively generate healthy flow of communication appropriate for each constituency.

9. Speak truth to others firmly, but with respect.

10. Am intentional about defining the personal impact I want to make on others, and regularly inventory whether or not I am doing so.

IN CONCERT

Our intent in discussing each of these four dimensions was to help you more deeply understand the power in them and to see how exceptional executives cultivate them. In practice, however, none in isolation has the ability to optimally sustain impact. Only when leveraged in concert with one another can they generate maximum power. It is in the understanding and effective development of these factors as an integrated whole that executives are enabled to truly rise to power, clearly distinguishing exceptional executives from just good ones.

To leverage the power in his Breadth, Dave West had to have deep connections both within and outside of Hershey. He had to make difficult choices and to have mastery of the context in which he competed. Mike Smith's broad understanding of the organization, deep contextual views of the business, and willingness to focus his organization on critical choices amplified the power in his connections. Marla's engineering background and multi-decade experience in the water sector in the developing world, her broad view of the end-to-end value chain of bringing water projects to life through local partners, and the deep connections she establishes with those partners and beneficiaries empower the laser-focused choices she makes that drive her unprecedented results. Not surprisingly, other observers of organizations are seeing similar patterns of capability coalescing at senior levels. A *Harvard Business Review* article titled "The New Path to the C-Suite" notes, "

> One theme that ran consistently through our findings was that requirements for all the C-level jobs have shifted toward business acumen and 'softer' leadership skills. Technical skills are merely a starting point, the bare minimum. To thrive as a C-level executive, an individual needs to be a good communicator, a collaborator, and a strategic thinker—and we think the trend toward a general business orientation over a functional orientation will continue.[43]

And so it will be for you as well. As you apply the power in Breadth, Choice, Context, and Connection, see them as interdependent dimensions that must work in concert. You may already have exemplary levels of capability in some areas but fall short in others. As you assess and prioritize the focus for your development, maintain a balanced view of how they are all working together. An overemphasis in one may lead to neglect and deficiency in another. For example, if you spend too much time building the contextual knowledge of your business and competitive landscape, you may inadvertently blur your perspective of how all of the pieces of your organization come together to deliver results for your business. Similarly, if you overemphasize building deep connections with stakeholders, it may later prove difficult to make and gain support for unpopular choices you have to make. You get the idea.

As we discovered and integrated these patterns from our research, we were struck by their remarkable elegance. Their power, in part, emanates from their utter simplicity accompanied by their profound collective impact.

As you incorporate these dimensions in your executive practices, keep that simplicity in mind. Don't needlessly overcomplicate them. And be patient with the process. They won't appear overnight. Remind yourself often that there aren't shortcuts and that acquiring and effectively wielding power is a career-long pursuit. There will be setbacks with each new role and altitude—a new setting demanding new Connections, more complex Choices, adjustment to Context, and further degrees of Breadth. Diligence is the price you pay to effectively rise to power. It demands never-ending adaptation. Embrace that truth, and you will not only enjoy the journey more, you will thrive.

J ORDAN TOOK A LOT OF hazing around the office the day after he returned from ringing the closing bell on Wall Street with Elise and key executives from Newrizon. The analysts' response to the partnership proved more positive than expected, with each company getting an optimistic nod from investors. The proof would be in the pudding.

Jordan held his leadership team meeting at the plant where the first molded packaging product with Newrizon's logo on it came off the line. Everyone raised a glass, in relief that they'd finally arrived at this day, in exhaustion for all it took, and in honor of the sacrifice it had required. The work of closing one legacy plant, reassigning any employees that could be to new roles, celebrating all of the early retirement parties, distributing the more than 120 generous severance packages, and the donation and conversion of the old building into a community center for the town was all behind them. Now the real work began.

"Getting here was hard enough," Jordan said to his team. "Succeeding here will be another matter entirely."

Dana Marshall, previously a sales VP for the East Division, presented the projections for the Newrizon partnership's first year. Jordan knew that after the fanfare of the signed deal faded, Huntington would struggle to sustain ongoing coordination across all of its functions to serve Newrizon well. In order to ensure the partnership's success, he put together a cross-functional team, a Newrizon Business Team, to run the Newrizon business. He gave it its own P&L and matrixed its members into their respective functions. Dana was the perfect person to lead the team, given she'd had experience in the supply chain and had a great track record of customer partnerships. Her team was off to a fantastic start and very excited by what they could accomplish, not to mention learn, on behalf of future specialty-packaging customer partnerships.

"This is by no means going to be a slam dunk, gang," Dana warned Jordan and her new peers. "While the prototypes all now have engineering specs for production, Newrizon continues to make modification requests. In the case of one design, our plant engineers are saying one of the lines will need retooling in order to produce it to spec. We're going back to Newrizon with a proposed compromise we believe will work and spare us the expensive re-engineering work, but who knows if they'll accept it. And this early into the partnership we definitely want to show well and accommodate them to the extent we can. If we have to take the cost hit in the first year, the numbers won't look nearly as pretty as we've projected. Jordan—we may need you to make a call to Newrizon to work some magic if we get pushback."

"Just say the word and I'll make the call," Jordan reassured.

Dana continued, "And a huge shout-out to Wayne and his people for the heroics they've delivered to get all of this up and running. I have no idea how they did it, but if it wasn't for them, we'd be in deep you-know-what."

Wayne laughed, "When you've been here as long as I have, you know who to go to for what, and who's gonna get 'er done. Finally cashin' in on thirty years of hospital visits, babies, funerals, holiday dinners, birthday parties, and 'Wayne, I really need this' whines . . . ain't nobody gonna say no to me now, I know too much!" They all laughed with Wayne as he felt proud of the contribution he and his folks had made.

"When can I get into that club?" Elise joked.

"Oh, you've got about ten years," Wayne bantered back.

Dana turned the update over to Elise as her slide came up on the screen.

"I'll be quick on this—you can see from the numbers the posi- tioning content we helped Newrizon with for their campaign is obviously working—we're exceeding plan by 22 percent. We had great data on their consumers that they didn't have. We were able to inform them of the importance of making critical product information more accessible than they'd first thought it needed to be. Needless to say, they're glad they trusted us. As some for- mer marketing lead once told me, 'Always know your customer's customer better than they do.'" She grinned at Jordan, who was rolling his eyes.

Jacinta gave a quick update on the search for Huntington's new CFO. "We're bringing back two candidates we saw early on for a third round—watch your calendars for some additional time with them. We really want this wrapped up by the start of the fiscal year." Kyle's departure six months ago was shrouded in mystery which was the cause of the awkward silence following Jacinta's announcement. Most assumed it was tied to the SEC scandal, but a few insiders suspected there was more to that story.

Jordan enjoyed a private moment of deep gratitude and sat- isfaction as he looked around the table at his team. It was hard to believe it'd been nearly a year since he'd become CEO. What a tumultuous year it had been. A montage of highs and lows played in his mind like a movie trailer: Mac's funeral, the SEC mess, count- less visits to customers and suppliers to apologize and restore trust, his struggle with addiction and painstaking recovery work he remained committed to, Andy's brilliant negotiation of Kyle's exit that got him what he wanted anyway—money in exchange for his agreement to hold confidential information in order to avoid further exposure of his own (thank God Andy kept thor- ough files on Kyle for leverage), the entire Newrizon saga, his son's high school graduation and college entrance, too many heated debates with Elise (now only in private), the plant closing and rib- bon cutting ceremony of the community center, and the myriad mistakes that taught him hard lessons alongside important wins he was proud of.

As his team filed out from the meeting, Andy stayed behind. "You know he'd be really proud of you, don't you?"

"Some days I wonder, Andy. I don't think about him as much as I did a year ago. I still miss him, but honestly there's just no time to wallow in it. And I know that's how he'd want it. I do know that without you I would never have survived this year. That's for damn sure."

"Well, I'm glad we're on this side of it and the nose of the plane is heading up now."

Jordan's phone buzzed. It was a text message from Carolyn. He got a little pale reading it. He looked up at Andy, who knew something was off. He held the phone up so Andy could read the text, which said, "You're not going to believe this, but Kyle is on the phone. He says it's important he speak with you. Will you take his call?"

Andy looked back at Jordan somewhat somberly. "Well, that can't be good."

CHAPTER EIGHT

POWERFUL ORGANIZATIONS THAT BUILD EXCEPTIONAL EXECUTIVES

THE SYSTEMIC LEVERS OF BREADTH, CONTEXT, CHOICE, AND CONNECTION

W E WOULD BE REMISS TO END *Rising to Power* having only looked at how individual executives become exceptional. The ability to continue leading effectively at the right altitude hinges on many things, not the least of which is the organization itself. If the organization is not actively committed to propagating exceptional executives, the ability of its leaders to reach and sustain Breadth, Choice, Context, and Connection will be hampered. Organizations must be intentional about designing and implementing the mechanisms required to multiply and unleash executive capacity across these dimensions. This final chapter focuses on how to create exceptional executives. While there are many organizational systems that can contribute either to the creation or the deterioration of exceptional executives, we will focus on the few we have repeatedly seen make a difference in enabling leaders to realize the power inherent in the dimensions of Breadth, Choice, Context and Connection.

TO CREATE EXECUTIVES WITH BREADTH, HARNESS THE POWER AT THE SEAMS

We wish we had a dollar for every time we've heard executives cite "organizational silos" as a major impediment to performance. The inability to coordinate work, or execute a critical initiative across organizational boundaries, is a common lament. Signs of excessive duplication of work, wasted resources, and sometimes catastrophic failure to transform are often rooted in issues related to a lack of coordination, information sharing, and synchronization of efforts.

The concept of boundaryless organizations is certainly not new. Jack Welch coined the phrase back in the early '90s as a way to push GE's culture to be more permeable across geographies, businesses, and functions. The speed and proliferation of information and the complexity of the market was outpacing the organization's capacity to anticipate and respond; the boundaryless organization was an attempt to reduce the rising costs of transacting business across a complex array of business lines and locations. While it had its merits, it was not practical as an organizational model. Boundaries are necessary to coordinate resources, clarify authority, and create the focus necessary to execute the business's strategy. They fuel the capacity to more effectively compete by separating essential from competitively differentiating work, which must be resourced and supported differently. They enable cost reduction through economies of scale when similar work is grouped. Unfortunately, when misplaced, they can also wreak havoc on speed, cost, and innovation by hindering natural synergies that only exist at an organization's seams. For example, if a business's major source of competitive differentiation is to provide low-cost solutions and products, then at the intersections of supply chain, manufacturing, and sales you would expect to see very tight coordination between what is being sold to customers and what is being made and shipped. Yet in many organizations vying for low-cost provider status, the tensions between these functions—often measured individually and against contradictory metrics—can make effective coordination difficult. A sales force driven to produce volume and margin can place demands on operations that they struggle to keep up with. In an organization where the major source of competitive differentiation is the iconic nature of their brand portfolio, the intersections of marketing, sales, and product development need to be highly interdependent to ensure the necessary degree of alignment between insights from consumers, the products being developed as extensions of the brand, and the architecture of the brand's core messages. Often, though, the different time horizons between marketing's more immediate messaging and product development's longer-term innovation cycles stress that seam. Border wars are further intensified when there are competing interpretations of what the insights are "really" saying—often propagated by salespeople who just want something new to offer their buyers. Cutting-edge technology as a competitive distinction puts tremendous pressure on the seams among engineering, R&D, and innovation and "solutions groups" who must bundle discrete technologies into commercially viable offerings. You get the idea.

An organization's competitive distinction is created by uniquely blending a set of capabilities that competitors find difficult to replicate. The challenge of effectively deploying those capabilities in service to the strategy, however, is that they are often bounded within and managed by discrete functions. It is at the intersections of these capabilities that the source of competitive advantage is found, and at these same intersections that the greatest organizational tensions and rivalries are produced. The irony here isn't lost on us. What ultimately makes it so difficult for organizations to effectively blend these capabilities into seamless sources of competitive performance? In our experience, the answer is in the prevalent, but flawed, assumptions of executives who lead multifunction organizations. They simply believe such linkages will happen "naturally" and that their role as "integrator" will suffice as the primary mechanism for blending key capabilities into great performance. Neither is ever true. The executive's role as integrator is important, but the linkages at critical organizational seams must be intentionally designed and managed if competitive advantage is to be harnessed and realized. Such naïveté is often compounded by deep-seated ambivalence about the degree of autonomy one has to relinquish to realize the advantages inherent at the seams.

As we saw Jordan do with the Newrizon Business Team, linking the seams across an organization, especially those that contain the "secret sauce" of strategic competitive advantage, is vital work for organizations and the executives who lead them. The purposeful configuration of discrete organizational capabilities in ways that yield the greatest results is what produces the Breadth that executives need to expand their end-to-end knowledge of the business. It enables executives to develop a broader perspective of how the pieces fit together.

We worked recently with the head of innovation for a large consumer goods company that was struggling to execute against a strategic plan that called for nearly 40 percent of top-line revenue over the coming three-year period to be derived from new product launches. The company had suffered several failed launches of products that gained little traction, and their capacity to commercialize even basic line extensions was limited. Marketing was incented to distribute solid content while keeping to a strict Advertising & Promotions budget. R&D was focused heavily on quality, since many of the products the company made were outsourced to offshore manufacturers whose quality standards often violated federal US standards. The consumer insights and analytics group held a great deal of power and controlled much of the study design and interpretation of results for both existing and potential new products. And manufacturing struggled to produce the volumes needed to hit revenue and ROI because of aging plants with limited capacity. In a determined effort to link these otherwise isolated capabilities, he brought together key leaders from across all four functional areas for several days of intense, structured conversations. He knew there was a blend of historic bad blood and a lack of understanding between the different groups for how each of their areas contributed to the strategy and the business. In a series of round-robin "summits" conducted for every seam, he made each pair of functions identify:

- the value their combined efforts yielded for consumers, customers, and the organization;
- where there was confusion over decision rights and where conflicts were getting in the way of execution;
- what aspects of the organizational strategy their combined efforts directly impacted;
- the ground rules by which they intended to shape their working relationship; and
- the priority actions they would begin taking *that day* to improve their coordination and contribution.

The results were astounding. The list of issues raised *and resolved* over these several days was impressive to say the least. Some capacity-draining challenges required longer-term action and investment to resolve. But many of the issues identified were simply the result of bad work processes, competing metrics, insufficient mechanisms to resolve conflict and finalize decisions, and a lack of shared understanding of how each function contributed to the results of the organization. The executive later said of this effort, "While it's terrific that we've got our pipeline moving more effectively now, and that our efforts to commercialize have far higher likelihoods of success, I think the greatest value of this work was the dozens of key leaders who now have a dramatically different understanding of their roles and contributions, and a far wider perspective on how we compete and make money. You can't put a price on that. Wherever they go in the organization now, their instinct to ask broader questions and have greater peripheral vision will be positively enhanced." If you need executives with Breadth, ensure that the adjacent spaces into which their part of the organization connects are properly linked so that everyone who must work together across those boundaries can solve problems, resolve conflicts, make decisions, and generate real business impact.

TO CREATE EXECUTIVES WHO MAKE IMPACTFUL CHOICES, DIRECT THE POWER OF GOVERNANCE

"Whose decision is it, anyway?" could be a great game show played in the conference rooms of most organizations. In lieu of clear governance, many companies suffer from too many priorities, muddy decision rights, bowling-for-dollars resource allocation processes, and "executive idol" approaches to key talent appointments. It's no wonder the capacity of executives to make focused choices and stick with them is challenged.

Governance, at its most elegant, is refreshingly simple. You need:

- the right people,
- equipped with the right data and authority,

- making the right decisions aligned against agreed-upon priorities,
- allocating the appropriate resources,
- determining the right steps to execute.

Sadly, most organizations fail to construct governance models closely linked to strategy execution. Truth is, the integration of strategic, financial, and talent processes that allocate authority, priorities, and resources in the service of executing strategy is one of the most profoundly differentiating activities a company can undertake. It is the very lever, when pulled, that can deliver the efficiency, effectiveness, and results that optimize a company's competitive positioning. Most organizations—of all sizes—tend to believe they have a governance model without ever having applied a comprehensive and intentional review of what it is and how it works. Some small and mid-sized companies think that governance is a concern for large organizations only. They operate more "organically" and pride themselves on being "an informal company." Informality is not effective governance. Regardless of whether you lead a start-up, a small-to-medium-sized business, or a large, publicly traded company, well-designed governance defines and promotes desirable behaviors in your organization and helps avoid negative ones. It helps clarify leaders' expectations, their spheres of power, appropriate performance measures, and the inner working of relationships between key stakeholders. If you want a simple definition, think of governance as the set of authority structures, roles, accountabilities, and processes by which critical aspects of the organization are managed and various groups of leaders gather to make and execute vital decisions. These include things like strategic prioritization; resource allocation; setting of targets and goals, and performance measurement around the enterprise strategy; the planning and building of P&Ls and budgets; managing the portfolios of products, clients, and talent; and long-term financial and strategy processes.

Well-designed governance ensures alignment and drives superior performance by enabling executives to make impactful choices as they guide the business, its units, its functions, and its investments. Just as there are symptoms of poor governance, companies that excel at organizational governance show strong performance in key areas. Their people are deployed to perform optimally, for example. Well-governed organizations fulfill their fiduciary responsibilities while mitigating risk. You'll see a clear alignment between business and operational objectives in these companies. These performance measures are themselves driven by the concrete things an effective governance model can provide. Core processes, policies, and plans can be defined for optimal organizational impact. Structure, accountabilities, and clear decision rights can be defined and established. Appropriate performance measures reflecting current strategy can be implemented. Information can flow to and from the right levels. Ineffective expenditures of time and resources can be sharply curtailed.

Even when effectively designed and operationalized, all governance models have some degree of imperfection. The complexities of organizational life and the dynamics of so many simultaneously moving parts would make static perfection impossible. Nonetheless, when it works well, the synchronization is impressive. One CEO client, pained by the lack of integrated planning processes and the proliferation of committees and task forces designed to work around all of the organization's bureaucratic processes, insisted on a governance overhaul. He wanted one set of metrics with a clear line of sight to the company's four business units, and he wanted the option of making resource trade-offs at the enterprise level, not just at the business level where they were currently made. He declared a moratorium on four distinct strategy and resource allocation processes, as well as the capital allocation team that was predominantly staffed and run by the largest business unit and had no representation from the smallest. He reformulated and streamlined the executive team and established an operating team that consisted of members of all four business unit leadership teams, and it was owned by him and the COO. Decision rights were clearly defined and distributed across these six governing bodies, and charters for each were established with linkages and synchronization of information flow between them. He established a forum to openly debate strategic priorities and quickly resolve major business problems, with one integrated data set that replaced dueling fact bases derived from an individual business unit's agenda. He enhanced the ability to manage the enterprise portfolio as an integrated business rather than a loose confederation of discrete businesses. He was able to leverage the supply chain, HR, and IT in ways that the old governance design prevented, both decreasing some bloated costs and raising the visibility of emerging talent that was previously obscured. Over the coming year, they were able to launch a major new product in one of the emerging business units into a new market and integrate an acquisition into the largest business unit, and they increased their talent retention by 38 percent, reversing a trend of unwanted defections. By the end of the first year, one of the BU leaders had to be replaced because of his inability to operate in the new world order—his need for severe autonomy having been greatly challenged by the transparency and coordination required of him. To be clear, cohesive governance designs, or redesigns, won't come without disruption. However, the gains they yield usually outweigh the pain of getting there if you are willing to stick with the process of change and resist pushback from the parts of the organization that are vested in protecting the old design because it serves some agenda or advantage for them. If you want your leaders executing against the right choices and a narrowed set of priorities, install governance systems that facilitate such choices.

REFLECTIONS ON THE RISE

1. To what extent does your organization intentionally work to link the seams across your organization? At what seams do you see tensions that undermine performance?

2. How effective is your organization's governance design? Where could decision rights, meeting designs, and data sources be more coherently defined and aligned?

3. What do you think has enabled Jordan and his team to hit their stride with Newrizon?

TO CREATE EXECUTIVES THAT MASTER CONTEXT, INSTITUTIONALIZE THE POWER OF MOBILITY

Silos and impermeable boundaries stifle an executive's Breadth, poor governance diminishes executive Choice, and the killer of an executive's capacity to master Context is insularity. If you want executives with deep knowledge of your business and competitive landscape, intimate knowledge of how your organization competes and wins, and extensive wisdom that they generously pass along to the next generation of emerging leaders, you have to systematically move them around the organization, around the industry, and around the world. Many high-performing organizations have executive talent management processes that put executives on rotational assignments throughout the organization domestically and globally. Some even include assignments outside the organization. The best way to deepen an executive's wisdom about the business, the industry, or the competitive dynamics is to move them around to different vantage points within the organization. Nothing creates more curious and empathic executives than taking an assignment in a business or function you've had to serve from elsewhere in the organization. They will be far more open-minded to contrasting views if they themselves have served on the other side of the table. Want great marketing executives? Make them spend two years in Sales. Want a great finance leader? Eighteen months in Operations will help. How can you build high-impact HR professionals? Poach your best leaders from your organization's customer service team and train them in HR. Want a world-class strategist? Send executives on assignment to work outside the industry, to work with suppliers, or to sit on boards of other companies. Want fantastic general managers? Spend ten years moving younger leaders throughout the organization's functions, business lines, and geographies, holding them accountable for clear contributions in each assignment. Some organizations take this too far and haphazardly move leaders through assignments too quickly. Our experience suggests that anything less than twenty-four months doesn't produce the contextual development needed to deepen the knowledge and appreciation of that aspect of the business.

Insularity happens when functions and business units become highly territorial about their talent, limiting the careers of top people by being unwilling to let them move around. Leaders who spend too many years in functional roles or single lines of business go native and become entrenched in one way of seeing the world. Too often, they fail to recognize their biases. Having deep knowledge of finance and accounting adds minimal value if you don't understand how the organization makes money and creates value in the market. The same is true for Human Resource knowledge—it is far more relevant and impactful when you have actually worked in the business for which you are trying to optimize talent. Designing great brands and brand content is far more powerful when you have interacted directly with and sold to the customers where your consumers shop. And you can make far greater impact on the end-to-end P&L of your business once you have actually done the work in each part, or at least most parts, of the end-to-end business. And there are real bottom-line implications for this. According to one study, "organizations with advanced and integrated talent management and mobility processes tied to business strategy outperform companies with little or no talent strategy by 32%."[44]

Talent management systems are critical to proactively preparing executives for successively broader, more complex roles, and they provide visibility to the talent available in the organization. Dana's preparation to lead the newly formed Newrizon team is evidence of this. Even more potent, however, is the personal investment senior executives make in scouting and cultivating promising up-and-coming executives. Listen to how this CEO of a global defense and technology corporation talks about the process of cultivating executives in his organization by intentionally moving them around and increasing their visibility to and by others:

> When you get out into the organization, and *really look* and *listen to* what people are doing, you realize there are all kinds of people with ideas about change, enthusiasm and energy, and doing great things. Contrary to what I was being told about a shortage of future talent, there wasn't a shortage of them at all. There's LOTS of talent. But it needs to be developed. The best way to develop it is to move it around. I am fortunate that I have many companies throughout the organization that I can move people around in. I saw the preparation of future executives as one of my key accountabilities. Not *just* mine of course. But if it was going to become a critical differentiator for us, and a deep part of our culture, I wanted to make sure it was one of my top priorities. At our executive team meetings we are constantly talking about executive development, what people are ready to move, and what we are doing to get others ready. I wanted increased visibility into the organization's pipeline of leaders. We created processes that allowed

me to have visibility to see other folks down in the organization. At first, it wasn't a conscious way to find leaders, it just happened. It was originally meant to accelerate change in the organization. In doing so, we made it possible for people who were willing to step up and make a difference to show us who they were. It expanded the audience with whom I normally met. More than just say hello, but hear what they were doing, see their creativity, dedication, and enthusiasm. And to make sure we had quality conversations, I knew I had to be in their world, not have them come to mine. It wasn't trying to "go around" the hierarchy. I found that the normal business review process is ineffective at creating places for conversation. It might tell you someone is a good presenter, but you don't get to meet people and understand what they are capable of.

Whenever there were major gatherings of leaders in various businesses or functions, I would travel to them all over the world—between four and six a year. I'd go there to thank people for being willing to learn more for the good of the company. I'd ask specific questions about how the change process was working in their part of the organization. By going to all those sessions it established a link between me and my potential future executives. When I got into the details of their initiatives, I could clearly see people who were committed, enthusiastic, working hard, and making progress. I realized that there are people at all levels of the company doing very interesting work, committed to making a difference and actually making great change, often in spite of management, to whom I'd otherwise have no visibility. The issue wasn't that we didn't have people, the issue was we didn't know who they were, and we didn't have a mechanism for making sure they were being moved around into assignments throughout their careers. So we greatly strengthened the management development process all throughout the organization by institutionalizing the practice of seeking out potential top leadership talent, and setting it on a path of cultivation around the world. And it is definitely working. Our stock price has seen double-digit EPS for the last several years, and I believe our performance has been directly impacted by how we've cultivated the hundreds of executives in the top layers of the company.[45]

If you want executives who master their context, diligently expose them to a diverse array of experiences and roles in the organization. Pay special attention to ensuring they are grounded in external realities. Have them serve on strategic planning processes that force hard looks at competitive, industry, and market shifts to ensure they can continuously adapt their views and approaches. Intentionally design their careers to assume roles that enhance their core expertise with perspectives of those they must serve or partner with. Build executives with world-class capacity to own your business context by purposefully moving them around and deepening them through a variety of rich, challenging, and high-impact assignments.

TO CREATE EXECUTIVES WHO EFFECTIVELY AND GENUINELY CONNECT, CULTIVATE THE POWER OF ORGANIZATIONAL NETWORKS

"If you aren't part of the underground, you'll never be able to get anything done." This was the counsel often whispered to new leaders at a global retailing powerhouse. The "underground" was the organization's hidden network of people to whom you could go to when you needed certain things done, access to critical information, resources for major projects, or advice on how to break down barriers that were getting in the way of executing important or high-risk strategies. The term "underground" alludes to the French resistance against the Nazis and the Vichy regime during World War II. The underground cells were networks of men and women who were repositories and distributors of intelligence and maintainers of escape routes. The men and woman of the underground hailed from a widely diverse set of socioeconomic, political, and religious backgrounds.

What's interesting about the metaphor is that it depicts a collection of vastly diverse people, who would normally have no reason to interact, united in a common organization engaged in high-risk activities for a greater cause beyond their immediate benefit. All organizations have some form of "underground." And much like the French Resistance, they create and depend on unlikely alliances coming together in the service of advancing the organization in ways that the formal organizational processes presumably cannot. The relationships formed in an organization's underground usually span many years and are characterized by "crucible" experiences—defining moments in the organization's history of make-or-break success—and, when observed, look much more like lifelong friendships than those of routine business colleagues. They eat lunch together, help solve one another's problems, exchange advice on how to work with difficult people, and genuinely enjoy being with one another. They take deep pride in the organization and its history, and while they will be the first to criticize the organization's idiosyncrasies, they will fiercely defend it when anybody else throws stones. When it comes to getting things done, they are able to collaborate in ways akin to an Olympic rowing team. The major limitation of these networks, of course, is the narrow, almost religious, exclusivity with which they function that prevents the majority of the organization from participating in and benefiting from them.

In the case of the retail organization mentioned earlier, most of the leaders who were appointed from the outside floundered, sometimes for years, because their access to the underground was limited, and invitation into the hallowed ranks was based on loyal tenure, stylistic fit with existing members (looking and sounding like them), and often dues-paying organizational hazing rituals. To be sure, the underground had its downsides, and some of them ugly.

The SVP of Retail Operations, on point to drive a great deal of growth for the corporation, recognized the need to import a lot of new talent. She asked us to help her "break the back of the underground" so that new leaders would have a level playing field on which to contribute and succeed. Our response surprised her. "Why on earth would you want to destroy such an amazing asset? Why not exploit it instead?" Our point was that it was hugely valuable in getting things done, and trying to dismantle an iconic, powerful, and yet invisible pillar of the culture was futile anyway. Why not try to harness it instead, and broaden access to it for *everyone*? It would require drafting several of its informal leaders, enlisting them into the cause of the organization's future, and inspiring them to use their informal power to do what it had always done—advance the cause of the organization. This time that meant enabling a large influx of new leaders to learn the ways of the underground more quickly and easily than had historically been the case. In essence, we weren't going to dismantle it. We were going to multiply it.

We've heard many organizations proudly describe themselves as relationship based. Usually we don't have to look too deep before discovering that nothing could be further from the truth. What we usually discover is that they are confusing a superficial sense of collegiality, or politeness, for genuine relationships. These common counterfeits often masquerade as meaningful collaborative partnerships, until of course they are tested. The simplest test of whether or not an organization fosters meaningful Connection among leaders is to follow the paths of decision conflicts. In most organizations, institutionalized collusion trumps healthy, open dissent as the way of dealing with conflict or disagreement. Executives politely nod in agreement in the room, and pocket veto, form unholy alliances, sabotage, and passive-aggressively undermine rivals outside the room. Once that becomes the norm, you can kiss any hope for meaningful connections good-bye.

Exploiting the natural fabric of organizational networks is what enables executives to have broad-reaching and deeply meaningful connections with bosses, peers, and direct reports over the life of their careers. This becomes especially important as executives move around and rise in organizations and those relationships need constantly to be redefined. Someone who was once a peer may reappear as a direct report or a boss in later assignments. Many organizations foster such networks through sponsoring corporate sports teams like softball leagues or soccer teams for employees, affinity groups such as Young Professionals or Asian American or Latin American Professionals, and so forth. Well-chartered cross-functional task forces consisting of leaders from across the organization assembled for specific initiatives often have the by-product of forming deep relationships that transcend the life of the initiative. One executive we've worked with for many years says of his work leading a sales transformation effort more than a decade ago, "The people I did that with are still some of the closest friends I have today. We speak regularly, exchange career advice, and call each other on birthdays, even though most of us don't work at that company anymore."

Don't discourage your organization's underground; feature it. When it takes on unhealthy forms, like "good ol' boys networks," "old timers," "the women's club," "the class of '99," or "the breakfast club" (all names of organizational networks we've actually seen), where cult-like exclusivity inhibits broad participation, address that. Work to open access to the network for others, while still honoring the relationships formed within the network itself. Most organizations have their cast of "usual suspects" to whom all of the prime assignments are given. That, too, is a form of underground whose access should be broadened to uncover hidden talent that might otherwise remain undiscovered. Resist the temptation to formalize such networks with charters, budgets, or leadership councils, or you will certainly kill them. (The retailer above wanted to do this as a way to gain control over the underground, but quickly realized how destructive that would be.) Celebrate their organic nature and allow their genuine capacity to shape great relationships to morph and adapt with the organization. If you want executives who form 360-degree connections as a regular part of how they lead, cultivate the power of the many informal organizational networks already in place within your organization and encourage widespread participation in them.

The power at the seams, the power in well-designed organizational governance, the power in purposeful executive mobility, and the power of organizational networks are amazing levers available to enterprises for cultivating exceptional executives. While many companies spend millions of dollars on executive development workshops, assessments, and reward systems, they are missing the power of some of the greatest mechanisms for cultivating executive talent that are right under their noses. Have the courage to shift some of the resources you know are not returning value to harnessing the power of these existing organizational mechanisms, and watch your cadre of exceptional executives flourish and multiply.

REFLECTIONS ON THE RISE

1. How effectively and intentionally does talent move around your organization? What have been the results?

2. Where do you see evidence of naturally formed employee networks in your organization? What value do they create? What challenges do they present?

3. How would you coach Wayne to help Huntington better leverage the network of veteran employees more broadly?

CONTROLLED BURNS

COMMITTING TO YOUR RISE BY LEAVING BEHIND WHAT GOT YOU HERE TO CREATE SOMETHING EXCEPTIONAL

Richard Sheridan, co-founder and CEO of Menlo Innovations, a premier software development company in Ann Arbor, Michigan, has enjoyed a distinguished career by any standard. He has risen to the top of renowned public companies, led major innovation projects, and been rewarded handsomely. And yet, he was miserable. In his provocative and inspiring book, *Joy, Inc.: How We Built a Workplace People Love*, he describes his journey to understand and address his own crisis of meaning.

> On the outside, I was still viewed as a great success, grabbing promotions and raises and greater responsibilities. . . . That didn't matter to me anymore, as I stared daily at my life of quiet desperation. There were long nights and weekends away from the family I loved, for me and the people who worked for me. Vacations were impossible to schedule. Projects were always in trouble, and then they were canceled. Disappointed colleagues yelled during difficult meetings. I believed that the only way out of my management quagmire was to fire half the

team, but I hated the hiring process, so that, too, seemed like a dead end. Quality issues delayed deployments. Customers complained incessantly about the delays and the results. My patience and love for the software game seemed to be finite after all. I had two choices: change the industry or get out. I chose change. . . . There had to be a better way to do things, a better way to work and manage a team. Though I had no firm idea what I was looking for, I was convinced there was a solution out there for my existential crisis.[46]

He goes on to define the organization he, and others, *would love* as one with joy.

Joy is designing and building something that actually sees the light of day and is enjoyably used and widely adopted by the people for whom it was intended. Tangible joy means delivering a product or service to the world that's so enjoyed, in fact, that people stop you on the street and say, 'Really, you did that? I *love* it.' The pursuit of joy within a business context is not about the pursuit of fame or profit. Humans aspire to a higher purpose. Teams desire to work on goals bigger than themselves. They want to have a lasting and valued effect on the world. They want to make their mark, not for the glory, but for the purpose of bringing delight.

Who wouldn't want to work in a place like that?

Sheridan further describes some of the monotonous, traditional organizational environments in which he suffered during his career. Tragically, most sound just like how people describe their organizations today. To succeed, however, Sheridan had to relinquish the safety of known methodology, the comfort and security of well-grooved paradigms, and the predictability of an approach that, while deeply flawed, was proven. To be sure, any transformational change of substance will demand sacrifice—giving up something known for the sake of something unknown.

Let's revisit Gallup's research on employee engagement. Roughly 70 percent—that's somewhere around *seventy million people* in the American workforce—are either not engaged, meaning they are just checked out and disinterested, or actively disengaged, meaning they are intentionally trying to undermine the organization. Only 30 percent of the American workforce is engaged at work. Seventy million people, mindlessly at best, trudging through their day. And odds are high you're leading some of them. Read. this. paragraph. again. slowly.

It is into this breach that executives are arriving. From that 70 percent, trust in leaders is at an all-time low. Throughout the book, we have deliberately hammered the point home about the epidemic of executive failures that have resulted in unprecedented levels of cynicism among American workers. We have done so because to realize any dramatic reversal in our global performance is absolutely predicated on a reversal of our leadership performance. Executive compensation levels for *failures* have repulsed the disappearing middle class. (As an example, Leo Apotheker, CEO of Hewlett-Packard for less than a year, was fired by the board but was paid more than $25 million, keeping the nearly $10 million he got a year earlier when he joined, as well as $7.2 million in cash severance and $18 million in stock.[47]) It's no wonder confidence in leaders is in an accelerated free fall with few signs of reversal, and it's not hard to see what's driving seventy million people to "quit and stay."

It doesn't take a rocket scientist to recognize that as a nation, and as a private sector, we're in real trouble. Presumably, you've read this book—especially if you've gotten this far into it—because you are intent on resisting the mediocre standards of leadership long accepted as customary fare and making a difference for those you lead and the organization relying on you.

And if that is the case, you have two very important questions to answer as you reach the close of our time together.

Do you believe you *should* make such a difference?

Do you believe you *can* make such a difference?

These aren't easy questions and both require deep consideration. We hope our perspectives, experience, and research have compelled you to answer yes to both. But to make this difference, to get us out of the dark corner into which we've backed ourselves and create workplaces of joy as Sheridan describes, we're going to have to give up a great deal of what makes us comfortable. Let's see how.

COUNTING THE COST: CONTROLLED BURNS IN THE SERVICE OF SOMETHING EXCEPTIONAL

All too rarely, we hear people say, "I love my job." Recently one person said this to us with such exuberance we couldn't help asking, "Why do you love it so much?" She said without pause, "Because it loves me back." No one would argue that the desire to give and receive love is foundational to the human experience. It is so fundamental to being human that we simply take the truth of it for granted, yet for some odd reason, organizations dangerously assume that this basic need to give and receive love somehow stays home when people come to work. What are the implications if the place where we spend nearly half our waking hours is bereft of the most fundamental need and desire we have?

What if we could more commonly say of the place where we spend so much of our lives, "It loves me back"?

What if when people got out of bed in the morning to get ready for work, they anticipated the experience of being loved and loving instead of anticipating the dread of being dehumanized? What if people didn't lose sleep terrified of a conversation they were going to have the next day with you, but rather could expect that even in difficult circumstances, you would show care? And what if they anticipated the exceptional contributions they would get to make alongside people with whom they shared fierce respect and delight? Many will dismiss these questions as inappropriate emotional focus for the capitalistic workplaces where productivity, cost reduction, and competitive advantage remain center stage. We kindly invite you to ask your HR executive for last year's turnover and retention cost analysis. Read the exit interview transcripts of those who left that you wish hadn't. These reports may offer you a different perspective.[48]

Can you say your organization loves you back? Can those you lead say that of you? Tonight, you can be sure there are people you lead sitting around dinner tables telling stories of their day. You are likely a central character in those stories on many nights when they return home to dine with family or friends. Do their stories reflect a sense that their job loved them back today, or something less desirable? Would you be proud to hear the story, or would you cringe? Would you have to defend yourself, dismissing their version of the story because you had good reason to act as you did?

Do you believe you *should* make a difference in how those stories are told?

Do you believe you *can* make a difference in how those stories are told? Deep down, we know that for someone we lead to title their story "it loved me back," there will be a hefty price tag for us as leaders. We intuitively understand we'll either have to invest heavily—of our time as well as other resources—or give something up, and that can be painful. You can be sure for Richard Sheridan to have produced a *workplace people love* demanded some real moments of sacrifice, what we refer to as "controlled burns."

Controlled burning, also known as hazard-reduction burning, is a technique used in forest management, farming, prairie restoration, and greenhouse gas abatement. Due to lightning and other natural events, fire is a natural part of both forest and grassland ecology, yet for years the United States has attempted to limit this natural phenomenon. It has cost us. Despite preventing billions of dollars of damage and loss of life, forfeited ecological benefits, and out-of-control forest fires that burn hotter due to buildup of fuels on forest floors, the use of controlled fires, usually done during cooler months, was fiercely resisted as a nuisance and feared risk by those whom it would most benefit. As a result controlled burning wasn't done in many communities for years.

Controlled burning is, in essence, fighting fire with fire. One could see why this forest management approach would not always make sense.

Our Navalent colleague Jarrod Shappell has done extensive thinking about the metaphor of controlled burns and their application to our lives. He writes,

> In order to see the benefits of fire we must ensure that they do not exceed the natural intensity and temperature that makes things beneficial. In other words, we must stop trying to suppress life's natural flare-ups, and embrace them, perhaps even create them, if we are to see the new life that will come from the purifying work of fire."[49]

Rather than waiting for catastrophe to strike from an out-of-control "fire" you inadvertently set through a choice, a behavior, a perspective, an ambition, or a lapse of judgment, set a controlled "fire" before you've destroyed more than you can imagine. (And for a reminder of what those risks may be, revisit chapter 5.)

Bluntly stated, pay now or pay later. If you genuinely want to become an exceptional executive, plan now for what it will cost you. Assuming you can become an exceptional executive while retaining all the comforts that propelled you to this moment sets your organization up for extravagant failure, and sets you up to be a cliché—another predictable statistic in the pile of data on failed executives.

For your rise to power to flourish, you must orchestrate your own controlled burns. There are privileges you enjoy; skills you've mastered; experiences that define you; fears disguised as "thoughtful and methodical" but experienced as paralyzing indecisiveness; insecurities disguised as "willing to rely on others' input" but experienced as over-inclusion and accommodation; resentment and anger disguised as "driven" but experienced as belittling; relationships you cling to; track records you're proud of—and not so proud of; product lines you've launched and brands you've built—yesterday's wins you keep trying to repeat; patents you earned, approaches you developed, publications in your name, and awards you've competed for—all which you incessantly remind people of; dogma you're known for; favors you've done . . . fill in your list . . . that have accompanied you thus far. Some may even have been instrumental in getting you here, . . . but may prove fatal if you take them any further.

For you to become an exceptional executive, you will inevitably have to abandon some things—beliefs, behaviors, skills, etc.—that are comfortable and to which you have long clutched. Things that in previous contexts were useful, perhaps wonderful, or simply benign, in a new context can be potentially destructive. These are the things that require a controlled burn.

In forests, controlled burning facilitates the germination of some desirable trees that require heat from fire to open their cones to disperse seeds, thus renewing the forests. New forest life requires forest death. At every successive altitude, you must intentionally forsake something from the past to gain something for the future. Your controlled-burn requirement could be as minute as an assumption you have about your business or team, or as substantial as an idiosyncrasy you've long dismissed as immaterial. If any of the messages on the previous pages have begun to penetrate, odds are you know exactly what your controlled burn needs to be.

Understandably, resistance to the prospect isn't completely outlandish. The concept of a controlled burn asks communities to have the faith to *voluntarily burn thousands* of acres right near their homes on the *off chance* it will prevent a hotter fire from burning their homes later. Similarly, voluntarily choosing to forfeit the immense advantages, comforts, and rewards you've long enjoyed *in the hope* something better will replace it and so *others* will benefit can be a hard pill to swallow.

And that's exactly what we're suggesting exceptional executives do. Harnessing the power of your Context, enhancing the power of your Breadth, mastering the power of Choice, and deepening the power of your Connections all typically lie just on the other side of a colossal leap of faith to forfeit something in the service of advancing something greater. This is the hallmark of an exceptional executive.

As you begin, or continue, your rise to power, the story of your leadership is being written through the organization in which you lead. Over time, like any good story, there will be both dark and triumphant moments. You will be both hero and villain. You will exercise power with brilliance, and you will know power failure. As Paul Maass reflected at the beginning of this book, the story of your rise to power will be told on the faces of those you have led. Your impact on the world, for better or worse, will be through them. And he modeled for us the power of choosing a controlled burn in the service of something exceptional. The chance of those you lead telling a joyful story of "it loved me back" may be directly predicated on the exceptional executive you become . . . in large measure through what you must first surrender.

To be sure, being an executive in today's organizations can be a brutal calling. It is not for everyone, and if you know now it's not for you, bless everyone, including yourself, by stepping aside or declining the opportunity.

But if you are up for the challenge, commit to making a great difference. Throughout your rise, you must believe you *can* and *should* leave your part of the world better than you found it. To do so, you must burn off anything that could thwart your rise for the sake of creating something exceptional. In the face of remarkably bleak leadership examples, spectacular abuses and perversions of power, and cynicism and deep distrust alongside herculean expectations of leaders, we fully appreciate how daunting the prospect of executive leadership can be. For your courage to even consider it, you have our profound admiration.

Turning the forceful tide of leadership insolvency and decay into something utterly magnificent will occur one choice, one interaction, one plan, one relationship, one rise to power, and one controlled burn at a time. And eventually, the cumulative effect will be felt across the world. Maybe that will be in our lifetimes, maybe it won't.

At Menlo Innovations, Richard Sheridan went first. He risked burning what had always worked in faith that something greater would appear. The results have been exceptional. And indeed, at many wonderful organizations in the world, exceptional executives like him are blazing the trail to transform their workplaces into marvelous communities of imagination, passion, courage, joy, and exceptional results. Places that "love me back."

Someone has to go first and lead the charge at your organization.

We pick you. You're perfect for the job.

In fact, we're confident you'll be exceptional.

FINAL APPROACH

Dear Huntington Shareholder,

Nearly seventy years ago, Linton Jacobs had a vision for a way to serve local manufacturers with more cost-effective industrial materials they could use in a wide variety of applications. In his barn, he developed, then eventually patented, a plastic-coated packaging material that allowed for local produce to ship longer distances and arrive fresher more reliably than had been the case with cardboard and more cost effectively than with wooden crates. Over the years, he and his friends produced multiple applications of that material to serve more than a dozen industries with more than three hundred products. When his son, Mackenzie Jacobs, took the helm nearly a quarter century ago, it was like a jet engine was strapped to Huntington's back. The growth we enjoyed was unprecedented. The acquisitions we did opened doors to markets and customers we would have never accessed before. Courageous risks, certainly not without our fair share of setbacks, paid off in the long run to help make us the company we are today.

As the newly formed Huntington Industries, parent company to Huntington Industrial Materials, Huntington Specialty Packaging, and Huntington International, celebrates its 70th birthday this year, we do so with enormous gratitude, humility, and joy for the journey we've been privileged to guide. We're now a diversified set of three thriving businesses serving unique markets with innovative offerings. We're proud to say all three divisions delivered impressive earnings this year, with our Specialty Packaging division leading the charge. Customers like Newrizon have enjoyed customized solutions that have uniquely served their customers and bottom lines. We're proud of these partnerships and look forward to more of them in the years to come. Our Industrial Materials division, which continues to loyally serve five rich customer segments, and our newly formed International division, whose primary focus has been our expansion in Latin America, both held their own this year, despite the economic headwinds and fluctuating currency challenges. This year, we also said good-bye to Huntington's original manufacturing plant, which for the last decade had exclusively produced some of our best-selling industrial material solutions. We celebrated the workers, the community, and their rich history with Huntington in a vibrant retrospective of all it had accomplished. And we ushered in our newest production and warehousing facility, a state-of-the-art, 140,000-square-foot facility located in the same town as our inaugural plant, bringing jobs and economic growth to the community that has served us so well for so long.

When we began our careers at Huntington, we never imagined the adventure we'd take. We're proud of the thousands of employees who make up Huntington Industries and grateful for the loyal customers who've been with us over the years, some as long as three decades. Our dedication to you couldn't be stronger.

And to our shareholders, we hope you feel proud of not just the returns on your investment in us, but of the company we've become. Our commitment to environmental stewardship through the Jacobs Foundation, the scholarships we've offered families in industrial communities, the economic advantage we've offered customers through our innovations, and our partnerships with great suppliers are all emblems of what we stand for, and the reputation we seek to uphold. Thank you for your financial loyalty and for helping Huntington retain the highest analyst ratings for the last four years. It is to you we proudly dedicate the pages ahead in this annual report showcasing this year's accomplishments.

Mackenzie Jacobs, or "Mac" as he was fondly known, had a quote hanging in his office: "There is no power on earth that can neutralize the influence of a high, simple and useful life."[50] He deeply instilled into us and the organization the truth that everything we did every day had to matter. The power behind our success was ultimately the result of the power we exercised to live good lives and to do great things for each other and those we serve. We have fiercely protected that principle at Huntington, and believe it to be truer today than ever. We trust you will see that reflected in the results we've achieved, the reputation we enjoy, and the aspirations we envision.

On behalf of all our Huntington colleagues worldwide . . .

With our grateful regard,
Jordan Neffron   Elise Russell
Chairman of the Board   President & Chief Executive Officer

APPENDIX

ADDITIONAL READING FROM *RISING TO POWER* ON DIMENSIONS OF POWER

The sections listed under each power dimension are a primary reference only. Each reading may touch on and involve the use of multiple dimensions of power. As you re-read each section you will come to better understand and appreciate their integral nature and recognize the optimal power that will result as you learn to effectively use them in concert.

	To better understand *Power in Breadth*, review these sections:	To better understand *Power in Context*, review these sections:	To better understand *Power in Choice*, review these sections:	To better understand *Power in Connection*, review these sections:
Chapter 1	• Extend your sense of time and embrace complexity (p. 39)	• The higher the rise, the harder the fall (p. 28) • Change the altitude of what you see and think (p. 36) • Resist the myth of the mandate (p. 37) • Summit Shock: Reconciling ideals with reality (p. 30)		• Monitor your internal monologue on arrival (p. 34)
Chapter 2	• Finding the Right Altitude (p. 47) • Playing your part well (p. 49) • Three Interdependent Systems (p. 50) • The Coordinating System (p. 53) • Understand the realities of scale and role (p. 59)	• The Strategic System (p. 54) • Get out of the weeds (p. 57)	• The Operating System (p. 51) • Pick your battles (p. 58)	• Give people space (p. 58)

	To better understand *Power in Breadth*, review these sections:	To better understand *Power in Context*, review these sections:	To better understand *Power in Choice*, review these sections:	To better understand *Power in Connection*, review these sections:
	• Leverage your knowledge of the organization w/o your biases (p. 78) • From seeing the parts to seeing the whole (p. 84)	• Get in Touch with your Inner Anthropologist (p. 67) • Gather disconfirming data (p. 70) • From the tyranny of the urgent to the art of the long view (p. 82) • Ensure your diagnosis doesn't turn into an indictment (p. 75)	• Synthesize learning into a shared set of "vital few" priorities (p. 71) • Extract yourself from the Coordinating system (p. 80) • From hyper-responsive to steady and focused (p. 83) • From doing it all to picking your battles (p. 84)	• Size up talent and build your team (p. 71) • Solicit and act upon personal feedback at key intervals (p. 72) • Build authentic relationships and allow people to get to know you (p. 74) • Determine if you are effectively blending in (p. 74) • Re-calibrate relationships with new and former peers (p. 77)
Chapter 3				

	To better understand *Power in Breadth*, review these sections:	To better understand *Power in Context*, review these sections:	To better understand *Power in Choice*, review these sections:	To better understand *Power in Connection*, review these sections:
Chapter 4	• Sifted data (p. 95) • Horizontal patterns (p. 111) • Cultural patterns (p. 112)	• Historical patterns (p. 110) • Economic patterns (p. 112)	• Clarify what you believe and value (p. 101) • Detect Patterns to Clear Up Organizational Distortions (p. 109)	• Larger than life (p. 92) • The megaphone effect (p. 93) • Aliens next door (p. 97) • Own your pathologies (p. 102) • Give other permission to name your triggers (p. 103) • Close the Gap between You and Those Distorting You (p. 103) • Know and understand your colleagues (p. 104) • Be loyal while avoiding accommodation (p. 105) • Be trustworthy and trusting, but not naïve (p. 106) • Develop self-awareness (p. 107) • Remain genuinely grateful and generous (p. 108) • Have climbing partners (p. 114) • Help others adjust their distortions (p. 115)

	To better understand *Power in Breadth*, review these sections:	To better understand *Power in Context*, review these sections:	To better understand *Power in Choice*, review these sections:	To better understand *Power in Connection*, review these sections:
Chapter 5	• Spin/hoarding (p. 147) • Havoc/Confusion (p. 149) • Redeeming Executive Power: The ultimate privilege (p. 153)	• The Conundrum of Power (p. 123) • Redeeming Positional Power (p. 135)	• Indecision (p. 133) • Accommodation (p. 134) • Redeeming Informational Power (p. 151)	• Exploitation (p. 139) • Counter-dependence/ Co-dependence (p. 141) • Blackmail (p. 147) • Stakeholder blindness (p. 142) • Indiscretion (p. 150) • Bribery (p. 140) • Redeeming Relational Power (p. 143)
Chapter 6	• Equity and Fairness (p. 165)		• Transparency and Justification (p. 166)	• Perfection (p. 161) • Clairvoyance (p. 168) • Accessibility (p. 169) • Inspiration (p. 170)

RISING TO POWER STATISTICAL METHODOLOGY

The following is an explanation of the methodology used in defining and analyzing the drivers of success in executive transition. Initially we analyzed verbatim comments captured from assessment interviews conducted on behalf of over one hundred executives. We used IBM SPSS Modeler Text Analytics, which identified the following seven factors:

1. Altitude & Systems
2. Character
3. Communication
4. Decision Making
5. Leading in Context
6. Problem Solving
7. Relationships

A more thorough ontology was then built to analyze these factors in more depth before proceeding with additional analysis.

Each interview document, typically forty or more pages, was classified using this ontology, and the resulting variables were analyzed using IBM SPSS Statistics. Additionally, we could then analyze and classify the variables that correlate most highly with both high performance and low performance. Several different techniques were used in order to make sure the classification was robust. Finally, to identify the variables that actually drive success in making transitions, we used several advanced analytics techniques, including linear and logistic regression, CHAID decision trees, and both parametric and nonparametric correlations.

Regression analyses were used to calculate the ultimate weights of the strengths and weaknesses as drivers of success. Log transformations were done on the ranking of the executives in the data set on both business performance and behavioral ratings. The strengths and weaknesses were introduced as flag variables indicating the presence or absence of a particular strength or weakness. Both stepwise and enter methods were evaluated with stepwise being used for final weighting of the drivers. Adjusted R Squared values for behavioral rating drivers ranged from 0.796 for the weaknesses to 0.964 for the strengths. Adjusted R Squared values for the business performance ratings ranged from 0.792 for the weaknesses to 0.967 for the strengths.

EXECUTIVE LEADERSHIP TRANSITION SURVEY INSTRUMENT

Thinking back on your first broad executive role, even if you are currently still in it, to what extent . . .

1. Did you have support from more experienced executives you could turn to for advice?
2. Did the people you led want more justification for your decisions than you felt was warranted?
3. Did the people you led ascribe motives to your choices that were very different from your true motives?
4. Did you find that decisions were more complicated and involved than you'd expected?
5. Did you play the role you thought you'd play in making strategic decisions?
6. Did you feel tempted to use the power that came with your role in the service of self-interest?
7. Have you felt held responsible for problems outside your control?
8. Did you find being an executive fun?
9. Did you understand the degree of challenge you would face?
10. Did formal processes intended to develop your leadership effectively prepare you for the realities of leadership at an executive level?
11. Do you feel that you have met the requirements of the role?
12. Were you prepared for what the role required?
13. Were you promoted into the role earlier in your career than you expected?

14. Did the organization see you as credible and able to successfully deliver the requirements of the role?

15. Did you find being an executive tiring?

16. Did the people you led rely on you to make decisions that they should have been making on their own?

17. Could the role have been easier if you'd gotten a more realistic preview of the job requirements?

18. Did you feel uncomfortable with the degree of power that came with the role?

19. Did the people you led want more of your time than you had available?

20. Did you feel lonely and isolated?

21. Did you feel that the impact you could have on your organization and those you led was a privilege?

22. Did you find it difficult to let go of the work you used to do?

23. Did the people you led place unrealistic expectations on you?

24. Were you able to build the necessary competencies through your career path to succeed at that level?

25. Did you find the wide influence you were able to have enjoyable?

26. Have you made the impact on the performance of the organization you'd hoped to make when you took the role?

27. Did you have realistic assumptions about what an executive role entails?

28. Have you had ongoing coaching and feedback to refine your ability to perform in an executive role?

29. Is the amount of power people ascribe to your position greater than the amount of power you actually have?

30. Do you feel that senior leaders tend to misuse the power that comes with the role?

31. Have your views changed about how senior leaders use or misuse power after becoming a senior leader yourself?

32. Do you spend your time dealing with the performance shortfalls of others?

33. Do you find that the degree of power that comes with a formal organizational role is different from what you expected it to be?

34. Has your experience of being an executive tested your abilities more than you'd expected it to?

35. Are you enjoying playing an executive role?

36. Does politics at the executive level undermine your ability to trust your peers?

37. Do you find the politics at the executive level negatively influencing your behavior?

38. Did other senior leaders place unrealistic expectations on you?

39. Have you adapted the level of detail you get involved in to match the demands of your role?

40. Do you treat the power that comes with your role as a privilege to be exercised thoughtfully?

Write-In questions

1. What is the one thing you wish you had been told prior to taking on an executive role that would have made your assimilation to the role smoother?

2. What is the one issue you find persistently challenges your leadership as an executive?

3. Which experience in your career best prepared you to assume an executive leadership role?

4. What have been your most important insights about using the power/authority that accompanies your executive role?

Demographics

- Gender
- Current Age ranges (26–30, 31–35, 36–40, 45–50, 51–55, 55–60, 61+)
- Age at time of promotion into executive ranks: (26–30, 31–35, 36–40, 45–50, 51–55, 55–60, 61+)

- Length of time in first executive role (less than 12 months, 1–2 years, 3–5 years, 5+ years)
- Total number of employees under your leadership in first executive role (<50, 50–100, 100–300, 300–500, 500+)
- Total number of employees under your leadership today (<50, 50–100, 100–300, 300–500, 500+)
- Career Tenure (years of total professional experience)
- Tenure with current company
- Number of companies worked for previous to current company

NOTES

1 Alvin Toffler, *PowerShift: Knowledge, Wealth, and Violence at the Edge of the 21st Century* (New York: Bantam Books, 1991).

Introduction: Wing Walking

2 Ken Favaro, Per-Ola Karlsson, and Gary Neilson, *CEO Succession Report: 12th Annual Global CEO Succession Study* (New York: Booz and Company, 2012).

3 Guido Stein Martínez and Javier Capapé, "The Factors Behind the Failure Rate of CEOs" (Barcelona, Spain: IESE [Institute of Higher Business Studies], 2009).

4 *High-Impact Leadership Transitions: A Transformative Approach* (The Corporate Executive Board Company, 2012).

5 Anne Huff Stevens, "The More Things Change, the More They Stay the Same: Trends in Long-Term Employment in the United States: 1969–2002" (NBER Working Paper no. 11878, 2005).

6 Willem van Zandweghe, "Interpreting the Recent Decline in Labor Force Participation," in *Economic Review: First Quarter 2012* (Federal Reserve Bank of Kansas City [www.KansasCityFed.org]).

7 Bob Johnson and Rob Oberwise, *Developing Global Leaders: A Guide to Managing Effectively in Unfamiliar Places* (New York: Palgrave Macmillan, 2012).

8 Daniel Goleman, "The Must-Have Leadership Skill," *Harvard Business Review* (October 14) – HBR Blog network (http://blogs.hbr.org/cs/2011/10/the_must-have_leadership_skill.html)

9 Any similarity to true events is merely coincidental. The patterns of organizational and executive behavior are indeed drawn from real life events.

Chapter One: Altitude Sickness

10 FLeon Festinger and J. M. Carlsmith, "Cognitive Consequences of Forced Compliance," *Journal of Abnormal and Social Psychology,* 58, 203–210 (1959).

11 Elliott Jaques and Stephen D. Clement, *Executive Leadership: A Practical Guide to Managing Complexity* (Oxford, UK: Blackwell Business, 1994).

12 Jennifer Reingold and Ryan Underwood, "Was 'Built to Last' Built to Last?" *Fast Company* (November 1, 2004), pp. 103–111.

13 Richard Gibson, "The Inside Scoop," *Wall Street Journal* (June 12, 2008): http://online.wsj.com/article/SB121321718319265569.html

14 Darren Rovell, "Behind the Counter: The Untold Story of Franchising," CNBC investigative report aired 02/13/2011; Josh Kosman, "Cold Stone Creamery Burning Mad at CNBC," *The New York Post* (December 28, 2010): http://nypost.com/2010/12/28/cold-stone-creamery-burning-mad-at-cnbc/

Chapter Two: Distinguishing Your Organization's Different Altitudes

15 David McCay, Patricia Larson, and Stan Larson, "'What E'er Thou Art Act Well Thy Part': The Missionary Diaries of David O. McKay," *Freethinker* (October 1999).

Chapter Three: Planning Your shift to the Strategic System

16 Steven Davis, "Executive Failure," *CEO Magazine* (April 6, 2006).

17 Ken Favaro, Per-Ola Karlsson, , and Gary Neilson, *CEO Succession Report: 12th Annual Global CEO Succession Study* (New York: Booz and Company, 2012).

Chapter Four: Altitudinal Distortions

18 Manfred Kets de Vries, *The Leader on the Couch: A Clinical Approach to Changing People and Organizations* (New York: John Wiley and Sons, 2006).

19 Harry M. Jansen Kraemer, Jr., *From Values to Action: The Four Principles of Values-Based Leadership* (San Francisco, CA: Jossey-Bass, 2011).

Chapter Five: Executive Power

20 Thich Nhat Hanh, *The Art of Power* (New York: HarperOne Publishers, 2008).

21 Jeffrey Pfeffer, *Power: Why Some People Have It and Others Don't* (New York: HarperBusiness, 2010).

22 Adam Kahane, *Power and Love: A Theory of Practical and Social Change* (San Francisco, CA: Berrett-Koehler Publishers, 2010). Both the Tillich and Jung references are used illustratively.

23 Vidula Bal, Michael Campbell, Judith Steed, and Kyle Meddings, "The Role of Power in Effective Leadership," a CCL white paper (The Center for Creative Leadership, Greensboro, NC, 2008).

24 These words come directly from our survey results; though we did not ask participants to distinguish between authority and power, nor do we see any benefit in doing so, it's clear the underlying assumption is one of caution.

25 Joe Trammell, "CEO Fail: The Roman Emperor CEO," *The American CEO.com* (April 25, 2013).

26 Hinke Groothof, Pieternel Dijkstra, and Dick Barelds, "Sex Differences in Jealousy: The Case of Internet Infidelity," *Social Psychological and Personality Science* 1: 353–360 (October 1, 2010).

27 Steven Appelbaum, Ana Marinescu, Julia Klenin, and Justin Bytautas, "Fatal Attractions: The (Mis)Management of Workplace Romance," *International Journal of Business Research* 7, no. 4 (2007).

28 Robyn Reilly, "Five Ways to Improve Employee Engagement Now," Gallup Business Journal (January 1, 2014); "The State of the American Workplace Report, 2010–2012," *Gallup Business Journal* online at http://www.gallup.com/strategicconsulting/163007/ state-american-workplace.aspx

Chapter Six: Managing Expectations

29 Becky Barrow, "Our Greedy Bosses," *The Daily Mail* (November 19, 2012).

30 Ferdinand Mount, *The New Few, or A Very British Oligarchy* (New York: Simon and Schuster, 2012).

31 www.peterbregman.com

32 Suzanne J. Peterson and Kristin Byron, "Exploring the Role of Hope in Job Performance," *The Journal of Organizational Behavior* 29 (6):785–803 (August 2008).

Chapter Seven: The Exceptional Executive

33 Barbara Kellerman, The End of Leadership (New York: HarperBusiness, 2012).

34 From *Bloomberg Business Week,* The Hershey Co. People: http://investing.businessweek. com/research/stocks/people/person.asp?personId=1202998&ticker=HSY.

35 Alyssa Abkowitz, "Netflix CEO Reed Hastings: The Secret of My Success," interview, reported in *Fortune Magazine* (January 28, 2009).

36 Amy Zipkin, "Out of Africa and Onto the Web," interview with Reed Hastings, *New York Times* (December 17, 2006).

37 James Marshall Crotty, "Netflix CEO Reed Hastings Blew 12 Billion in Market Cap. Why Should we Listen to Him about Education[?]" from *Forbes.com* (May 3, 2012): http://www.forbes.com/sites/jamesmarshallcrotty/2012/05/03/netflix-ceo-reed-hastings-blew-12-billion-in-market-cap-so-why-should-we-listen-to-him-about-education/.

38 Boris Veldhuijzen van Zanten, "Inspiring Entrepreneurs: What Netflix CEO Reed Hastings has learned in his business career" from *The Next Web* blog (September 13, 2013): http://thenextweb.com/entrepreneur/2013/09/12/inspiring-entrepreneurs-reed-hastings-netflix/.

39 "Netflix tests new price tiers for streaming video service" from the *Las Vegas Sun* (December 31, 2013): http://www.lasvegassun.com/news/2013/dec/31/netflix-tests-new-price-tiers-video-service.

40 Water1st International: http://water1st.org/.

41 From Market Watch Investing: www.marketwatch.com/investing/stock/nFLX/charts.

42 Dan Heath and Chip Heath, *Decisive: How to Make Better Choices in Life and Work* (New York: Crown Business, 2013).

43 L. Kevin Kelly, and Bryan MacDonald, "The New Path To the C-Suite" from *The Harvard Business Review* (March 2011): http://hbr.org/2011/03/the-new-path-to-the-c-suite/ar/1.

Chapter Eight: Powerful Organizations That Make Exceptional Executives

44 "The State of Global Talent Management Survey" from "The Definitive Guide to Talent Mobility," http://pt.slideshare.net/Softscape/sum-t-wptalentmobility. SumTotal 2010 based on a combined aggregation of twelve business and HR operating metrics.

45 Ron Carucci, *Leadership Divided: What Emerging Leaders Need and What You Might Be Missing* (San Francisco, CA: Jossey-Bass, 2006).

Epilogue: Controlled Burns

46 Richard Sheridan, *Joy, Inc.: How We Built a Workplace People Love* (New York: Portfolio Penguin, 2013).

47 David Goldman, CNNMoney.tech (September 22, 2011).

48 First appeared in Ron Carucci and Josh Epperson, *In Future in-Formation: Choosing a Generative Organizational Life* (Parker, CO: Outskirts Press, 2009).

49 Jarrod Shappell, Control Burns and the Purifying Work of Fire, unpublished white paper in progress.

50 Booker T. Washington

For more information, contact us at:
Info@navalent.com
800-818-0297
www.navalent.com

navalent

powering your transformation journey

INDEX